THE SHAPING OF ENGLAND

HISTORIES BY ISAAC ASIMOV

THE GREEKS

THE ROMAN REPUBLIC

THE ROMAN EMPIRE

THE EGYPTIANS

THE NEAR EAST

THE DARK AGES

THE SHAPING OF ENGLAND

THE SHAPING OF
ENGLAND

BY ISAAC ASIMOV

HOUGHTON MIFFLIN COMPANY BOSTON

1969

078135

To my parents,
in their Golden Wedding year

CONTENTS

BEFORE THE ROMANS

THE BRITISH ISLES

In the year 1900, the island kingdom of Great Britain was the strongest power on earth. Regions on every continent, making up one quarter of the earth's land surface and of its population, were subject to Queen Victoria of Great Britain. Its navy could defeat any enemy or combination of enemies. Its language was spread over the world and was spoken more widely than any other language in existence.

When, in the decades following 1900, Great Britain's power declined and it was no longer the leading nation of the planet, its place was taken by the United States of America, a land which had originally been colonized by Great Britain, which spoke the language of Great Britain and which lived under a system of law and government inherited from that of Great Britain.

How was it that Great Britain reached its pinnacle of success and power? After all, for thousands of years, while other parts of the world were rich and civilized, the British Isles were thinly populated, poor and barbarous, and nothing about them — nothing at all — seemed to give any promise of future greatness.

The story of how the British success came about is a long one and not all of it can be told in this book. We can, however, make a beginning and see how the island and its population were molded under the blows of successive waves of invaders until, nearly a thousand years ago, they arrived at their present state — and were never, thereafter, conquered again.

The chief scene of this tale is the "British Isles," a group of islands lying off the northwest coast of Europe, with a total area of 120,000 square miles, or about the size of our state of New Mexico.

Making up three-quarters of the whole is the island of Great Britain, with an area of 89,000 square miles (about the size of Utah). In ancient times, it was known to the Romans as "Britannia" and in English, this becomes "Britain."

Why is it now "Great" Britain, then? That is because, some fifteen centuries ago, some of the islanders fled across the stretch of water that separates it from Europe, seeking refuge from barbarous invaders. They settled in the northwest corner of the nation we now call France and the place of their refuge became a kind of smaller Britain.

This is reflected in the name of that region now. It is "Bretagne" in French and "Brittany" in English. In Latin it is "Britannia Minor," meaning "little Britain." After that, the island from which the refugees had come had to be called "Great Britain" to distinguish it from the little Britain on the Continent.

There are some ways in which the island is indeed "great" even in size. It is the largest island off the European shores, and it is the eighth largest island in the world. Through much of its history, it lay off the coast of a Europe in which large nations

could not be kept together and which was therefore divided
into rather small ones. The island of Great Britain, under
such conditions, made up a nation of respectable size. Indeed,
the nation that made its mark in early modern times did not
occupy the entire island at all, but only the southern three-
fifths of it.

To the west of Great Britain is a second major island, only a
third as large. To the Romans it was known as "Hibernia" and
to ourselves as "Ireland." It was doomed always to remain
under the shadow of the larger island.

Some twelve thousand years ago, the area was just emerging
from the most recent "Ice Age." All of northern Europe, including the land which later became the British Isles, was
then covered with a thick layer of ice. Slowly, the glacier retreated as the climate warmed, and by 10,000 B.C. the land
emerged, chilly and wet, and not at all an attractive place for
settlement.

The island was still joined to the European continent in those
early days, and whether the land was attractive or not, men
drifted in. The skin-clad hunters of the Stone Age followed the
animal herds northward as the ice retreated.

The British region remained part of the continent for several
thousand years. Far to the east, small farming communities developed in Canaan and in the highlands north of the Tigris
River in western Asia, and the first patchy centers of civilization
appeared on earth*; but in the new land to the northwest, nothing better than the sparse settlement of roaming hunters was
yet to be found.

Slowly, the climate improved as the dark pine forests spread
northward and the summers grew more balmy. And as they
did, the glaciers that still existed to the north continued to melt.
The sea level rose, the land area shrank, and by 6000 B.C. the
rising waters had cut off Great Britain from Europe and Ireland from Great Britain.

* see my book "The Near East" (Houghton Mifflin, 1968)

The waters of the Channel now rolled to the south of Great Britain, that of the Irish Sea to the west and of the North Sea to the east.

Left to themselves on the islands were the early Stone Age inhabitants, whose remnants may still be found today in the form of polished stone tools and pottery. They seem to have had domestic animals and to have worked flint mines.

Their position was improved in that the islands would now have to be invaded by sea, a more difficult task than a mere overland trek. This was to be the saving of the inhabitants on numerous occasions right down to the present day, and it gave them a sense of security the peoples of the continent could rarely enjoy.

Salvation could not always be depended on, however. The islands were to see numerous invasions by sea, and some of them were successful.

THE BEAKER FOLK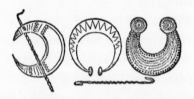

We can see the earliest of these invasions only dimly. Not long after 2000 B.C., the "Beaker Folk" invaded Great Britain. They are called that because they left behind distinctive drinking cups, or beakers. They also brought with them onto the island the arts of weaving and of metallurgy. The latter was important, for the Beaker Folk used bronze weapons where the previous inhabitants had had nothing better than stone. With superior weapons, the invaders managed to establish their domination.

The Beaker Folk must have been something more than merely one group of barbarians taking over from a somewhat more primitive group of barbarians. They have left relics behind that are infinitely more impressive than beakers. These consist of circles of large, flat rough-hewn stones, standing on end.

The most famous of these is called Stonehenge (stone'henj), and is located near the town of Amesbury, about seventy miles west of London. It consists of two concentric circles of huge rocks, the outer circle being 105 feet in diameter. The individual rocks are sixteen feet high and six or seven feet wide. Thirty of them, standing upright, made up the outer circle with thirty more lying flat over them. Only thirty-two of the original sixty stones of the outer ring are there now and only half of those are still upright. The missing stones were probably broken up and used for building purposes by the surrounding people of later centuries. The inner circle consisted of smaller stones, of which only eleven are still standing. Even what remains is still an impressive sight.

Analysis of a bit of charcoal found at the site, by modern dating methods, leads us to suppose that Stonehenge was erected about 1750 B.C. Oddly enough, though, the first record of any mention of Stonehenge by the people of the island dates back only eleven centuries.

By that time, the islanders had no notion of the enormous age of the structure (which was already over two thousand years old). Nor did they know why it had been built, nor how. They felt it must have been built, by magical means, through the wizardry of the legendary Merlin.

As a matter of fact, we are not much better off than the islanders of eleven centuries ago. No one is yet at all certain how the Beaker Folk managed to work with those huge stones, considering the tools they had at their disposal. Nor are we sure what the purpose of the circles was. It has been fashionable to suppose that Stonehenge and other stone circles scattered over the British Isles were used for primitive religious ceremonies, but we have no real evidence for it. Mostly, this thought arises because we usually can't think of anything else that it might be used for.

In 1963, however, the Anglo-American astronomer Gerald Hawkins, of Boston University, advanced the daring notion that stone circles like Stonehenge were actually primitive astronomic observatories. Making use of what was left of the structure (including not only the large stones but also various stone-filled pits), Hawkins showed that one could locate the rising sun at the summer solstice and predict the occurrence of lunar eclipses.

It is hard to believe that primitive people could be so sophisticated in astronomic lore, but it is even harder to believe that all the things Hawkins can demonstrate arise out of mere coincidence. The circle, it would seem, had to be planned with astronomy in mind. To be sure, the motive for following the movements of the Sun and Moon so exactly would very likely have been connected with religious rites and, if so, Stonehenge is indirectly involved in religion after all.

Nor were the Beaker Folk completely isolated from Europe despite the salt water that now girts the island. They traded with the rich civilizations of the eastern Mediterranean. One might wonder what such relatively unadvanced people as the Beaker Folk had to offer the already luxurious centers of population in the east. The answer is: metal.

For a thousand years and more, bronze had been the key to war. It is much tougher and stronger than leather; much less brittle than stone. It was better than any other metal which could be obtained in quantity. A bronze-equipped army could usually beat one without bronze, and do so without much trouble. The Beaker People themselves had demonstrated this when they entered Great Britain from the European continent. For any war-making group, then, a major problem would be that of insuring an adequate supply of bronze.

Bronze is a mixture of two metals: copper and tin. Neither is extremely common, but there were good sources of copper available to the civilized nations rimming the eastern Mediterranean. The island of Cyprus, in the northeastern corner of the Mediterranean Sea, was one such source, and the very name "copper" is supposed to be derived from the name of the island.

Tin was another matter. Not only is it generally rare, but it is found in concentrations sufficient for profitable mining in only a few parts of the globe. The small quantities available in the eastern Mediterranean were soon gone and sources had to be found farther afield. (In modern times, the most important sources are in southeast Asia and in central South America, and both of these were out of the question for the early civilizations of the Mediterranean.)

Leading in the search for new sources of tin were the Phoenicians, a people who inhabited the eastern shores of the Mediterranean (and who were the "Canaanites" of the Bible). They were the most daring navigators in the world during the time when the Egyptian Empire was at its height and when the still barbarous Greeks were fighting under the walls of Troy.

These Phoenicians scoured the Mediterranean from end to end. They did more; they moved out through what we now call the Strait of Gibraltar and ventured into the Atlantic Ocean itself — the first civilized people to do so.

Somewhere out in the Atlantic, they found a source of tin on islands they called (according to the Greek historian Herodotus) the "Cassiterides." Since the Greek word for tin is "kassiteros," we can refer to them as the "Tin Islands."

It is generally agreed that the Tin Islands are what we now call the Scilly Islands (sil'ee). These are a group of about 140 small islands (only about six square miles in area all together) lying thirty-five miles west of the southwestern tip of Great Britain. The Beaker Folk lived there, to be sure, and remnants of stone circles can be found. (One of them, about twenty feet across, is found on the island of Samson.)

There is little tin on the isles now but there is some on the section of Great Britain that lies nearest. This is the region known as Cornwall, and although the Cornish tin mines have been exploited for some three thousand years, they still produce small quantities.

Between 1500 B.C. and 1000 B.C., when the Phoenician ships were sailing across the ocean to Great Britain, the Scilly Islands and Cornwall must have been busy places. After 1000 B.C., when the importance of bronze declined, with the discovery of ways to extract iron, the tin trade fell off and the importance of Cornwall withered.

Memories must have lingered on of a time when the southwestern tip of that peninsula contained a thriving town, and legends arose to explain why that town no longer existed. The section between the Scillies and the tip of Cornwall (the legends said) was once dry land and made up the kingdom of Lyonesse. It figured in the legends of King Arthur as the home of one of the most famous of the knights, Sir Tristram, and has long been one of those twilight lands of romance that can be found in storybooks but not on the map. It is my suggestion, then, that Lyonesse is but the vague memory of the Tin Islands.

One might suppose that Great Britain would have been dragged into the circle of civilization, at least just a little way, as a result of this trade, but that was not so. The Phoenicians were intent on keeping their monopoly. Only they knew where the Tin Islands were; thus, they could keep tight hold of the bronze supply as nowadays nations would want to keep tight hold of uranium supplies. Great Britain's trade had a very narrow base, therefore, and once the importance of bronze dwindled, what small gains its people had made slipped away.

THE COMING OF THE CELTS

While the Beaker People were erecting their stone circles

and trading their tin, trouble was brewing for them on the continent.

In central Europe, about 1200 B.C., there lived a group of peoples whom the Greeks called "Keltoi." That was probably a version of a name which the particular tribes the Greeks met called themselves. The name may have come from a word meaning "courage" in the native language; they were calling themselves "the brave ones," in other words. The name becomes "Celts" (Kelts) in the English language.

An alternate name, possibly from the same source, is "Galli," which reaches us from the Romans, and which to us has become "Gauls."

The Celts gradually spread out west and east and by 1000 B.C. occupied most of the land we now call France. In ancient times, this land was called Gaul after its Celtic inhabitants.

Not long after 1000 B.C., bands of Celts crossed the strip of sea separating the British Isles from the Continent. (At the narrowest, this strip of sea is only twenty-two miles wide, and this narrow bit of water is now called the Strait of Dover.)

Eventually they gained a permanent foothold in the southeast corner of the island, and slowly spread out. They had an advantage over the Beaker Folk in that they brought with them the new war metal — iron. Iron was much commoner than copper and tin were, and iron formed weapons that were harder, tougher and better than bronze. Iron was as superior to bronze as bronze had been to stone.

The one great disadvantage of iron was that it was more difficult to extract from its ores than copper and tin were. It was not until some time after 1500 B.C. that the proper technique of iron metallurgy was developed in the regions south of the Caspian Sea. Slowly knowledge rippled outward, and with the Celts it reached Great Britain which then entered the "Iron Age."

By 300 B.C., Celtic tribes were in full control of almost all the island of Great Britain. Some of the tribes eventually passed on to Ireland, too.

Not only did the Celts bring iron with them; they also brought with them important improvements in daily living — the use of wood for floors and doors, for instance, and such minor amenities as razors for men and cosmetics for women.

Celtic towns grew to respectable size, considerably larger than anything that had been seen previously. The largest, perhaps, was on the site now occupied by Glastonbury, in the southwestern portion of the island, ninety-five miles west of London.

The Celtic languages are a branch of the great Indo-European group of languages. These have a common grammatical basis and an easily followed variation in fundamental vocabulary, and are spoken through wide stretches of Europe and Asia from the British Isles to India.

One Celtic dialect that spread out over Great Britain is known as "Brythonic." This name was undoubtedly derived from the name which the tribe that spoke it gave to themselves; and it eventually gave rise to the word "Britain." In speaking of the Celtic inhabitants of the island, I will refer to them as "Britons."

The Celtic invaders of Ireland spoke another Celtic dialect called "Goidelic." The version of this word which survives today is "Gaelic."

By the time the Celts had gained control of the British Isles, they had reached their period of maximum power in Europe. Not only had they taken over most of Britain and Gaul, they had spread westward through Spain and eastward as far as the regions we now call Poland and Rumania.

They even poured across the Alps and invaded Italy. In 390 B.C., the Gauls (as the Romans called them) took Rome itself. To be sure, Rome was merely a small town in central Italy at the time. It had not as yet made any mark on the world, and had for some three and a half centuries been doing nothing more than fighting it out with neighboring towns as undistinguished as itself. The Gauls eventually left and Rome recov-

ered* but northern Italy remained Celtic for several hundred
years more.

Over a century later, Gauls raided further east, penetrating
the very centers of civilization. In 279 B.C., they pushed into
Greece, slaughtering and ravaging. Groups even crossed the
Aegean Sea and penetrated the peninsula of Asia Minor. Finally, they were defeated and settled down in the central regions of that peninsula. Those regions came to be called
"Galatia" or "land of the Gauls." *

That, however, was the Celtic high point. Enemies were
gathering both from the direction of civilization and from that
of barbarism.

The Romans, having recovered from the sack of their town
by the Gauls, had gone on with amazing speed to establish their
control over larger and larger sections of Italy. By 270 B.C.,
when the Gauls were settling in Galatia, Rome had already
made itself master over all of Italy south of the Celtic section.

The Roman armies were by now too well organized for the
more primitive Gauls to resist. By 222 B.C., the Romans had advanced to the Alps and had absorbed the Celtic regions in
northern Italy.

Meanwhile, there was, in the region we would now call
northern Germany and Scandinavia, another group of tribes
which did not speak any of the Celtic dialects. Their language
was also Indo-European but belonged to another sub-group.
They were the Germans.

The Celts, in their own expansion, had not been able to
take the German lands, but had surrounded them on all sides.
As time went on, though, population pressure forced the German tribes to push southward. The Celtic lines held at first but
the pressure was inexorable.

By 100 B.C. the Celts in eastern Europe were being overcome

* see my book THE ROMAN REPUBLIC (Houghton Mifflin, 1966)
* see my book THE GREEKS (Houghton Mifflin, 1965)

and the Germans had moved as far to the west as the Rhine
River. Across the Rhine, the Germans and the Celts faced each
other. What made the position particularly uncomfortable for
the Celts was that to the south, the Roman power had
now swallowed almost all the Mediterranean lands.

Even at this point of crisis for the Celts, Britain remained
secure. As was the case so often in the history of the island,
the twenty-two-mile stretch of open sea that made up the
Strait of Dover was a super-moat, keeping off all casual
enemies.

To be sure, daring voyagers from the civilized lands of the
Mediterranean occasionally visited Britain, so that it wasn't
entirely lost to view.

One famous visit took place about 300 B.C. It was that of
Pytheas of Massalia (the modern Marseilles).

Massalia was the westernmost outpost of Greek civilization,
and it was in continuous competition with the great Phoenician
colony of Carthage on the north African shore. The Carthagin-
ians were no strangers to the open Atlantic, and finally Pytheas,
the most daring of all the Massalian voyagers, followed them
there.

Pytheas was the first Greek to emerge from the Mediterranean, and he apparently explored the northwestern coasts of
Europe in some detail. He wrote up an account of his voyages
which is, unfortunately, lost to us. We know of them only by
references in later authors who, for the most part, did not take
Pytheas seriously, but thought him to be the type of traveler
who comes back to astonish the naive home folks with tall tales
that can't be checked.

Actually, what we can find out about his accounts seems very
often to have been quite accurate, as nearly as we can tell. He
apparently visited Britain and noted the fact that they threshed
their wheat in closed barns rather than in the open air as in the
Mediterranean lands. This must have seemed odd and even
laughable to the Greek readers of Pytheas' account, but it made

a lot of sense. After all, the damp and rainy weather of Britain made open-air threshing highly impractical. Pytheas also mentioned the Britonic habit of making beer and ale out of cereals and of drinking fermented honey (mead). This, too, would have been an interesting oddity to the wine-drinking Mediterranean peoples.

But what is left us of Pytheas' accounts tells us nothing about the actual tribal organizations of the island, nothing about personalities, or about government, religion or society.

JULIUS CAESAR

Although Britain may have felt secure in the decades after 100 B.C., it could not have remained indifferent to events in Gaul.

Britain traded freely with Gaul. The two regions were drawn together by common language and customs, and were kept friendly by the fact that oceanic separation prevented them from encroaching upon each other's territory. When the sky darkened for Gaul, it had to cloud over for Britain as well.

The beginning of Gallic troubles came with a warlord who had arisen among the Germans, one whom the Romans knew as Ariovistus (ar''ee-oh-vis'tus). He united a number of tribes under his rule and then led his warband into Gaul in 71 B.C. For a dozen years, his influence spread as he defeated one after another of the disunited Gallic tribes.

At first the Romans looked upon him as an ally. They considered the Gauls their hereditary enemies (they had never forgiven the Gauls the sack of Rome in 390 B.C.), and the enemy of one's enemies is a friend. Ariovistus, however, was entirely too successful and, in consequence, Roman regard for him rapidly cooled.

Furthermore, one of the leading Romans of the time was Caius Julius Caesar. Caesar was a man of vaulting ambition who had everything he needed to rule the vast Roman realm except a military reputation and an army loyal to himself. These he intended to develop and Gaul seemed the place to do so.

In 58 B.C., he led the Roman legions into Gaul, and there he revealed himself (rather unexpectedly) to be a military leader of the first rank. He defeated the Gauls, then marched against Ariovistus, defeated him as well, threw him across the Rhine, then crossed it himself in pursuit.

It was Caesar, in the book he wrote about these campaigns, who first mentioned the "Druids." This was the name given by the Celts to those among themselves who were the repositories of what learning existed in their society. The Celts were not yet literate and the Druids retained the oral traditions of their people, putting them into swinging poetry for easier memorization. (The Druid tradition of poetry remains even today among the Celtic remnants in Europe, such as the Welsh and Irish.)

Naturally, they were a priesthood, for their learning and their understanding of the movements of the heavenly bodies gave them, in the eyes of the common people, a knowledge of how to placate the gods and foretell the future.

The Romans later suppressed the Druids, and by no gentle means, because they represented the national traditions of their people and were the center of anti-Roman movements. The Romans felt they could not keep the conquered Celtic regions quiet nor adequately Romanize the population unless they destroyed the Druids. As an excuse, they maintained that Druidism was extraordinarily evil, involving black magic and human sacrifice.

Because of Roman writings on the subject, we think of Druidism today as a dark and brutal religion and many imagine Stonehenge to have been built as a shrine at which their evil rites might be practiced. Yet it is quite likely that Druidism was no worse than other primitive religions and as for Stonehenge, that was built a thousand years before the first Druids appeared in Britain.

And what little of the Druidic tradition survived the Romans was completely wiped out after the coming of Christianity. It comes about, then, that we know just about nothing concerning Druidism except what we are told by its bitter enemies.

The Britonic* tribes were not so blind as to be unaware that Caesar was conquering Gaul, and that this would be a tragedy for them for several reasons. In the first place, Gallic trade might be diverted southward toward Italy and that would leave Britain the poorer. Secondly, a strong Roman force lining the opposite shore of the Channel would be a standing threat to Britain. Finally, there must also have been sympathy for fellow-Celts under the heel of an oppressor. (It is all too easy to forget that there are emotional motivations in history as well as economic ones.)

The Britonic tribes, from their sanctuary behind the Channel, did what they could to encourage rebellion among the conquered Gauls, and to send whatever help they could. Thus, when the Veneti (a Gallic tribe in what is now Brittany) revolted in 56 B.C., Caesar found clear evidence of Britonic help. Caesar put down the revolt, but was annoyed.

He was in no real mood to conduct an elaborate campaign across the Channel. If the Gauls rose behind his back (as they were quite likely to do) he might have trouble getting back in time and might even find himself isolated on a hostile and mysterious island. And yet to allow the matter to rest without doing anything would be to encourage the Britonic tribes to make trouble in Gaul indefinitely.

---

* The usual adjective would be "British" but that refers to the modern kingdom of Great Britain and I prefer to use "Britonic" for the Celtic land of Roman times.

Caesar therefore planned a quick raid; nothing serious or permanent. He just wanted to bloody the Britonic nose and teach the islanders to keep hands off the continent.

In August, 55 B.C., he ferried two legions (ten thousand men) across the Strait of Dover and landed them on the Kentish coast, along the extreme southwest of Britain. (The name Kent is from the Britonic tribe "Cantii" who then dwelt there. At least Cantii is the Roman version of the name. Canterbury, the most famous of the Kentish towns, is "town of the Cantii.")

Caesar's raid was not at all successful. The Britonic warriors reacted violently and the rough seas threatened the safety of the beached Roman ships. After three weeks, Caesar was glad enough to take his men back to Gaul, with an embarrassing number of casualties and nothing much to show for them.

The situation was now worse than it would have been if Caesar had done nothing at all. The Britons felt they had defeated the Roman general and were now bolder than ever in their interference in Gaul. Caesar would have to try again and this time, despite the risks, he had to use a force big enough to accomplish something.

In 54 B.C., he crossed the Channel again, with a fleet of eight hundred ships and no less than five legions, including two thousand cavalry. The Britons dared not dispute the landing of such a host but retired, and Caesar had his foothold.

It was next necessary for Caesar to drive inland and force the capitulation of enough Britons to make it quite clear to the islanders that they were defeated and that Rome was not to be trifled with. The Britons fought valiantly but were driven back, step by step, to the Thames (tems) river, the largest in southern Britain.

The territory immediately north of the Thames was under the rule of a Britonic tribal leader, Cassivelaunus (kas"ih-veh-loh'nus), the first islander to distinguish himself in history by name.

Cassivelaunus fought resolutely against the Romans, practicing a scorched earth policy when he retreated, and tried to persuade the Kentish tribes to burn the Roman ships. His skill and resolution did not avail against Caesar in the end, however, and he was forced to capitulate.

Once again Caesar returned to Gaul. He had spent a spring and summer in Britain this time. He had not left any occupying force, or even the smallest garrison, so that the Britons were as free as ever they had been before.

But he had left something behind, at that — the Roman name. Caesar had accomplished his purpose; he had showed the Britons what the legions could do, and they had been forced to bow their heads to the eagles. Gaul would be left alone now, or at least more nearly alone than it would have been otherwise.

And it was. Gaul was rapidly Romanized and became one of the pleasantest provinces of the realm. The Celtic language and law gave way to Latin, and Britain found itself isolated from the continent not only by the Channel but by an ever-widening gulf of cultural difference.

2

ROMAN BRITAIN

THE ROMAN CONQUEST

And yet what immediately followed Caesar's invasions was not so bad for Britain, if nationalist emotions can be overlooked. Roman rule over Gaul was enlightened, and the Gauls were much better off under the Romans than under their own chaotic tribal system.

As it turned out, the Britons could trade with the new Gaul as they had traded with the old. What's more, they could trade to better advantage, for the riches of civilization now poured into Gaul and from there into Britain. In fact, the southern tribes of Britain began to adopt a Roman coloring themselves and Latin inscriptions appeared upon their coins.

The difficulty was that the situation could not remain as it was. The Britons considered themselves free and independent, but the Romans felt that Caesar's second expedition had made Britain a kind of Roman protectorate and there was always the temptation for them to occupy the land.

Shortly after Caesar's death, Rome had become a kind of monarchy with Caesar's great-nephew Augustus at its head. Augustus bore the title of "Imperator" ("leader") which has become "Emperor" in English — so that we may speak now of the Roman Empire.*

Augustus had some vague plans for occupying Britain, but there was much to do in pacifying and reorganizing a Roman realm that had been racked by fifteen years of civil war after Caesar's conquest of Gaul. Furthermore, there was fighting against German tribes east of Gaul and that was far more pressing than the matter of a distant island. So what with one thing and another, Augustus never got around to dealing with Britain. Nor did his successor, Tiberius.

The third emperor, Caligula, was more seriously tempted, thanks to a piece of internal Britonic politics.

The most powerful chieftain in southern Britain during this period was Cunobelinus (kyoo″noh-beh-ligh′nus) who had maintained a careful friendship with Rome and had formed an alliance with Augustus. (An alternate version of his name is "Cymbeline." William Shakespeare wrote a play by that name, which was set in the Britain of this period, but which was, of course, quite unhistorical.)

But no ruler, however cautious, can guard against intrigue in his own household. Cunobelinus' son, Adminius (ad-mih′-nee-us), having rebelled, was defeated and sent into exile. In A.D. 40,† he crossed into Gaul and eventually made an offer to cede Britain to Rome if Roman troops would take him back

---

* see my book "The Roman Empire" (Houghton Mifflin, 1967)
† Years that follow the birth of Jesus are often given the initials A.D. ("Anno Domini" or "year of the Lord") to distinguish them from the years B.C. ("before Christ"). In this book, almost all dates are A.D., and I will henceforth give them as mere numerals.

to his own land and place him on its throne. He would then, apparently, be content to rule as a Roman puppet.

The Emperor Caligula was a vain youngster who had had a nervous breakdown of some sort and had become quite dangerously mad. He found it amusing to send an army to the northern coast of Gaul, but was not really interested in the arduous task of crossing the sea and campaigning in the island. The empty gesture was enough for him.

Cunobelinus died in 43, however, and was succeeded by two sons who were much more anti-Roman than their father. At least the Romans said they were, and found a useful puppet against them in the person of a Kentish chieftain named Verica. He had long lived in Rome and went through the motions of putting in an official plea for help. This gave the Romans a chance to invade Britain under the pretext of helping an ally. Under Claudius, the fourth Emperor of Rome, who had succeeded Caligula in 41, the full-scale conquest of Britain began at last.

In the very year of Cunobelinus' death, the Roman general Aulus Plautius and forty thousand men followed Caesar's old route of nearly a century before and landed in Kent. Rapidly they subdued the area south of the Thames, killing one of Cunobelinus' sons and leaving the other, Caractacus (kuh-rak'-tuh-kus) to carry on the fight alone.

The Romans were intent on making this an actual occupation, and when they forded the Thames River they established a fort and a garrison at the spot. This developed into a town the Romans called Londinium and which later became London. It is a safe bet that no one in the Roman army could possibly have imagined that the time would come when that fort would grow into the largest city in the world and would rule over territories three or four times as large as the Roman Empire at its widest.

Claudius himself made a trip to Britain (the first Roman

Emperor to appear on the island) to receive the surrender of a number of the tribes.

Caractacus had to abandon his capital at Camulodunum (kam"yoo-loh-dyoo'num) some forty miles northeast of London. Camulodunum was then made the capital of the new Roman province of Britain and it came to be called Colchester (from Latin words meaning "colonial camp").*

Caractacus fled to what is now southern Wales, but was finally captured in 51 and sent to Rome as a prisoner. His family went with him and he was well-treated by Claudius who was not at all a bad emperor.

Slowly and laboriously, under a succession of generals, the Romans extended their hold, pinning down each area by establishing a fort garrisoned by a few hundred legionaries.

A work of conquest is always hastened and made easier if the conquered people are well-treated and if the fact of defeat is not rubbed too sharply into their skins. Such enlightened behavior is, however, sometimes too much to ask. Soldiers naturally detest an enemy which, by the very nature of their losing fight, must rely heavily on traps, ambushes and terrorism, and often the soldiers can't distinguish between resisting natives and friendly ones anyway.

That was the case in 60 to everyone's loss. At that time, the tribe of the Iceni (igh-see'nee), in the area just north of the Roman capital at Colchester, was under the rule of a leader who maintained himself as a humble and loyal Roman vassal. He died that year without a male heir, leaving two daughters and his queen, Boudicca (boo-dik'uh).† The dead father had taken the precaution of leaving part of his wealth

---

* In later legend, "Old King Cole," of nursery-rhyme fame, was supposed to have ruled there and the town was supposed to have been named for him, but that is just a story.
† She is better, but less accurately, known to later generations as Boadicea (boh"ad-ih-see'uh).

to the Emperor Nero, the successor of Claudius, in the hope
that this would win his family favored treatment and that his
daughters would be allowed to rule over his land.

To the Roman governor, however, it seemed that the land
should become Roman outright, since there was no male heir.
All the property was taken and the daughters of the old leader
were, according to the story, brutally mistreated. When the
Queen, Boudicca, objected, she was whipped.

Boudicca, brooding over the injustice of it all (and surely we
can't help but sympathize with her) waited until a good part
of the Roman army was off in the western hills, subduing the
tribesmen there. She then spurred her own and surrounding
tribesmen into a wild rebellion against the Romans.

The Britonic rebels burned Colchester and utterly destroyed
London, slaughtering every Roman they could find and many
of the pro-Roman Britons as well. Roman reports (possibly ex-
aggerated) placed the number of those killed at seventy thousand.

Boudicca, defeated at last by the returning Roman army,
killed herself, but the entire Roman structure in Britain was
shaken to its core. The island that had seemed pacified was
clearly not at all so and all the work had to be done over again.
The task was made all the worse by the fact that Nero's rule was
ending in chaos and that for a time, Roman internal politics
were going to make full-scale military action impossible.

THE NORTHERN LIMIT

Rome settled down in 69 when Vespasian seized power and
made himself emperor. He was a capable general who had
served under Aulus Plautius in 43 in the campaign that first

established Roman power in Britain, so he knew the island.

It was 77, however, before he felt secure enough on the continent to spare a large army for Britain. In that year he sent Gnaeus Julius Agricola (uh-grik'oh-luh) to Britain. He had been a very capable general who likewise had had experience on the island, for he had fought there during Boudicca's rebellion.

Agricola found Britain reasonably pacified by then, but he labored to smooth the way toward its Romanization and to extend the Roman sway northward. He conquered all of western Britain and led his armies north as far as the Tay River, in what is now central Scotland.

The only tribes left unsubdued in the entire island were in the northernmost highlands, the poorest and least desirable portion. This did not represent a large area and Agricola well knew its limits for he had sent his fleet on a voyage of circumnavigation of Britain.

Agricola himself dreamed of completing the conquest of all of Britain and even of neighboring Ireland, but Domitian, the younger son of Vespasian, who became emperor in 81, thought otherwise. The northern highlands, he guessed, would be next to impossible to subdue (all later experience showed he was right) and if they were taken, Rome would have very little for its pains. In addition, there were problems with barbarians on the Danube which were much more immediate and important.

In 84, therefore, he recalled Agricola with the northern highlands still unconquered and initiated a strictly defensive policy in the island.

The northern tribes were called "Caledonians" ("Caledonia" remains a poetic name for the northern third of the island to this day). They were pre-Celtic in race although there was, by then, considerable Celtic admixture.

Agricola had defeated the Caledonians in 84 at Mount Graupius, an unknown site. This has come to be misspelled as Gram-

MAP I
Roman Britain

CALEDONIA (SCOTLAND)

Grampian Mountains

Tay River

Firth of Forth

Antonine's Wall

Firth of Clyde

Hadrian's Wall

IRELAND

Eboracum (York)

Lincoln

ROMAN BRITAIN

ICENI

CAMBRIA

Camulodunum (Colchester)

Verulanium
Londinium (London)

Stonehenge
Thames River

KENT

Glastonbury

CORNWALL

Strait of Dover

Scilly Islands (Tin Islands)

FRANCE

pius, and it has given its name to the Grampian Mountains that run in an east-west curve about seventy miles north of modern Edinburgh.

The defeat merely sent the Caledonians scurrying deeper into the mountains, and they continued to be a source of periodic disturbance to the Romans. Even while the southern three-fifths of the island remained quiet, as many as forty thousand soldiers had to stand constantly at bay in the north.

The slow but steady Roman bleeding in northern Britain became more and more difficult to endure as the Empire found its troubles increasing everywhere. To be sure, the Emperor Trajan had conducted great campaigns in the east in the years immediately after 100 and had won spectacular victories, adding sizable pieces of territory to the Empire. This, however, had been a kind of last gasp, and the Roman army in Britain had to be stripped so that more men could be sent east. The task of holding off the Caledonians became harder than ever.

Trajan's successor, Hadrian, visited Britain in 122 for a personal view of the situation.

Hadrian's policy was the direct opposite of Trajan's. He was a man of peace and he wanted only to establish a defensible frontier which could be kept intact with a minimum of effort.

He decided therefore to fortify the Britonic frontier in the most direct possible way. He would build a wall across the island and, to do so with the least effort, he chose a point where the island was quite narrow. This is along the east-west line from what is now the city of Carlisle to what is now the city of Newcastle, a distance of about seventy-five miles. This meant a strategic withdrawal of a hundred miles from the extreme northern limits subdued by Agricola.

This fortification, "Hadrian's Wall," was a substantial one indeed. It was built of rock, was from six to ten feet thick, fifteen feet high, and had a broad ditch in front. Observation towers were interspersed along it and it was backed by a line of sixteen forts.

For a while, this new strategy was eminently successful. Cal-
edonian attacks fell to nothing and behind the wall Britain
experienced a profound peace. Cities grew larger, and London, which had become the chief port and trading center of the
island, attained a population of fifteen thousand. Five thousand miles of Roman roads sprayed out of London in every
direction and the upper classes built villas on the Italian style
with bathrooms and courtyards. (The remains of five hundred
villas have been uncovered by modern diggers.)

Indeed, the Romans eventually felt confident enough to wish
to push northward once more. Under Hadrian's successor, An-
toninus Pius, the legions advanced again.

Some ninety miles beyond Hadrian's Wall, two opposing
arms of the sea, the Firth of Forth and the Firth of Clyde cut
deeply into the island. Between them is a thirty-five-mile stretch
of land running from what is now Glasgow to Edinburgh. In
142, a new wall was built across this stretch ("Antonine's
Wall"). It was by no means as elaborate as Hadrian's Wall,
and was built of packed earth rather than rock. But it, too, had
a ditch in front and forts in the rear.   .

Antonine's Wall was, however, a little too far forward. It
could not be maintained easily and the Caledonians were able
to puncture it and make considerable trouble.

Then, too, the assassination of Emperor Commodus in 192 let
loose a troubled period of civil war in Rome, as had the assassination of Nero a century and a quarter before. This time the
civil war was much longer and much worse, and Britain was
directly involved.

The general in charge of the legions in Britain, Decimus Clo-
dius Albinus (al-bigh'nus) was one of those who aspired to
the imperial throne. He led much of his army into Gaul in
an effort to enforce his claim and was met there by Septimius
Severus (see-vee'rus), another general. Severus won out in
197 and became emperor but in the meantime the northern
reaches of the province of Britain (with its army in pursuit of a

will-o'-the-wisp in Gaul) had fallen into complete chaos. In
the half-century since Antonine's Wall had been built, Hadrian's Wall had been allowed to fall into disrepair and now the
Caledonians had little trouble in penetrating both.

Severus and his sons were forced to lead an army into Britain
and there undertake punitive expeditions against the Caledonians in 209. The old general saw clearly enough that Rome
would have to pull in its horns. Antonine's Wall was abandoned
forever. Severus ordered Hadrian's Wall refurbished and
strengthened and made it the frontier once and for all.

Having seen to this, he retired, worn out and sick, to Eboracum (the modern York) and there, in 211, he died. He was
the first Roman emperor to die in Britain.

THE INNER LIMIT

After Severus' time, the Caledonians disappear from history. Replacing them were a people called the Picts. This
name seems to be derived from a Latin word for "painted"
and some historians think it may refer to their habit of painting
or tattooing their bodies. This is not certain. The name Pict
may simply be the Latin way of saying some native name of
unknown meaning. It may be, too, that the Picts and Caledonians were essentially the same racially, but that one tribe
replaced another as dominant and that the change in name
resulted.

In addition, the northern portion of Britain was invaded by
Celtic tribes from northern Ireland at about this time. These
new tribes were called Scots by the Romans and it is they who
have given their name to modern Scotland.

The confusion in the north lightened the pressures on Ro-

man Britain and gave it nearly a century of peace. This peace
was the more precious since the Empire underwent a long
period of anarchy, with competing generals tearing at the fab-
ric of the realm and barbarians ravaging the outskirts. The
Channel saved Britain from suffering its share of that misery.

More and more Roman did that portion of the island under
imperial control seem to become. So Roman did it seem, in
fact, that centuries later the islanders retained a dim memory
of their land as not only under Roman control but as Roman in fact. The Romans had tried to connect themselves with
the superior culture of Greece by inventing their descent from
Aeneas, a hero of the fallen city of Troy. And in later centuries
on Britain, long after the Romans were gone, there arose the
legend in Britain that a great-grandson of Aeneas, named Brutus, fled Italy and came to Britain, which received its name
from him. He founded a city called "New Troy" which eventually became London.

This is sheer fantasy, of course, arising from the memory of
the Romans, and from a desire to claim noble descent, and also
from the sheer coincidence that "Britain" is somewhat similar
in sound to the common Roman name "Brutus."

It is important to remember that despite appearances, the
Romanization of Britain was not really thoroughgoing. In other
Celtic provinces, such as those of Spain and Gaul, Romanization was complete. The Celtic language and culture vanished
and when, in later centuries, German barbarians broke down
the Roman structure in the west, these western provinces clung
to Roman ways and the Roman language for long centuries.
(Even today, French and Spanish are clearly descended from
the Latin and are examples of "Romance languages.")

Britain was farther from Rome and separated from it by the
sea. It was less extensively colonized by non-Britons. What's
more, it had at its borders something that neither Spain nor
Gaul had; it had a reservoir of fanatically independent Celts,
who kept their language and tradition inviolate, and whose

very existence must have seemed a standing reproach to nationalistic Britons.

It is not surprising then that Romanization was to be found chiefly in the cities and among the upper classes. As it happens, it is the cities and the upper classes that make the most noise, but beyond them was the countryside and the peasantry, and among them a mute Celticism continued as a kind of unbreakable inner limit to the Roman advance.

Even religion probably served the Celtic resistance. To be sure, the native Druidism declined while Roman cults were imported, as were eastern religions such as Mithraism from Persia and the worship of Isis and Serapis from Egypt. However there was one eastern religion that was unpopular with the Roman authorities and it may have appealed to some of the Britons for that very reason. The religion was Christianity.

The origins of Britonic Christianity are completely lost in legend. According to the later legend-makers, St. Paul and St. Peter visited Britain, but this can be dismissed out of hand.

A more elaborate legend involves Joseph of Arimathea, a wealthy Jew who was friendly to Jesus. His appearance in the New Testament story takes place after the crucifixion when he asks Pontius Pilate for permission to remove Jesus from the cross. With the permission granted, Joseph removed the body, wrapped it in fine linen and deposited it in his own tomb.

Legends naturally multiplied about the figure of this charitable man. He was supposed to have been imprisoned for forty-two years and during that interval was kept alive by the miraculous influence of the "Holy Grail." This was the cup from which Jesus had drunk wine during the Last Supper and in which Joseph had caught Jesus' blood during the crucifixion.

Eventually Joseph was released by the Emperor Vespasian and (all this according to the legend) took with him not only the Holy Grail, but also the spear with which Jesus had been wounded while on the cross. In Britain, Joseph founded an abbey at Glastonbury and began the conversion of the Britons.

Naturally, there is nothing to this legend, which was elaborated centuries after the supposed time it had happened by the monks at Glastonbury Abbey. Still there is no question that Glastonbury Abbey is one of the oldest centers of Christian worship (if not the oldest) in Britain, whether it was founded by Joseph of Arimathea or not. It is interesting that Glastonbury, the one-time great Celtic center, should be thus open to Christianity, and it makes it tempting to suppose that this foreign, Roman-derided religion was one more way for the Celts to maintain their resistance to things Roman.

The general Roman instability which occupied much of the third century came to an end in 284, when a strong general, Diocletian, made himself emperor. He decided that in order to bear the burdens of empire properly, there had to be two emperors, one in the east and one in the west, and each ought to have an assistant and destined successor, called a "Caesar."

The Caesar in the west was Constantius Chlorus. One of his tasks was to seize control of Britain, which, at the time, had been under the power of a dissident general for a decade. Constantius Chlorus performed that task in 297 and thereafter the island remained his favorite seat of government.

At the time of Constantius' appointment to the rank of Caesar in 293 he was married to a woman named Helena, whom he had met as a serving girl in Asia Minor. He had a young son by her, a son named Constantine. One of the conditions of Constantius' appointment, however, was that he divorce Helena and marry the stepdaughter of the western emperor. This he did.

Under his mild rule, Britain was fortunate indeed and was spared a strenuous ordeal. In 303, Diocletian was induced to institute the last and most severe of the persecutions which the Christians underwent at Roman hands. By this time, the Christians had grown to number nearly half the population in the eastern reaches of the empire and the pagans must have felt it was a matter of wiping them out now or seeing them take control.

In the west, however, the Christians were much fewer in number and in Britain they made up perhaps no more than one in ten of the population. Constantius Chlorus, though no Christian, was a tolerant man, and saw to it that Diocletian's edict against the Christians was simply ignored. There was no persecution in Britain.

Partly because of this, Constantius was remembered with favor by the later inhabitants of the island. His first wife, Helena, later became a saint and in her old age (legend says) she visited Jerusalem and there found the true cross on which Jesus had been crucified. The further legend grew up in Britain that she had been a Britonic princess and a daughter of no less a person than Old King Cole himself — a rather amusing promotion for a servant girl from Asia Minor.

Despite Constantius Chlorus' mildness the first martyr tale in Britain is placed in his time. It involves a Christian convert named Alban born in Verulamium (ver"yoo-lay'/mee-um), a town twenty miles north of London. It had been an important early center of Roman power and had been one of the cities burned in Boudicca's revolt. Alban is supposed to have been martyred during Diocletian's persecution. Near his tomb in Verulamium, first a church and then a monastery was built and about these there formed the nucleus of the modern town of St. Albans.

The tale of Alban is also quite doubtful, but soon Britonic Christianity was to come into the light of undoubted day. In 314, a council of bishops was held at Arles in southern Gaul, to settle one of the doctrinal disputes that were then exciting the Church fathers. The records show clearly that Britain was by then organized into bishoprics, for no less than three Britonic bishops were in attendance, one from London, one from Lincoln and one from York.

THE ROMANS LEAVE

In 305, Diocletian and his co-emperor in the west abdicated. In the drawn-out struggle for the succession, Constantius Chlorus tried to take part, but he was fatally ill and in 306 he died in York, as had Septimius Severus nearly a century before.

Constantius' son Constantine was at the imperial court, where he was being held as polite hostage for the good behavior of his father. He manged to escape, though, and to reach Britain just before his father's death. The Roman troops at once proclaimed him emperor.

He returned to the continent with an army, won victory after victory and by 324 was sole emperor over the united Roman realm. By that time he had made Christianity the official religion of the empire and in 330 he founded a new capital, Constantinople.

Through the fourth century, Rome sank steadily but managed, somehow, to hold its own by dint of an ever more intense effort against the German barbarians who, from their base east of the Rhine and north of the Danube, constantly threatened the empire. Even Britain, relatively secure from continental invasion, was open to forays from the Picts and Scots, who infiltrated across Hadrian's Wall and who, moreover, raided its coasts by sea.

Rome roused itself to make one last effort to stabilize the situation in Britain. In 367, the Emperor Valentinian sent his ablest general, Theodosius, into Britain. There he defeated the Picts, reorganized the Roman forces, and marched in triumph into London. During his short stay on the island, Theodosius placed the Roman administration on a sound footing once more and then left for service elsewhere. He was executed in Africa as a result of some petty intrigue, but his son, another

Theodosius, became emperor in 379. He was to be the last great emperor over a united Roman Empire.

After the death of the Emperor Theodosius in 395, the western portion of the Empire began its final collapse. This began with an invasion of Italy by a German warband.*

The desperate Roman leaders managed to defeat the first armies that invaded Italy, but only at the price of calling in the legions from the provinces, thus throwing them open and defenseless to other invaders.

In 407, the Roman legions of Britain (the last organized Roman troops in the west outside Italy) embarked for Gaul. This was not so much an attempt to save the empire as it was a plot by the general of those legions who wanted to take advantage of the chaos to make himself emperor.

He failed to do so, but for Britain it didn't matter whether he failed or succeeded. What counted for the island was that the Roman troops had left Britain and were never to return. Four and a half centuries after the first Roman soldiers had stormed ashore in Kent under the banners of Julius Caesar, the last Roman soldiers left Britain forever on an ignoble errand.

The Britons were thrown on their own resources, fighting off Picts and Scots as best they could. Region after region was devastated and the Roman skin peeled off. As the wild Celts poured into Britain, the older ways, never entirely forgotten, reasserted themselves.

The Latin language gave way to Brythonic again. Civilization receded, even Christianity faded; Britain became Britain again, almost as though the long Roman episode had never been.

* see my book THE DARK AGES (Houghton Mifflin, 1968)

3

THE COMING OF THE SAXONS

THE CELTIC RETREAT

The details of the backward slide into barbarism are lost to us. With the passing of the Romans and the destruction of the Roman veneer, no reliable contemporary was left to write history, no one to bear witness.

We must suppose, though, that the Picts and Scots did not roll southward unopposed. The Britons of the south may have returned to their Celtic heritage but even so they would fight for their lives and their material possessions, for their higher level of culture and their higher standard of living, against the barbarians of the north.

What battles were fought, what deeds were done, what disasters were suffered, we cannot say for certain. The best we have to go by is the material in a book called "Excidio Britanniae" ("The Ruin of Britain") written about 550 by a priestly historian named Gildas.

The accuracy of the history is rather doubtful as it seems to have been written for the purpose of pointing morals — that is, to show that the wicked are justly punished for their sins. (This has its place, but it is not the way to write objective history, for it becomes too tempting to twist things to point up the moral more sharply.) Furthermore, some historical references are clearly wrong, as when Gildas states that both Hadrian's Wall and Antonine's Wall were built about 400.

In any case, taking the tale for what it is worth, Gildas says that about 450, Britonic leaders despaired of holding off the northern barbarians. They sent for help to the Roman general, Aetius, pointing out that they were caught between the barbarian Picts and the inhospitable ocean and must be either slaughtered or drowned. (An early case of being between the devil and the deep sea.) Aetius could offer no help, which is not surprising, for although he was just about the last competent general the Romans were to have in the west, he had his hands full, and more than full, with the Goths and the Huns.

A Britonic leader named Vortigern (vawr'tih-gurn) is then supposed to have been forced to look elsewhere in sheer desperation. Since the south had failed, he turned east.

East of Britain is the four-hundred-mile wide North Sea. On the other side are shores which are now occupied by the nations of Denmark and West Germany. In the fifth century, there was a tribe of Germans dwelling on the Danish shore who called themselves "Jutes." The peninsula which they inhabited, stretching northward toward modern Norway and Sweden and forming the mainland territories of Denmark, is still called Jutland to this day in English. (It is "Jylland" in Danish.)

South of the Jutes, in the part of modern Germany lying just south of Denmark (Schleswig) lived the Angles, and to their west along what is now the northern coastline of West Germany, lived the Saxons.

It was to these German tribes that Vortigern is supposed to

have sent his plea for help. In particular, he appealed to the brothers, Hengist and Horsa, who ruled over the Jutes. (Some people think that since Hengist and Horsa mean "stallion" and "horse," the whole story can be dismissed as legendary, but maybe not. Personal names can often be odd.)

The Jutes answered the call with alacrity and in 456 landed in Kent. (The somewhat later historian, Bede, makes this crucial date 449.) Just half a century had passed since the old Roman masters had left the country and now the new Germanic masters had arrived, for what followed is surely what was to have been expected. Foreigners who are called in to help one side in an internal struggle almost invariably destroy both sides and take over for themselves. It is perhaps the clearest lesson history teaches, the one most frequently repeated and perhaps the least frequently learned.

What happened, according to the legend, is that Vortigern agreed to marry Hengist's daughter, Rowena, and a great marriage feast was held to celebrate the friendship and alliance of the two peoples. At the feast, the Britons were carefully encouraged to drink deeply and were then slaughtered by the Jutes, who took over Kent and made it their own.

Other Germanic tribes were not long in following them. In 477, a band of Saxons passed through the Strait of Dover, leapfrogged the Kentish territory of the Jutes and landed on the southern coast of England. There they established what was to be the southernmost of three Saxon kingdoms, Sussex ("south Saxons"). Soon after another band landed still farther west to found Wessex ("west Saxons"). North of Kent, Essex ("east Saxons") was founded. (Essex and Sussex still remain as the names of English counties.)

Considerably later, about 540 or so, the Angles were founding a series of kingdoms north of the Thames. They landed first in the land of the Iceni, where once Boudicca had raised her standard of revolt four centuries before. There they founded what came to be called East Anglia. To its west was eventually founded Mercia, a word related to "march" which means "border land." Mercia was, for a long time, the border land against the Britons to the west.

The northern boundary of Mercia was the Humber River, an estuary that cuts deeply into the eastern coast of Britain. North of the Humber was Deira (day'ih-ruh) making up the eastern portion of what is now Yorkshire. North of Deira was Bernicia, which extended to the Firth of Forth, deep in modern Scotland.

Of the three groups, the Jutes, although first in the field, were apparently weakest. Their period of power petered out soon after 600 and Kent, where they established themselves, retains its old name, so that the Jutes are almost forgotten.

The Angles and Saxons remained prominent and indeed were closely related in language and customs so that, to all intents and purposes, they may be regarded as a single people. In modern times, the term "Anglo-Saxon" was invented to refer to them for that reason. Nothing like this compound term was ever used in their own time, however.

The four Anglian kingdoms were larger than the rest and were at first dominant over the others. At the time when the new masters of the island became known to the Continental lands, it was these Anglian kingdoms which were prominent and in the Continental writings there is therefore reference to the "land of the Angles." This became "Angle-land" or, as we would now say, "England."

This was the name used for the land by the Angles and Saxons themselves and they called themselves "English." I will not, however, use "English" to refer to the new Germanic masters of the island for that has close associations with a later time when still another invasion further altered the culture of the island.

To keep the flavor of this particular period of the island's history, I shall speak of the Germanic peoples as "Saxons," using the term to include Angles and Jutes as well.

This is justifiable, first because before the next invasion was to take place one of the Saxon kingdoms was to come to dominate the land. Secondly, the Britons in the west used "Saxon" as a general term for their Germanic enemies, perhaps because their sharpest battles were with the men of Wessex. We pick up the term from the still-popular Celtic legends that tell tales of this period of history.

The name, England, is properly used, of course, only for those portions of the island which came to be dominated by the Angles, Saxons and Jutes. The northern two-fifths of the island remained largely Celtic (albeit with considerable infiltration from the south) right down to modern times and formed the kingdom of Scotland. It infuriates Scotsmen to this day to have the entire island referred to as England. The island is Great Britain, and only the southern portion is England. (The Scottish term for the men of the southern kingdom — Sassenachs — is a form of the word "Saxon.")

The Britons, then, as return for their plea for help (if indeed that plea were really made) now found themselves fighting an enemy even more fierce and dangerous than the ones they had faced before.

They fell back westward slowly, fighting the Saxons bitterly every step of the way as once, four centuries before, they had fallen back northward before the Romans. For the most part, the Britons suffered defeat after defeat, though they kept fighting indomitably. At least once, however, they experienced an important victory.

Gildas describes a great battle, fought about 500, at a place called Mons Badonicus. The exact site is not known but wherever it was (possibly along the upper reaches of the Thames River) the Britons won a smashing victory and gained a respite for a generation.

Gildas describes the Britonic leader as having been one Ambrosius Aurelianus, who, from the name, was probably a Romanized Britain. Ambrosius must have instantly become a

Britonic hero, and his memory lingered on and grew brighter with the telling and re-telling. A later Britonic writer, Nennius, who lived about 800, harked back to this old tale of glory.

In Nennius' version, which was naturally further removed from reality than Gildas' had been, Ambrosius was transmuted into a wizard servant of Vortigern who helps him oppose the Saxons. Leading the Britonic forces in actual battle is someone named Arthur who fights twelve battles against the Saxons, the last being that of Mons Badonicus, and wins them all.

From this, by still further exaggeration and romantic invention, the great legends concerning King Arthur and his knights of the Round Table were established, tales that have maintained their hold upon our imagination down to this very day, with the latest popular version being the musical comedy "Camelot." *

Eventually, however, and despite the check at Mons Badonicus, the Saxons resumed their advance. In 577, the Saxons reached the Bristol Channel and split the Celts into two portions.

The hilly peninsula to the north was called "Wealhas" by the Saxons. The term meant "land of the foreigners" and it has come down to us as Wales. Its inhabitants are the Welsh. It seems unfair to use the name since it was the Saxons rather than the Welsh who were the foreigners at that time, but it is too late to do anything about that now. The Welsh themselves call themselves "Cymri" (kim'rih), a name related to the Cymric people, who were closely related to the Brythonic tribe.

South of the Bristol Channel was a region called "Cornwealhas" by the Saxons, a name meaning "the foreigners on the

---

* Camelot is the legendary capital of Arthur's kingdom. Its site is unknown because it may never have existed. The legend-making monks of Glastonbury, always fascinated by the Celtic past, placed Camelot at Cadbury Hill, only a dozen miles from the abbey. This may have been a way of establishing a pilgrimage attraction for the financial benefit of the abbey.

headland." This has become "Cornwall." (Sometimes, in earlier times, Cornwall was known as "West Wales" while Wales
itself was "North Wales.")

Still other Britons had been driven across the Channel
(which after this time can be called the "English Channel")
to northwestern Gaul, where the peninsula once called
Armorica became Britanny.

In Cornwall, the Celtic stand was to be a dying one. Little
by little the Celts were pushed farther back into the southeast
corner until by 950 they came completely under Saxon control.
The Cornish dialect of the ancient Brythonic tongue held on
for centuries more but by 1800, Cornish was extinct.

Wales itself was another story. It held out against the English for centuries and even when it was forced to submit, it
never entirely gave up its national self-consciousness. To this
very day Wales, with an area nearly that of Massachusetts
but with only half the population of that American state, retains its distinctive culture. The Welsh language is still spoken
by over half a million people (though it seems to be in a state
of decline).

For this reason, Wales cannot be considered part of England. If the entire region south of the Scottish border must be
spoken of, it is properly termed "England and Wales."

To summarize, then: In the fifth and sixth centuries, the island of Britain underwent an experience that was unique
among the erstwhile Roman provinces. Elsewhere, the Germanic invaders did not displace the older population but settled among them as a ruling minority. As a minority, they
gradually accepted the language and at least a form of the
religion of the conquered.

Not so in the case of the Saxon invasion of Britain. In that
island, the older population was rooted out altogether or en-
slaved and made Saxons of. In the portions of the island controlled by the Saxons, the old language died out utterly. The
only trace of the Celtic tongue in England were some place-

names. Kent, Devon, York, London, Thames, Avon and Exeter
stem from the Celtic. Cumberland, in northwestern England
is "land of the Cymri."

Aside from that, the new dominant language in England
was a completely Germanic language. This has been referred
to as "Anglo-Saxon," but the competing term "Old English" is
now apparently preferred. Furthermore, the Saxons retained
their pagan beliefs and Christianity died out utterly in England.

Of all the Roman provinces, only Britain was thoroughly
Germanized and de-Christianized.

THE CELTIC PRIESTS

But Great Britain is only the larger of the two chief islands
making up the British Isles. What of Ireland?

That remained thoroughly Celtic, more thoroughly Celtic
than Britain could possibly be, for Ireland had never even felt
the touch of the Roman legions.

Yet if the Roman soldiers had not crossed the Irish Sea, the
Roman priests did. It came about this way . . .

Just about the time that the Roman soldiers were leaving
Britain, a Britonic theologian named Pelagius was advancing
a view of Christianity which was considered heretical by many
leaders of Christian thought on the continent. As Pelagian
views were spreading in Britain, the Church felt it necessary
to take action.

In 429, Pope Celestine I sent Bishop Germanus of Auxerre (a
town in Gaul, eighty miles southeast of Paris) to Britain to
argue against the heresy. In the course of his journey, he made
a short trip to Ireland, where he preached the Gospel, then
passed on to northern Britain where he died.

Germanus' brief stay in Ireland had accomplished nothing directly but it had broken ground. Ireland had been brought to Christian attention and a greater missionary was soon on hand.

This greater missionary was Patricius (a Roman name meaning "noble"), better known to English-speaking people by the shortened version, Patrick. He was to become the beloved St. Patrick of Irish tradition, the patron saint of Ireland.

Patrick's life is obscured by legend but the usually accepted version is that he was born about 385 in some as-yet-unidentified place in Britain. This is sometimes used as a way of irritating Irishmen, in a joking way. St. Patrick, they are told, is an Englishman.

Of course, that is not so. To be an Englishman, Patrick would have had to be a Saxon, and he was born two generations before the first Germanic invaders landed in Kent. He was a Briton, and as Celtic as any Irishman.

While still a teenager he is supposed to have been picked up by raiders from Ireland and carried off a slave to that land. After a few years' enslavement, he managed to escape by ship to Gaul, where, alas, the German tribes had just been pillaging their way from one end of the province to the other.

Patrick received an education in central Gaul, under Bishop Germanus. After Germanus had made his brief excursion into Ireland, Patrick was sent, in 432, to try again.

In northern Ireland, Patrick achieved conversions and organized churches. It is likely that his successes were modest. After all how much could one missionary, however gifted, do in a wild and lawless pagan country? Later legends, however, expanded his deeds into a heroic one-man conversion of the entire island. He is supposed to have died on March 17, 461, and that day has been celebrated ever since as "St. Patrick's Day."

In the century that followed St. Patrick's death, Christianity continued to spread in Ireland and began to take on a distinctive tinge of its own. The Saxon occupation of the east and south of Britain interposed a pagan barrier between Ireland (along with what remained of Celtic Britain) and continental Christianity.

Irish Christianity developed in its own way, therefore, and introduced a number of differences that seem trivial to us today but were of immense importance to the thought of the time. To mention the two most frequently cited differences, the Irish shaved the heads of monks differently than did the Christians of the continent, and they calculated the date of Easter according to a system of their own.

A distinctive "Celtic Church" therefore came into being in the sixth century. In some ways, the Celtics were more fortunate than the Roman Church of the time. The western portion of the European continent was sinking into abysmal darkness because of fresh invasions of Germanic tribes, such as the Franks and Lombards. Learning almost disappeared in Gaul and Spain and grew dim even in Italy.

Ireland, however, was secure against all the Germanic tribes, even against the Saxons. For three centuries after Patrick's death learned men could labor in peace, copying books, studying and interpreting Scripture and, in general, keeping scholarship alive. The Irish priests even managed to pick up Greek somehow and for several centuries, they remained the only Westerners who still held the key to that ancient language. It was Ireland's golden age.

The Irish, having never been under Imperial Roman rule, did not develop the bishoprics which had formed all over the continental Church in imitation of Roman secular administration. Instead, the Irish clergy lived in communities and formed monasteries, so that their religious leaders were abbots, not bishops.

About 521, Columba (koh-lum'buh) was born in what is now Donegal county in the north of Ireland. He became a Celtic monk, the greatest of all, and under his guidance, the

Celtic Church entered into a vigorous missionary existence. He founded churches and monasteries in considerable numbers, and in 563 with twelve disciples erected a church and monastery on Iona, a tiny island not more than six square miles in area off what is now the western coast of Scotland.

Iona became the inspirational center of the Celtic Church. Using it as a base from which to penetrate the northern sections of Britain, Columba began to convert the wild Picts to Christianity. (At about this time, a Christian missionary named David, of whose life virtually nothing is known, is supposed to have revitalized the fading Christianity of the Britons in Wales. David is still the patron saint of Wales.)

Columba was succeeded by another vigorous Celtic missionary, Columban, who was born in 543 in Leinster, in the south of Ireland. Where Columba had converted Celts, Columban aspired to wider fields. In 590, he left Ireland for Gaul, where the savage Franks (who, however, were good members of the Roman Church) were in full control, and where the very name of Gaul was, in consequence, to give way to France.

Once in France, Columban began to establish monasteries everywhere he went and to spread the doctrines of the Celtic Church.

On the continent, however, Columban ran into difficulties. In the sixth century, Benedict of Nursia had founded monasteries in Italy, and by the time Columban was roaming the continent, these Benedictine monasteries were spreading over western Europe in flourishing fashion.

Following Roman doctrines, the Benedictine monasteries had the advantage, for they were tightly organized and disciplined where the Celtic monasteries were decentralized.

In 590, what's more, the very year in which Columban began his penetration of the continent, a new Pope, Gregory I, the Great, was elected. He had been a Benedictine monk himself, and as Pope made use of monks in his administration. He brought the full weight of the papacy to bear on the side of

the Benedictines, and the one-man-attempt of Columban had
to crumple.

A gathering of bishops condemned Columban for the disputed points of doctrine, and Columban had to begin a running argument that lasted for years and which he was bound
to lose. He was finally forced into Italy, where he founded another monastery in defiance, and then died in 615.

After that the Celtic Church was confined to the Celts and
could find no place on the continent. If it was to expand, it
would have to do so at the expense of paganism.

Clearly, the closest field for expansion was among the pagan
Saxons — but, as it happened, the Roman Church was interested in them as well.

MISSIONARY FROM THE SOUTH

The crucial event in connection with the Christianization of
England took place in Rome, but it had its beginning in northern England. In the mid-sixth century, the two Anglian kingdoms of Deira and Bernicia were being established. In those
unsettled times, continuing wars made it certain that there
would be a steady supply of captives who could profitably be
sold as slaves. (Indeed, in early Saxon times, England's great
export commodity was just that — slaves.)

In the 590's, while Gregory I was Pope, several lads from
Deira had been brought to Rome and placed on sale there.
The Pope himself passed by and saw them. Struck by their
rosy complexions and long yellow hair, Gregory stopped and
demanded to know of what nation they were.

"They are Angles," he was told.

"Not Angles, but angels," he said, in a pun that is equally

valid in the Latin he spoke and in the English in which it is given here.

Finding that the Angles were pagans and not wishing so handsome a race of people to be lost to salvation, Gregory began to lay plans to send a missionary to England. For the purpose he chose Augustine, a monk in a Roman monastery, and sent him northward.

Augustine did not go to Deira, the land of the slave boys. He went instead to Kent, the portion of England nearest the continent and a place where, in any case, matters seemed at their most promising.

Kent was, of course, the section where the first Germanic tribes had landed. It had been settled by them a full century at the time of Augustine's coming and it was the most prosperous portion of England at the time. To the west of Kent, the Saxon kingdoms fought the Welsh, and to the north of Kent, the Anglian kingdoms fought the Scots. Kent, for the while, could enjoy peace.

The first Kentish king who stands out with comparative clarity is Ethelbert,* who came to the throne in 560. He was a pagan, but he could scarcely have been ignorant of the existence of Christianity. There must have been Britonic slaves in the kingdom and these might be Christian. Celtic missionaries would be found here and there in England.

But the Celtic church was at a disadvantage in Kent. Of all the sections of England, it was farthest from the Celtic centers in Ireland and Iona, and closest to the Roman centers in France. Indeed, in 584, Ethelbert married a Frankish princess, and she was Catholic. Ethelbert allowed her to practice her religion and to bring priests into the land. He remained pagan

---

* The various Saxon names are often spelled with an initial "Ae" as "Aethelbert." To our eyes, the names look simpler if the "Ae" is replaced by either an "E" or an "A," according to which fits the pronunciation better, and I will do so in this book. The prefix "Ethel" means "noble," by the way.

himself but certainly after that Christianity could no longer remain strange to him.

Then, in 597 Augustine, the missionary from the south, landed in Kent with a party that included forty monks. He brought with him, too, a letter from Pope Gregory addressed to Ethelbert as "King of the Angles." This title was used under the influence, perhaps, of the Anglian slaves who had so impressed the Pope. In any case, it set the precedent for the continental habit of speaking of the region as "Angle-land" and, therefore, our own "England." Had Gregory seen slaves from one of the Saxon kingdoms, would we now be calling the land of Shakespeare and Churchill "Saxland"?

Ethelbert greeted the missionaries politely but cautiously. At first, he insisted that Augustine preach out of doors where the possibly dangerous Christian magic would be diluted. Afterward, as no bad effects seemed apparent, he allowed the party to use the church that had been at the disposal of the Kentish queen and her priests.

Augustine founded a monastery in Ethelbert's capital at Canterbury. In 601, Pope Gregory appointed Augustine bishop, and head of the church in all England. Augustine thus became the first "Archbishop of Canterbury" and from that day to this, the Archbishop of Canterbury has been considered the highest ecclesiastic in England.

Ethelbert finally allowed himself to be converted. This was an important development, for Ethelbert's power reached outside Kent over the neighboring regions of Essex and East Anglia. Under his protection, then, Augustine was free to spread his doctrines far afield. When Augustine died about 607, the Roman form of Christianity had been firmly planted in southeastern England. Bishops had been appointed over Rochester, in western Kent, and over London, as well as over Canterbury.

Ethelbert's long reign (he ruled for over half a century, from 560 to 616) meant a period of stability that further worked in favor of the progress of Christianity. So did Ethelbert's firm attempt to establish an ordered society. He published a written code of laws, for instance, the first to be seen in England. The law code was particularly useful in that it provided a carefully fixed series of fines for offenses up to and including murder. This replaced the random system of revenge in which a wronged person did as much wrong in return as he could, thus laying himself open to re-revenge and to the blood feuds that do so much damage to the social structure of primitive societies.

Beyond Ethelbert's sway, even at its broadest, was the Saxon kingdom of Wessex in the west, and the Anglian kingdoms of Deira and Bernicia in the north. Deira (from which had come the slave boys so admired by Gregory) had as its first great king a chieftain named Elli.

Elli came to power about 560 and reigned successfully for a full generation. Under him, Deira broadened its territories. Colonists were sent out in 586, who penetrated the central sections of Britain and established Mercia, which quickly gained its independence of Deira.

In 593, Elli died, and Ethelfrith, who then ruled over Bernicia, promptly invaded Deira and took over the kingdom. Elli had a son, however, named Edwin, who managed to get out of Deira in time. He fled for refuge to the brother-kingdom of East Anglia.

Ethelfrith was a successful ruler who defeated the Scots and Welsh handily, but he could never feel truly secure while Edwin, the "rightful king" of Deira, remained at large.

The pressure was on Redwald, king of East Anglia, from both sides. Edwin did what he could to gain Redwald's support for a move northward, while Ethelfrith offered bribes and threatened force to get him to give up Edwin.

While Ethelbert of Kent lived, matters remained as they were. Ethelbert's influence was for peace and his hand was heavy over East Anglia. In 616, however, Ethelbert died, and with him Kentish supremacy died, too, never to return.

The vacuum left by Ethelbert's death, apparently filled Redwald with ambitious dreams. He was suddenly anxious to strike out for himself and by some doughty blow gain the newly opened chance at the supremacy over all England.

As for Ethelfrith, Ethelbert's death made it possible for him to move southward, in 617.

Luck was against him, however. In the interest of speed and surprise, he struck southward with a small force, but found Redwald, who was on the point of marching northward quite independently, facing him with the entire East Anglian army.

Ethelfrith discovered the enemy's overpowering advantage in numbers too late for a safe retreat. Rather than surrender, he fought a battle at the Idle River, which ran between the two kingdoms. East Anglia won, of course, and Ethelfrith was killed.

The East Anglian victory placed Edwin on the throne of Deira and Bernicia and the two kingdoms remained united thereafter. Because the whole of the double kingdom was north of the Humber River, it came to be called "Northumbria."

If Redwald expected that the victory would indeed make him dominant over England with Edwin as his puppet, he was mistaken. Edwin was as strong a ruler as his enemy, Ethelfrith, had been. He defeated the Welsh, extended his rule far to the west, and under him, Northumbria soon came to be the most vigorous of all the kingdoms in Germanic Britain. (This period of domination of the Anglian nations after the death of Ethelbert of Kent, confirmed the continental habit of speaking of "Angleland" and made sense of it. The name "England" was fixed beyond eradication by this time.)

In 625, Edwin demonstrated the new importance of Northumbria by marrying Ethelberga of Kent, the daughter of the great Ethelbert. Ethelberga was a Christian and she brought with her an aged priest, Paulinus, who had been with Augustine in his missionary labors in Kent. Now, once again we witness the efforts of a Christian queen to convert her pagan husband. (This happened among the Germanic leaders many times in early Christian history; the pacific doctrines of the Church had a much greater appeal, in the beginning, to women than to men.)

Edwin was swayed, not so much, perhaps, by the arguments of his wife and of Paulinus, as by a series of other events as follows:

Of the Saxon kingdoms to the south, the one least desirous of admitting northern supremacy was Wessex. The ruler of Wessex decided to demonstrate this by concerting a plot to assassinate Edwin. He sent an ambassador to Northumbria who, in addition to the usual polite speech, carried a poisoned knife. While delivering his message to Edwin, he drew the knife and sprang. Only the quick action of a Northumbrian official, who interposed his own body and lost his life, saved Edwin.

Naturally, Paulinus at once pointed out that the God of the Christians had saved his life for the sake of his Christian queen. Edwin, impressed, promised to undergo conversion if he defeated Wessex (with whom, after the attempt at assassination, he was obviously at war) and returned safely. This he did, and in 627 he and his principal noblemen accepted conversion.

Christianity, in its Roman form, having previously established a firm hold in the south, now established one in the north. Edwin's capital, York, where he was baptized (and where Septimius Severus and Constantius Chlorus had both died centuries before) was made the site of a bishopric with Paulinus as first bishop. In all the succeeding centuries the Archbishop of York has remained the second ecclesiastic in England, with only the Archbishop of Canterbury outranking him.

Edwin was, by now, the most powerful ruler England had yet seen, and held sway over the largest territory. Far to the north he built a castle on the Firth of Forth to guard his northern boundary against the Scots. Tradition has it that around this castle there grew up a town that was eventually known as Edinburgh ("Edwin's town").

THE SECOND ROMAN CONQUEST

But all was not yet sweetness and light for England. There was Christianity in the north and south, but in between there yet lay a large stretch of paganism. This was Mercia, the erstwhile Deiran colony, but now a powerful kingdom in its own right, and under the rule of a demonic chieftain named Penda.

Penda is a curious character. He was an ardent pagan and despised Christianity, yet made no effort to stop Christian missionaries at work in his realm. Apparently, he thought that true men would be immune to Christianity and that anyone who gave in to it was a weakling not worth the saving. Furthermore, he seemed to love battles for their own sake and made little effort to follow them up with conquest. An occasional piece of slaughter seemed all he needed; nothing more.

Edwin's conversion to Christianity seemed a good reason for a battle. Penda had consolidated his rule over Mercia in 628, the year after that conversion, and he began the war at once. Nor did he hesitate to form an alliance with a Welsh prince, Cadwallon.

Cadwallon was a Christian, but he was a Welshman, too, and was eager to repay Edwin and his Northumbrians for the defeats they had earlier inflicted on the Welsh. If to do so meant to ally himself with one who was both a pagan and a "Saxon," that was just an item. As for Penda, anything that would make a battle more of a free-for-all was fine for him.

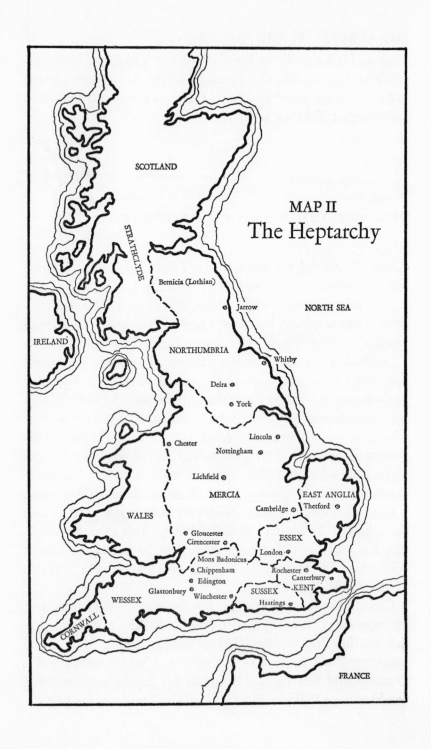

MAP II
The Heptarchy

SCOTLAND

STRATHCLYDE

Bernicia (Lothian)

Jarrow

NORTH SEA

IRELAND

NORTHUMBRIA

Whitby

Deira

York

Chester

Lincoln

Nottingham

Lichfield

MERCIA

EAST ANGLIA

Cambridge

Thetford

WALES

Gloucester
Cirencester

ESSEX

London

Mons Badonicus

Chippenham

Rochester

Canterbury

Edington

Glastonbury

Winchester

SUSSEX

KENT

WESSEX

Hastings

CORNWALL

FRANCE

In 632, Edwin was brought to bay at Hatfield, thirty miles south of York. He suffered a great defeat and was killed. His fifteen-year reign thus came to an end.

With savage delight, Cadwallon then began a systematic devastation of Northumbria. The evils that befell the land must have convinced the population that conversion to Christianity was a mistake and that the old Nordic gods were punishing them for their infidelity. Paulinus and those with him had to flee York, and all of Northumbria relapsed into paganism, as six years of Christianity were wiped out.

But now the pendulum swings again. When Ethelfrith had usurped Elli's kingdom, Elli's son, Edwin had fled south for refuge. When Edwin retook the kingdom, Ethelfrith's sons fled north for refuge.

One of those sons, Oswald, had been converted to Christianity; but in the north, it was Celtic Christianity that dominated, thanks to the work of Columba. Oswald became a sincere Celtic Christian and even spent some years at Iona.

In the confusion that had followed Edwin's death, Oswald returned to Northumbria and in 633 managed to kill Cadwallon in battle.

(Cadwallon was the last Britonic leader to take the offensive against the Saxons. For centuries afterward the Welsh were to maintain a successful resistance, and there would be times when it would seem they were about to establish their independence once and for all; but their posture remained purely defensive from the time of Cadwallon's death to the last important Welsh wars seven centuries later.)

Under Oswald, it almost seemed that the days of Edwin were restored. Even Christianity was brought back, albeit in its Celtic version. Oswald allied himself with Wessex by marrying a daughter of its king and seemed for the moment as powerful as Edwin had been.

But Penda was still there, ruling over Mercia. Again he prepared for war and a rousing battle, and history repeated itself. In a battle between Mercians and Northumbrians in 641, Northumbria was again defeated and its king again killed.

But history kept right on repeating. Oswald had a brother, Oswiu, who now seized the Northumbrian throne and, to make his position more acceptable, married a daughter of Edwin. In this way he hoped to unite the old ruling houses of Deira and Bernicia and remove the perpetual threat of civil war from Northumbria. He even allowed the southern half of his dominions, Deira, to be ruled, viceroy fashion, by Oswine, a prince of the house of Edwin.

And, anxious to avoid the fate of his predecessors, Oswiu made every effort to placate that ever-fierce pagan warrior Penda. He turned over one of his sons to Penda as a hostage. He allowed his daughter to marry one of Penda's sons (and that son was converted to Christianity as a result). Now he offered tribute and the actual recognition of Penda as over-lord.

The old pagan shrugged it all off. He had amused himself with victories over Wessex and East Anglia and by 654 he felt that it was Northumbria's turn again, and mere surrender by Northumbria was not going to be allowed to spoil his fun.

Oswiu, very much against his will, was forced to fight and battle was joined somewhere near the city of Leeds. This time, Penda found himself with exactly one battle too many. The Northumbrians, beaten twice in 632 and 641, now fought with the fury of despair and the Mercians sustained a notable defeat. Penda was killed and with him died the last hope of paganism, for Penda's Christian son succeeded to the Mercian throne.

From then on, England was safely Christian and the last remaining pagan ruler, the King of Essex, was converted at Oswiu's persuasion.

But which variety of Christianity was to prevail? Celtic or Roman? The north was Celtic, the south Roman. The battle was by no means even, however. Celtic Christianity was backed by the Scots and Irish who did not bulk large in the world of the time. Roman Christianity had the continent behind it, the prestigious kingdom of the Franks and the even more prestigious papacy.

Oswiu himself, the most powerful Celtic Christian in history (from the secular viewpoint), was uncertain. His wife was of the Roman belief and her influence on him was strong. The priests of the two competing sects disputed each other with acrimony and threats of hellfire and it was enough to make anyone nervous. What if he were on the wrong side?

In 664, therefore, Oswiu called a gathering of bishops — a "synod" — to meet at Whitby, a coastal city forty miles northeast of York. Here he listened patiently to the arguments of both sides over such things as the style of monkly tonsure. Ought monks shave the middle of their heads, leaving a rim of hair all around in imitation of Jesus' crown of thorns? Should they, instead, leave a tuft of hair in the middle as was the Celtic practice (and perhaps that was a Druid survival)?

The Celtic priests quoted Columba in great detail, but Oswiu was much struck by the statement of the Roman bishops who claimed they followed the Pope, who was the successor of St. Peter — the same St. Peter to whom Jesus had said (Matthew, 16:18-19) ". . . thou art Peter, and upon this rock I will build my church . . . And I will give unto thee the keys of the kingdom of heaven."

Oswiu turned to the Celtic bishops and demanded to know whether this was true. The Celtic bishops had to admit that the verse was correctly quoted. "In that case," said Oswiu, "I must adhere to the followers of Peter, lest when I die and go to heaven I find the gates closed against me by the holder of the keys."

The sorrowing Celtic bishops were forced to leave the kingdom and find refuge in Scotland and Ireland.

England had undergone a second Roman conquest, this time in the religious sense. English missionaries, preaching the Roman variety of Christianity, followed the retreating Celtics, and little by little Celtic Christianity dwindled. In 716, Iona itself — a century and a half after Columba — joined Rome, and thereafter the Celtic Church lingered on in increasingly moribund condition till its last flickers died out in the eleventh century.

4

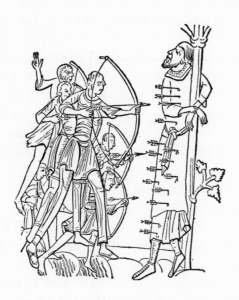

THE COMING OF THE VIKINGS

ENGLISH CULTURE

The Christian victory had not been without cost. The years of
Penda's triumphs had been destructive indeed and the structure and organization of the Church required repair and revi-
talization.

What was needed was a competent Archbishop of Canterbury, one who could take firm hold and by whose leadership
the Church could be made strong and solid. Oswiu of Northumbria and Egbert of Kent, representatives of northern and
southern England respectively, were at one in their search
for him.

Such a man was finally presented to England by Pope Vital-
ian. The papacy was, at that time, still under the control of the
Eastern Roman Emperor, and it is not surprising that the
Pope turned to the east. There he found one Theodore of Tar-

sus, a Greek churchman born in the same city in Asia Minor in which, six and a half centuries before, the Apostle Paul had been born.

Theodore was brought to England under the care of Benedict Biscop, a Northumbrian nobleman. The easterner became the seventh Archbishop of Canterbury in 669 and things began to hum at once. He organized church councils so that bishops everywhere might know exactly what they were to do. One council, which he called together in 673 at Hertford (about twenty miles north of London) was the first at which bishops from all over England were represented.

Theodore reformed abuses and brought religious practices into line with papal doctrine. He divided England into conveniently sized bishoprics, replacing the previous rather haphazard pattern. Even once-pagan Mercia was divided into five bishoprics. Theodore's work succeeded in advancing the concept of a unified England for the first time.

The young English Church almost at once began to produce men of learning and inspiration who would serve as its ornaments.

The first English literary figure was Caedmon (kad'mon), a Northumbrian who did his work sometime between 660 and 680 in the time of Oswiu and of Theodore of Tarsus. His story is told by a historian who was born in Caedmon's lifetime, and what is found in that account represents our total information concerning him.

According to the story, Caedmon was an illiterate herdsman who once attended festivities at which each guest was asked to sing in turn. Caedmon knew no songs and retired in humiliation. That night he dreamed he was ordered to sing by some stranger and he found himself composing poetry that he remembered after he had awakened. He retired to a monastery at Whitby, where the abbess recognized his suddenly discovered talent and kept him there as a kind of "poet in residence."

Copies exist of the poem he is supposed to have composed

in his dream. So do a number of the other poems attributed to him, all on religious themes. It is arguable how many of the "Caedmon poems" are really by Caedmon, for he was reported to have had many imitators (as any bold innovator is bound to have). Whether by Caedmon or not, these verses are extremely valuable relics of Old English poetry.

The historian through whom we know the tale of Caedmon is Bede who, like Caedmon, was a Northumbrian. He was born in 673, when Caedmon was actively composing poetry at Whitby, and entered a newly founded monastery before he was ten. This monastery was at Jarrow, about sixty-five miles northwest of Whitby and near the modern city of Newcastle. The monastery had been founded in 682 by Benedict Biscop, the same who had escorted Theodore of Tarsus from Rome to Canterbury.

Bede studied under Biscop and lived as quiet and satisfying a life as it was possible for a man to live in those days. He remained in the monastery all his life, indulging in his literary labors to the very day of his death. He became a priest and might eventually have been promoted to abbot, but this he refused, fearing that the administrative duties would deprive him of time for his beloved writing.

Because of his priestly office, he was given the courtesy title of "venerable" so that he is commonly known as "the Venerable Bede." The adjective merely means "respected" and is equivalent to our modern title of "Reverend." Because "venerable" has come to be applied to old men particularly (who, because of their age, are to be respected) legends arose that Bede lived an extraordinarily long time. This is not so. He lived to be over sixty, dying in 735, and while that is long for that period of history, it is not extraordinary.

Bede's greatest work and the one for which he is best known is *The Ecclesiastical History of the English Nation* completed in 731, and because of it he is called the "father of English history."

The book is remarkable in several ways. For one thing, he dated events from the birth of Jesus, rather than from the supposed date of the creation (as was then fashionable). In this respect, the rest of Europe eventually followed him. Then, too, Bede's attitude toward history was quite admirable. He researched his work carefully, sifting critically through the various legends. He even sent a monk to Rome to search through the century-old archives of Pope Gregory I for any letters concerning England.

He summarized also the state of scientific knowledge in his time. The scraps of knowledge available to him were pitifully meager, but considering the darkness that was descending on western Europe, every bit of light, however dim and flickering, was extremely valuable. Bede recorded the fact that the earth was a sphere and noted that tides were caused by the moon. He was the first to make a point of the fact that high tide did not occur everywhere at once and that tide tables had to be prepared separately for each port.

Bede was particularly interested in the question of the proper method for calculating the date of Easter. This is understandable since it was an important difference between the Celtic and Roman Churches and since Bede lived in a time when the dispute between the two in Northumbria itself was still a warm memory.

He gathered together the necessary astronomical information for the purpose and noted that the day of the vernal equinox had slipped forward in the Julian calendar. (This was the first clear evidence that the Julian calendar, established seven centuries earlier by Julius Caesar, was not quite perfect — but it was to be eight more centuries before a slightly different and better calendar, the one we use now, was worked out.)

He wrote many commentaries on the Bible and on the day of his death managed to finish a translation of the Gospel of

St. John into Old English. Unfortunately, that translation has not survived.

Bede was fiercely anti-Celtic, perhaps naturally so in view of the recentness of the dispute. His English history did its best to minimize the work of the Irish missionaries and as long as Bede remains our chief source of early English history, our knowledge of the Celtic Church must remain dim and, probably, distorted.

Born in 673 — the same year in which Bede was born — was Wynfrith. He was a man of Wessex in southwestern England, near the town of Exeter. He, too, entered a monastery in early life, took the name of Boniface ("good deeds") and came to be one of the learned men of his generation. His field of endeavor, however, lay outside England.

Western Christendom was in dire peril on the Continent. The Frankish kingdom had spread out now over all of Gaul and much of what is now western Germany. It was a large area and was inhabited by warlike men, but it was poorly organized, ravaged by civil war, and far gone in ignorance and decay. Yet upon its shoulders alone fell the support of the Roman Church.

To the northeast of the Frankish kingdom were independent German tribes, mostly pagan. To the southeast, Italy was falling under the heel of a group of Germanic invaders, the Lombards, who adhered to a Christian heresy, Arianism.

Worst of all, a new religion, Islam, had been preached in Arabia by a prophet named Mohammed in the time of Edwin of Northumbria. Islam had spread rapidly throughout western Asia and across northern Africa, carried on the victorious banners of Arabic armies. Now it had actually crossed into western Europe and its armies were subjugating Spain and were beginning to threaten the southwestern flank of the Franks.

England was far removed from Spain and from Italy and

could do nothing about the Islamic and the Arian dangers. It was, however, merely the width of a sea removed from the German pagans. Already an Englishman had endeavored to do something about that paganism. A Northumbrian, Willibrord, who had studied in Ireland in his youth, had traveled to Frisia (the modern Netherlands) which is located due east of southeastern England, across 120 miles of the North Sea. There he founded a bishopric in what is now Utrecht.

Willibrord had merely scratched the surface, however, and in 716, Boniface went to Frisia determined to do more. Thus began nearly forty years of labors, all through pagan Germany, and in the Frankish kingdom as well. Among the Franks, he became the most powerful ecclesiastic of his time.

Boniface is rightly known as the "apostle to the Germans" for by the time he came to his end as a martyr in 754 (at the hands of a group of still-pagan Frisians) he had established churches through much of pagan Germany, had reorganized the last remnants of a continental Celticism that had persisted since Columban's labors a century before, and had secured a vast area for the Roman Church.

THE RISE OF MERCIA

The number of Germanic kingdoms in England during this period of its history was not fixed, but by the year 700 there were seven, and it is this number which seems most characteristic. The entire period is sometimes referred to as the "Heptarchy" (from Greek words meaning "seven governments") in consequence.

Four of the kingdoms were crowded into the southeast portion of the island and were (from north to south) East Anglia, Essex, Kent and Sussex. They were small and, through much of this period of English history, were of little moment — except for Kent's brief period of supremacy under Ethelbert in the sixth century.

The rest of England was divided among the remaining three kingdoms: Northumbria, Mercia and Wessex (again going from north to south). These three were the relatively large kingdoms and each was kept at the peak of warlike efficiency by the honing action of constant wars against the Scots and the Welsh. Each might reasonably aspire to domination over the Heptarchy, and, indeed, each took its turn.

Northumbria was first to do so in the decades just preceding and succeeding 700. It was then clearly in the fore both politically and culturally.

Its role in arranging the Synod of Whitby was, however, its last important act of domination over England generally. The ravages of Cadwallon and the repeated invasions of Penda had weakened it, and it was slowly declining while Bede at Jarrow was writing his history.

Mercia, on the other hand, was gaining strength. In 716, the year in which Boniface left for Europe, Ethelbald (eth'el-bawld), a descendant of a brother of old King Penda, became King of Mercia and at once began to extend his power. Bede, in his history, stated that at the time of writing (731), Ethelbald controlled all of England south of Northumbria. Perhaps he was led to think so by the fact that Ethelbald, in his letters, vaingloriously called himself "King of Britain" but this was an exaggeration.

Mercia was by now as Christian as the rest of England and Ethelbald was as Christian as any king of his time, which meant he wasn't very much of a saint. Boniface wrote a letter to Ethelbald from Germany, for instance, urging him to live more virtuously and to have fewer mistresses. He had to admit, though, that Ethelbald was very generous in his gifts to the Church (and that, then, as always, covered a multitude of sins).

Ethelbald did not actually try conclusions with fading Northumbria, partly because the south was not entirely pacified. He claimed lordship over Wessex, but Wessex refused to be persuaded that was so. In 752, there was war between the two kingdoms and Wessex defeated the Mercian forces.

There is a tale that in the fight with Wessex, Ethelbald betrayed personal cowardice and shrank from a challenge to personal combat with Cuthred, the King of Wessex. This may just be an excuse put forward by certain conspirators among his own Mercian subjects. They plotted his assassination and finally accomplished that goal in 757.

After some months of confusion, the Mercian nobles managed to agree upon Offa (awf'uh), a distant relative of Ethelbald, as the new king. He turned out to be the greatest Mercian of them all.

He reestablished Mercian control over southern England more firmly than such control had existed under Ethelbald. He took an army into Sussex and Kent in the 770's and when he had made certain there would be no back talk from that direction he was ready to attack Wessex.

In 777, Offa defeated the army of Wessex on the Thames near Oxford and forced them to recognize his overlordship. Nevertheless, he made use of methods other than force, too, for in 789, he married one of his daughters to the King of Wessex, thus forming a marital alliance. Another daughter was later married to the King of Northumbria so that his influence was spread over every kingdom of the Heptarchy.

Even so, England was not truly a single nation but under Offa it made its closest approach to that goal up to that time.

As the outstanding English king of his time, it is to be expected of Offa that he would take up the battle against the Welsh. Even he did not venture to pursue the ever-resisting

Welshmen into their hill country (it was always a lot easier to go into the Welsh mountains than to come out alive), and truly there was little point to doing so. The Welsh could no longer possibly pose a real threat to the English. The worst and most they could do was to conduct terror raids, and Offa's only intention was to put a stop to that.

He took a leaf out of the strategy of the Roman Empire and built an earthwork wall, north and south, along the Welsh frontier from end to end (except for such parts as were so wildly forested as to be impassable in themselves). Wales was thus marked off roughly along its present boundaries, and traces of "Offa's Dike" ("dike" is an old word meaning "wall") still exist today.

Offa was the first English monarch to make an important mark outside the island. Midway in his reign, the Frankish kingdom came under the rule of Charlemagne (Charles the Great). Charlemagne was the most powerful monarch of the Middle Ages and ruled over the greatest realm, but Offa, in closing a trade treaty with the great king, dealt with him on equal terms.

Offa might not have been able to carry this off if the English Channel had not existed, for Charlemagne's Frankish kingdom was much more powerful than Offa's Mercia was. However, Charlemagne had no navy and the Channel did exist.

Offa was even able to make his power felt with the Pope himself, who at that time was Adrian I, a good friend of Charlemagne. It seemed to Offa to be rather derogatory to Mercia that the Archbishop of Canterbury should be supreme over the English Church. That was only a relic of Kentish supremacy, now nearly two centuries out of date. Offa wanted an archbishopric in the Mercian town of Lichfield (about fifteen miles north of the modern town of Birmingham). The new archbishop would be in charge of the Mercian Church, while Canterbury would confine his jurisdiction to the southeast.

Pope Adrian had to give in to this demand in 787, although

MAP III

England
in the Time
of Offa

Iona

Edinburgh

NORTH SEA

IRELAND

Jarrow

Whitby

NORTHUMBRIA

York

Hatfield

Humber River

Lichfield

EAST ANGLES (EAST ANGLIA)

Offa's Dike

MERCIA

EAST SAXONS (ESSEX)

WALES

Hertford

London

Rochester
Canterbury

WEST SAXONS (WESSEX)

Oxford

KENT

WEST WALES

SOUTH SAXONS (SUSSEX)

FRANCE

the new arrangement was not to survive Offa's death by long. (The story goes that Adrian offered resistance to the idea at first, whereupon Offa coolly suggested to Charlemagne that the Pope be deposed and that a Frankish Pope be installed in his place. Perhaps Adrian thought Charlemagne might be tempted to do this, and when Charlemagne quietly suggested to Adrian that he humor Offa, the Pope hastened to do so.)

Internally, Offa's outstanding achievement was the establishment of a national coinage. He had probably gotten this notion when he took over Kent, which was already putting out coins. They in turn got the notion from the Franks who had begun a national coinage in 755. Offa's coins, however, were much more beautifully executed than the crude items put out among the Franks, and clearly indicated the fact that England led western Europe in culture at this time.

This is made even clearer in connection with the life of Alcuin (al'kwin).

Alcuin was a Northumbrian, born in or near York about 732, shortly before Bede's death, and while Ethelbald of Mercia was at the height of his power. Alcuin studied at York, in a school which at that time was unparalleled in western Christendom. He himself became a paragon of learning, whose equal could not be found on the continent, and in 778, he became head of the school.

In 781, in the course of a visit to Rome, Alcuin met Charlemagne. That Frankish monarch was acutely conscious of the miserable state of learning in his giant kingdom and was only too aware of the fact that without educated men to administer it, the kingdom would have to fall apart (as eventually, after his death, it did). He was eager to start a government-sponsored program of education but he lacked the necessary educators to carry it through.

He was greatly impressed with Alcuin and at once offered him a position at the Frankish court, asking him to supervise the proposed educational program. Alcuin accepted and re-

mained among the Franks for the rest of his life, never returning to England.

Alcuin performed giant labors, teaching court officials,
founding other schools, and writing instructional material for
them. He modified the Church law as it then existed in Italy,
adding practices common among the Franks, and doing it so
reasonably and well that the modifications were accepted in
Rome.

He abandoned earlier Frankish styles of writing which were
incredibly sloppy and could scarcely be read. Instead, he de-
vised a new system of writing small letters that took up less
space on the precious parchment and were infinitely clearer.
The design was so good that the first printers, six centuries
later, adopted it. Alcuin's letters are still used today as "small
letters." The Romans had had only "capital letters."

Alcuin had lit a candle in the darkness of the Frankish kingdom and it never quite went out. He is the brightest and most
influential figure in this period of English cultural supremacy over Europe, but that supremacy was destined to be short-
lived indeed. A horror from the North was about to fall upon
all western Europe and upon the British Isles particularly.

THE NORTHERN FURY

At the time of Offa's death in 796, after a successful reign of
forty-two years, Mercia was at the very peak of its power, but a
small alarm bell had already sounded the knell of doom. A
new round of barbarian invasions was about to start, was, indeed, already making its first thrusts, and — in part — from
the same narrow peninsula where the old ones had originated.

While the Jutes, Angles and Saxons, had occupied the peninsula we now call Jutland and the coasts to the southwest, the
islands to the east, together with the southern tip of what is
now Sweden, were inhabited by a Germanic tribe known to us
as the Danes.

When large numbers of the Jutes, Angles and Saxons departed for Britain in the fifth and sixth centuries, the Danes expanded westward into the vacuum left behind. Their descendants still dwell there in the land we now know as Denmark.

In the large peninsula north of Denmark, there lived the Norwegians on the side fronting the Atlantic Ocean and the Swedes
on the side facing the Baltic. The three nations together may
be referred to as Scandinavia.

All three nations have had a long and vital seafaring tradition, for they have long coasts; and in the case of the Norwegians and Swedes particularly, the cold northern climate makes
agriculture difficult and fishing is a prime source of food.

Beginning in the eighth century, the ocean became more
than a source of food to these "Northmen." It became a high-
way to loot and adventure. Why this was so, we can only guess.
Population increase made it difficult for the Northmen to find
enough to eat at home, and some of them would naturally look
for better places overseas. Another solution would be to fight
each other so that one tribe might take over the land and resources of another. The loser would then have no choice (those
of them that survived) but to go overseas.

The first raiding parties that traveled over the ocean to attack other coasts found the loot plentiful and the resistance
weak. Once they came back with tales of that sort, why,
naturally, it would encourage others to do the same, for the love
of loot, adventure and the sheer pleasure of swinging the
sword.

The Swedes, facing eastward, ventured into the vast plains
of eastern Europe and outside the limits of this particular book.

We will concern ourselves only with the Danes and Norwegians. To their victims, they were the Northmen; to themselves they were "Vikings," meaning "warriors."

The Vikings had been exposed to Christianity, to be sure. In sporadic raiding in the sixth century, they picked up Christian captives. And about 700, Willibrord, who had founded Christianity in the Netherlands, paid a brief visit to Denmark. He didn't accomplish much there, but he did bring back some thirty Danish boys to be brought up in the Christian religion among the Franks.

Later on, when Boniface had completed his task of proselytizing the Germans, the German areas were used as a base for more elaborate missionary journeys into Scandinavia. If anything, though, these had a negative effect, for a strong pagan reaction resulted.

The first Viking raid against England of which we have any record was in 787 against Thanet, a region (then an island) at the tip of Kent. It wasn't much of a raid as those things developed later, but it was a portent of terrible things to come.

It was not long thereafter that Viking ships were attacking the northern portion of Britain with great effect. The Vikings took over the smaller islands to the north and used them as bases from which to make more or less extended landings in Pictish and Scottish territories. By 795, they had made their first landings in Ireland.

Through the next two centuries they bathed the islands in blood and terror. At first, they raided only the coasts; then they moved their ships up the rivers. At first, they raided only in good weather; then they learned to land in winter, wait for it to pass and press inward when the weather warmed again.

No raiders ever had easier pickings. The Vikings ships were the best one could find anywhere in the Atlantic. Indeed, the other nations of western Europe had no ships to speak of at all. The Vikings could sail or row freely along the European coast and choose their targets at will and at leisure. The Christian victims could only wait in panic, hoping that their river or their section of coast would not be selected and muttering the special prayer put into the litany of many churches at this time: "From the fury of the Northmen, good Lord, deliver us." The good Lord rarely did.

The victims were in such panic over the tales they had already heard and the Vikings themselves were so terrible in appearance (some were so battle-mad they fought unarmored in a kind of bloody ecstasy, and these were called "berserkers") that there was scarcely heart for any resistance at all.

The aggressive paganism of the Vikings made matters still worse. Whereas churches and monasteries might serve as refuges and sanctuaries against ordinary armies, the Vikings were actively impelled, by their own religious feelings, to do their worst to such Christian structures. The fact that churches and monasteries usually offered more loot than other buildings encouraged this procedure.

In Ireland, the effect of the Norse raids was devastating. Ireland's culture was wiped out, her Golden Age extinguished, and she was reduced to a barbarism that was not entirely lifted for a thousand years. The remnants of the Celtic Church in the south perished and when Christianity was to flower again on the island it would be in its Roman form. Only in Scotland did the last remnants of the Celtic Church remain.

In 838, the Norse seized a section of Ireland's west central coast, and Dublin (which is now the capital of the Irish Republic) was founded in 840 as a Viking military post. The sites of Waterford in the south and Limerick in the west were also seized.

The Vikings expanded their holdings and gradually settled down to become a long-term part of the Irish scene. It was the first successful invasion of Ireland in historic times and, even so, it only touched the coasts. The interior of Ireland, while badly damaged and reduced to near-anarchy, remained entirely Irish.

As for Scotland, its response to the Viking raids was union.
Kenneth MacAlpin, who held supremacy over the Scots, was
accepted in 844 by the Picts as well, and became Kenneth I
of a united Scotland.

Kenneth I was crowned at Scone (just north of the modern
city of Perth). It was the old Pictish capital, and Kenneth made
use of it as a gesture to make his own Scottishness more palatable to the Picts. As an added touch, he brought a stone to
Scone which, according to legend, had been the very stone
which served Jacob as a pillow on his journey north to Syria.
It had been while Jacob was sleeping with his head on that stone
that he dreamed his vision of angels passing from heaven to
earth and back. Kenneth I was crowned while seated on the
Stone of Scone and all later Scottish kings were similarly
crowned until the Stone was taken away by an English conqueror four and a half centuries later.

The first nucleus of the Kingdom of Scotland was small and
weak. To the north were provinces and islands held by the Vikings; to the south was Northumbria stretching well into the territories we consider Scottish today. Nevertheless, it was the beginning of a kingdom that was to endure for seven and a half
centuries, resisting all English attempts at conquest, until
when the island of Great Britain was finally united, it was in
peace, and with a Scottish king, not an English one, on the
united throne.

THE RISE OF WESSEX

The richest prize in the British Isles was England, of course,
and it was vulnerable. After Offa's death, Mercia's strength
had been quickly dissipated. Different claimants for its throne

fought among themselves, and the other kingdoms of the Heptarchy, which had been quietly subservient to Offa, struck quickly for their independence.

As a result, Offa's attempts to make England a great power, to be reckoned with by the Franks and the papacy, fell apart. In 802, Pope Leo III abolished the Archbishopric of Lichfield and made that of Canterbury supreme over all England once more. In 808, Charlemagne, who had once been forced to treat with Offa on equal footing, could now extend a kind of protectorate over the English kingdoms, forcing Northumbria to take back a king they had exiled.

Meanwhile, the Viking raiders were cautiously reconnoitering the English coast. In 794, the old Northumbrian monastery at Jarrow, where Bede had worked so happily nearly a century before, was sacked and destroyed. About 800, Viking ships landed in Dorset on the southern shores of Wessex and did some slaughtering.

But, fortunately for England, Wessex was now coming into its own as a new champion. Kent, Northumbria and Mercia had each in its turn assumed supremacy and had each in its turn declined. It was the turn of Wessex now. It was perhaps geographically sensible that this should be the case. The Viking raids fell most strongly on those sides of the island that faced Scandinavia — the north and east. Wessex, as the southwesternmost of the Anglo-Saxon kingdoms was farthest removed from the menace and was the one most likely to survive the initial shock of a great attack and the most likely to be able to mount a counterattack.

Wessex, which had been founded about 500, and which had expanded as a result of painful victories over the Welsh, was the most vigorous of the three Saxon kingdoms. It never accepted the overlordship of any of the other kingdoms of the Heptarchy without a hard fight. It fought Ethelbert of Kent, successfully, in 568, and Penda of Mercia, with less success, nearly a century later, after it had turned Christian.

Despite the defeat by Penda, Wessex continued to spread at the expense of the Welsh. By the time Ine (igh'nuh) became King of Wessex in 688, it controlled all the territory south of the Thames from the vicinity of London to the border of Cornwall.

Ine stabilized the internal structure of Wessex and ordered the preparation of its first written law code. (This is particularly important since the legal system of modern England and therefore modern America descends from that of Wessex.) He also organized Wessex into two bishoprics one of them at his capital, Winchester, which is in south central England, sixty miles southwest of London.

In 726, Ine abdicated in order to visit Rome and end his life in the odor of sanctity. That end came almost at once and he did not live to witness the supremacy of Mercia. Wessex resisted that supremacy, as it always did and, as mentioned earlier, Cuthred of Wessex defeated Ethelbald of Mercia.

After Offa of Mercia died, a new personality made itself felt in Wessex. This was Egbert, the son of a king of Kent, and a member of the royal house of Wessex as well.

Offa had earlier driven him out of Wessex, preferring another and probably more tractable member of the royal house to rule over the kingdom. Egbert escaped to the Franks and served under Charlemagne for three years. Then, in 802, when the King of Wessex died, he hurried back, and as the one remaining scion of the royal family was proclaimed king.

Under Egbert, Wessex began to expand again. He pushed the Welsh in Cornwall to the limit and annexed virtually all their territory, leaving them only a few isolated strongholds whose loss was only a matter of time. The small southern kingdoms, Kent, Sussex and Essex, fell into his lap without a struggle and East Anglia called for his help in a fight they were having against Mercia.

Egbert defeated the Mercian army in 823 and by 829 had overrun all of Mercia and had even forced Northumbria into accepting his overlordship. For a while, with his power at this height, he was virtual master of all of England.

To be sure that peak was not retained. The Mercian king managed to regain at least the northern portion of his dominion and Northumbria paid only lip service, but even so Egbert controlled all of southern England tightly and from that point on the Wessex supremacy over the Heptarchy was fixed.

But that overlordship was an empty one, for the Viking nightmare was intensifying and the question was scarcely which kingdom would rule England but would there be an England to rule at all?

By 835, Viking successes in Scotland and Ireland had emboldened the raiders to the point where they fell on England itself in force. Their target was an island at the mouth of the Thames River, where they gathered loot against virtually no resistance and sailed away triumphantly. The next year a still larger raid at the mouth of another river was met by soldiers of Wessex, who, however, ran away at the first fierce onslaught of the wild barbarians with their horned helmets, loud cries and berserker rage.

Egbert, humiliated, called a meeting of his chief subordinates in London and angrily concerted measures for defense. These had to await another Viking descent and that was not long in coming. This time the Vikings landed on the coast of Cornwall, where the Welsh population of the region, rankling at their defeat by Egbert, were perfectly willing to join the pagans in an assault on Wessex.

Again the Vikings were met by the forces of Wessex, but this time the king was there in person. The Vikings were faced boldly, beaten back and forced to flee to their ships. Egbert had shown that the Vikings were human after all and could be beaten. Not long after, in 839, he died — but not before he had established Wessex' greatness.

Egbert's success stung the Vikings badly and gained for Wessex a measure of relief. That, however, merely meant that the raiders turned to other regions and the eastern shores of England suffered the worse for it.

Egbert's success was a tragedy for the Franks too, for the Vikings, turning aside from England, gave the Frankish shoreline their full attention for the first time. Cities such as Hamburg, Utrecht, Paris and Bordeaux were bloodily sacked. The Vikings even followed the Atlantic coastline down to Spain, where they sacked Seville and entered the Mediterranean. Europe bled everywhere along its rim.

Eventually, Viking self-assurance was restored, even with respect to Wessex. There Egbert was dead and his son, Ethelwulf, was on the throne. Ethelwulf was a pious man who seemed to be no warrior. In 851, therefore, the Vikings attacked. Three hundred fifty ships, each crammed with warriors, approached the mouth of the Thames and began to move upstream. They had paused to sack Canterbury and when they reached London, they sacked that. The king of Mercia attempted to stop them but his forces were cut to pieces and he had to flee in ignominy.

The Vikings turned south where the forces of Wessex were waiting, under the leadership of Ethelwulf himself. Once again, as a dozen years before, the Wessexmen, under their monarch's eyes, defeated the Vikings and sent them howling. This battle is supposed to have been the worst defeat the Vikings suffered in the field in the entire course of their raids.

It is a curious thing, in fact, that the small kingdom of Wessex (small in comparison with the great realms of the continent) was the only land anywhere in Europe to oppose the Vikings with resolution in the fierce days of their raids, and inflict a number of heavy defeats upon them in open battle.

Ethelwulf gained great prestige as a result of this victory and the supremacy of Wessex over the Heptarchy was confirmed. Ethelwulf, still more priest than warrior at heart, took the opportunity of the respite gained by this victory to indulge in his life's ambition. He wanted to visit Rome. He took his fourth son, Alfred, with him and left his eldest son, Ethelbald, as regent in his place.

On his way back from Rome, he visited the court of Charles the Bald, a grandson of Charlemagne, who reigned over the western half of his grandfather's Frankish empire; that is, over France. It is further evidence of the prestige of Ethelwulf that Charles the Bald, who had been notoriously unsuccessful in his own attempts to fight off the Vikings, was willing to give the English king the hand of his daughter, Judith, in marriage.

When Ethelwulf came home, though, he found his son Ethelbald so firmly in control of the throne that, rather than precipitate a civil war that would certainly place England in the hands of the Vikings, he stepped out of the picture, contenting himself with the rule over the eastern kingdoms of Essex, Kent and Sussex and leaving his son the king of Wessex itself. He died in 858.

Each one of Ethelwulf's four sons now ruled Wessex in turn as the skies continued to darken over England. In 860, a band of Vikings landed on the Wessex coast, surprised Winchester itself and sacked it, but were later defeated by a hastily gathered force. Ethelbald died in that year, and Ethelwulf's second son, Ethelbert, took over and reigned till 865.

During his reign a Viking raiding party landed on Thanet at the tip of Kent (the place which had suffered the very first such raid three-quarters of a century before). The people of Kent, in terror, offered a bribe to get the Vikings to leave. The Vikings agreed and set a good high figure, which the Kentishmen desperately scraped together. Having taken the money, the Vikings laughed good-naturedly and proceeded to ransack and ravage eastern Kent anyway for anything else they could find.

In 865, when Ethelwulf's third son, Ethelred, became king, the Viking raids finally reached their climax. Indeed, they were no longer raids but became a full-fledged invasion.

The story begins with Ragnar Lodbrok, the first Viking raider to be known by name, but a person whose story is encrusted with legend and concerning whom so many contradictory tales are told that it is impossible to tell what, if anything about him is true.

He is supposed to have been a king of Denmark who, in the course of a raid on Northumbria, was captured and put to death in some gruesome manner. (One version is that he was cast into a pit of poisonous snakes.) His last words were that the "cubs of the bear" would avenge him.

Those cubs were his sons, Ivar and Ubba. Back in Denmark, they got the news of their father's death and swore revenge. Gathering a large force, they landed in East Anglia in 865. There was no resistance and they wintered in the land, awaiting reinforcements.

Those reinforcements came in 866 and for the first time there was a full-scale Viking army in England, rather than a mere raiding party. (At this point, though, we need not speak of Vikings. Previously, the raiding parties had come from no surely ascertained point of origin and it is difficult to tell whether they were Danes or Norwegians. Here, however, it was definitely a Danish army and we can call it that.)

The Danes left East Anglia, marched north and took the city of York. The Northumbrian army was beaten, the Northumbrian king taken and put to death with atrocious tortures. It was the end of the Northumbrian kingdom.

In succeeding years, the Danes subdued Mercia and East Anglia, establishing colonies with the intent of taking over the land permanently. All of England outside the realm directly ruled over by the King of Wessex was now virtually under Danish control.

The Heptarchy was ended and only Wessex remained to prevent a total Danish conquest.

5

THE SAXON TRIUMPH

ALFRED THE GREAT

As far as the Danes were concerned, Wessex was to remain
independent only as long as it would take the invaders to get
to it. In 871, the Danes reached the upper Thames in the vicinity of Reading and the Wessex army under Ethelred (accompanied by his younger brother Alfred, the one who had once
visited Rome with his father) faced them. Again, the Wessex army defeated a hitherto undefeatable force, though later
legend gave the credit to Alfred, who led the charge when the
Saxon king was engaged in helping with the celebration of the
Mass.

The Wessex victory was, however, not decisive this time.
The Danes rallied and received reinforcements. In another
battle, fought two weeks later, the Wessexmen were forced to
retreat and Ethelred was fatally wounded.

Ethelred had young sons, but Wessex was in mortal danger and it was simply unthinkable to have the land ruled by a child when an adult member of the family, a proven warrior, was available. Therefore, Ethelred's younger brother, Alfred (the fourth and youngest son of old Ethelwulf) came to the throne in 871, at the age of twenty-three.

The situation was dark. The Danes were not yet in complete control of England, to be sure. In the far north, a portion of Northumberland held out and the western half of Mercia still maintained itself. Yet neither remnant could offer a serious threat to the triumphant Danes. Only Wessex, controlling the land south of the Thames, remained intact, and heavy Danish blows had just about exhausted it.

Immediately after Alfred's accession to the throne, the Danes tried to take advantage of the possible confusion attendant on the beginning of a new reign by invading the land. They marched far south of the Thames and defeated Alfred at Wilton, some twenty-five miles west of Winchester. The Danish victory was not a cheap one for them, however, and Alfred, falling back cautiously, kept his army alive.

But he knew he could not go on for long. He had to have time to reorganize, time to prepare — time, time, time, at any cost. So he offered to buy peace, to bribe the Danes to leave him alone for a while. The Danes, for their part, were not entirely anxious for war, at least not with the resolute men of Wessex who, even in defeat, inflicted damage enough. They accepted the money and spent the next few years consolidating their hold on the rest of England. They put a final end, in 874, to the Mercian kingdom, driving its last king from the throne, only eighty years after the death of the great Offa.

Alfred had the time he needed now, and one thing his quick mind saw was the need for a navy. It was sea power that gave the Vikings their triumph, sea power that took them here and there along the coast, enabling them to swoop down anywhere at will and to escape any time at will. They could supply a host or outflank an enemy army. In fact, while their victims had no navy of their own, the Vikings might lose skirmishes but they could always return. They could never really be defeated.

It might seem then that those who lived in terror of the Vikings would realize the necessity of building a navy; of meeting the Vikings' ships before they could land; of cutting off those parties that did land. Oddly enough, the victims did not think of it, or else were so unused to the sea that they feared it as much as they did the Vikings.

Alfred was the exception. The Saxons had once been sea rovers (how else had they reached the island of Britain) and there was nothing to prevent them from sailing the sea again but a failure of will. Alfred therefore set about constructing a navy, producing the first feeble whisper of what was eventually to become the world's strongest sea power.

Eventually, when the Danish truce began to wear thin and raids were beginning again on a small scale, Alfred's navy moved. In 875, his ships put to sea and, in a naval battle, actually managed to defeat the Danes. Perhaps this is not surprising, for if the ships were new, the sailors were not amateurs. They were not Wessexmen, but Frisian mercenaries (pirates would be a better word) hired by Alfred to man his ships. He won a second naval victory the next year after a storm had happened to wreck part of the Danish fleet.

The most powerful Dane at the moment was Guthrum, the center of whose power was in what had once been East Anglia. Stung by Alfred's sea power, he determined to smash Wessex once and for all.

Unfortunately, Alfred was caught napping. In January, 878, the King of Wessex was at Chippenham, fifteen miles south of the Thames. This was a favorite residence of the Wessex kings, but it was close enough to the frontier to be rather dangerously exposed at this time. Ordinarily, perhaps, the armed men quartered in the city would have been on guard, but now all was forgotten in the gay festivities of the Christmas-New Year holiday.

The pagan Danes were not involved in any such holiday and Guthrum managed to bring a large force to the very walls of the city before the alarm could be spread. By then, it was far too late. The Danes broke through the gate and there was a fearsome slaughter. Alfred himself barely managed to escape with a small force.

For a while, Wessex was prostrate and the Danes occupied virtually all of it. No organized Wessex army could be found to face them and Alfred himself was hiding in the swamps and forests of Somerset, just south of the Bristol Channel. The last Saxon king in England was reduced to guerrilla warfare and the ultimate Danish triumph seemed at hand.

There is a very famous story of Alfred at this low point in his career, one that is as well-known to young Englishmen as the story of George Washington and the cherry tree is to young Americans — and perhaps no more true.

The story goes that at one point Alfred's fortunes had sunk to so dismal a pitch that he was forced to conceal himself in the hut of a cowherd, who did not know his guest's identity — except that he was some warrior fleeing from the Danes.

The cowherd's wife had no great liking for him, since he would bring death to them all if he were discovered by the Danes and grumblingly put him to work watching the cakes (some sort of griddlecakes, actually) she had set to heating over the fire. She gave him meticulous instructions as to what to do to keep them cooking properly. Alfred nodded his head absently and then fell to thinking of ways and means of recouping his all-but-lost kingdom, never noticing that the cakes were burning.

The good woman did, though. She came rushing in and cried out in despair, "Look, man, the cakes are burning and you do not take the trouble to turn them; when the time for eating them comes, then you are active enough."

Poor Alfred bowed his head to the storm, admitting the justice of the complaint. The picture of the King reduced to so low a state as to be forced to endure the scolding of a cowherd's wife is very dramatic to anyone who knows (as all Englishmen do) that he rose to be the greatest of all the Saxon monarchs and justly earned the title of Alfred the Great. (Indeed, it is possible the story was invented to point up the drama, for it can't be traced back to a period earlier than two centuries after it had supposedly happened.)

In actual fact, Alfred was doing far more than skulking and hiding. He established a fortress in the more inaccessible bogs of Somerset (a landscape which nowadays is, of course, thoroughly tame) and from it harassed the Danes and slowly collected men.

Another legend even tells that in order to get reliable information concerning Danish plans and the disposition of their army, he himself assumed the disguise of a minstrel and invaded their camp, amusing them with his songs and patter and discovering all he wanted to know. (A modern TV adventure serial could scarcely improve on that.)

It was only five months after the flight from Chippenham that Alfred had built enough of an army and understood enough of the Danish position to venture an attack of his own. In the late spring, he surprised the Danes at Edington, not far south of Chippenham, as earlier they had surprised him. He was even more successful, for he defeated them and penned Guthrum and a number of his men in their fortified camp.

Guthrum was faced with the choice of starvation or surrender, and he chose the latter. He was helped in this by the fact that Alfred chose to drive an easy bargain. In this, Alfred was probably very wise. If he demanded too much, he would have driven Guthrum to desperation and if Guthrum were slaughtered, there would be vengeance from other Danes soon enough. Easy terms, on the other hand, might win Guthrum to a policy of peace.

KINGDOM OF PICTS AND SCOTS

NORTHUMBERLAND

Jarrow

IRELAND

KINGDOM OF YORK

Dee River

DANELAW
DANISH MERCIA

MERCIA

EAST ANGLIA

NORTH WALES

ESSEX

London

Thames River

Chippenham

Canterbury

KENT

Edington

Wedmere

Winchester

WESSEX

SUSSEX

SOMERSET

DORSET

CORNWALL

Bristol Channel

MAP IV
England in the Time of Alfred

Alfred therefore asked only that Guthrum evacuate Wessex and offered to recognize Danish occupation of most of the rest of England. The division of England into Danish and Saxon halves followed a generally northwest-southeast line, from the mouth of the Dee River to the mouth of the Thames.

The Danish portion came to be known as the "Danelaw," the region, that is, that followed the laws and cutoms of the Danes. It included what had once been the kingdoms of Northumbria, East Anglia and Essex, together with the eastern half of Mercia.

Still Saxon was Wessex itself, and what had once been Sussex, Kent and western Mercia. These were not separate kingdoms, however. Only one Saxon kingdom remained, or was to remain in future. Alfred was not King of Wessex, but King of England; in a very real sense, he was the first King of England, even though he ruled over only half of the territory that was eventually to form England.

In making this treaty, it is quite possible that Alfred saw that the division set up was quite an arbitrary and unimportant one. The Danes were not very different from the Saxons. They came from the same territory from which the Saxons had originally come. They spoke very nearly the same language and had very nearly the same cultural heritage. It was very likely (and in the end it turned out to be so) that Dane and Saxon would fuse indistinguishably and that the two would, before long, form a common kingdom.

The one difference that might hamper this was religion, for the Danes were still pagan, and this difference Alfred strove to eliminate. As part of the peace settlement, Alfred insisted that Guthrum turn Christian.

Guthrum agreed (perhaps his sympathies already lay in that direction). He submitted to baptism with Alfred himself as his sponsor and he accepted the new and more Christian-sounding name (to Saxon ears) of Athelstan. After that, Christianity spread with reasonable speed among the Danes and never again was England to witness pagan domination of any part of its territory.

The Danish problem wasn't utterly solved, to be sure. There were Danes in England outside Guthrum's sway and occasional raids took place. Alfred's firm handling of these incidents increased his prestige, which reached a peak when he decided that he needed London as a firm bulwark against such raids, and, in 886, took it and began to fortify it strongly.

It was after this that the boundary of the Danelaw was made official and the treaty put into written form. It is called the Treaty of Wedmere after the town where the agreement was made — a town near Alfred's old place of refuge in his days of burning the cakes. By and large, Guthrum held to the treaty.

After the events of 878, Alfred had long enough intervals of peace to concern himself with internal affairs. The Danish ravages had disorganized the financial and legal structure of his kingdom and he set about rebuilding that. He made a careful study of the Biblical laws outlined in the Old Testament and studied also the earlier law codes put out by men such as Ethelbert of Kent, Offa of Mercia and Ine of Wessex. He then published a code that, in his view, summarized the best of these.

Naturally, the state of learning and scholarship in England had faded dreadfully under the disasters of the past century. From being the cultural leader of Europe, producing such men as Bede and Alcuin, England had become an intellectual wilderness. This was of great concern to Alfred, who was himself one of the minority of kings who was a genuine scholar.

He collected learned clerics from his own dominions and from abroad, inviting scholars from among the Franks as, a century before, Charlemagne had invited scholars from among the English. Since Latin was then known to but few Englishmen, Alfred labored to translate those books with which he felt everyone ought to be familiar from Latin into Old English. Some of the translation he made himself; notably (according to tradition) a translation of Bede's history of England.

Like Charlemagne, Alfred also established schools at court where boys might learn to read and write.

When Alfred died in 899, after a reign of twenty-eight years, England was well on its way upward. It was strong once more, where it had been almost dead at the start of his reign. It had an efficient government, where it had been reduced almost to anarchy; and the danger of illiteracy had been vanished.

Alfred was buried at Winchester to the sorrowing of the nation. His mild rule had earned him the genuine affection of his people and he was long remembered as the great Saxon hero through the dark days that were yet to come.

ACROSS THE OCEAN

Although the battle of Edington marks the turn of the tide as far as the Viking assault on England was concerned, the Vikings were not yet finished elsewhere. France, which had no king as resolute or as capable as Alfred, had to endure a great siege of Paris between 885 and 887, at the very time that Alfred was taking London to cap his triumph.

The Vikings went on to score triumphs of a more admirable sort over the impersonal forces of nature. After all, they were not merely ravenous monsters intent on destruction, torture and death. Many of them were colonists looking for land. And once the Vikings settled down, they showed a rare capacity to adapt themselves quickly to civilized ways and a remarkable attitude for the development of efficient government. (Nor must we forget that their descendants in modern Norway, Sweden and Denmark have organized what are surely among the most civilized and decent societies in the world.)

Combine the need for land with the fact that the Vikings were among the most daring explorers ever known, and it is not surprising that, in their small open boats, they braved the northern seas and began to find new lands in a western movement the rest of Europe was not to follow for six more centuries.

This westward movement was encouraged by political developments at home. The Norwegian chieftain Harold the Fair-Haired began his rule about 860 and, if the chronicles are to be trusted, remained in power for the incredible length of seventy years. He established his power over numerous Viking clans and forced their leaders into exile.

One of these exiles, a Norwegian chieftain named Ingolfur Arnarson, set sail in 874 and landed in Iceland, an island 650 miles west of Norway and 500 miles northwest of the northern tip of Britain.

It was not an entirely new land. Some have suggested that Pytheas of Massalia, the Greek explorer of twelve centuries before, had sighted the island and named it Thule (thoo'lee). Of course, it isn't at all certain that the land Pytheas called Thule was really Iceland. He probably circumnavigated Britain and it is much more likely that he located the Shetland Islands, 125 miles northeast of the tip of Britain, and gave them that name.

We are on safer ground in granting the initial fame of discovery to the Irish. Celtic monks, seeking new places for missionary expansion after their defeat in England, seem to have located the Faeroe Islands (fair'oh), 250 miles north of Britain, not long after the Synod of Whitby.

About 790, when the Viking fury was beginning to break over Ireland, other monks, possibly based on the Faeroes, reached Iceland itself, only three hundred miles northwest of the Faeroes.

Neither the Faeroes nor Iceland are easy lands in which to live and the Irish did not remain permanently in either place.

They died or left, and by 800 both places were bare of human habitation. It was the Vikings who then recolonized them and who were the first to establish permanent settlements there. The inhabitants of the modern Faeroes and of Iceland are the descendants of those early settlers.

Iceland was used as a base for still further explorations. Icelandic navigators brought back tales of land to the west and in 982, an Icelander, Eric Thorvaldson, better known as Eric the Red, undertook to sail west in search of it. He had just been sentenced to exile for some reason or other and felt that this would be as good a way as any other to pass the time.

He came to Greenland which, at its closest, lies two hundred miles northwest of Iceland. Greenland had certainly never been reached by Europeans before (except for fugitive sightings by earlier Icelanders).

Greenland is the largest island in the world but it is one huge wasteland, covered as it is almost entirely by an immense miles-deep glacier, a final relic of the Ice Age. Only Antarctica is bleaker than Greenland.

Eric tried to get past the floating ice, so he sailed southward to the tip of the island and then turned up the southwestern coast which is the least bleak portion of the island. The northern climate was generally a bit milder in that century than it is now and Eric judged the southern portion of the island to be fit for habitation. By 985, he returned to Iceland to collect colonists and gave them a sales talk that must have been the equal of anything a real estate operator could do today. He even had the incredible gall to call that vast expanse of frigidity Greenland, as a way of convincing people it was overgrown with vegetation. It still carries that ludicrous name today.

Eric gathered his colonists and in 986 headed west with twenty-five ships. Fourteen ships made it and a colony was founded on the southwestern coast near the island's tip. Actually, the latitude was more southerly than that of Iceland, but whereas Iceland gets the tag end of the warm Gulf Stream, Greenland gets the frigid Labrador Current. Nevertheless, rather incredibly, the Viking colonists hung on and stubbornly persisted for many generations.

Indeed, Greenland was a base for still further explorations. In 1000, Eric's son, Leif Ericsson (also called Leif the Lucky), who had been visiting Norway, was returning to Greenland. He tried to hit the southern tip of the island but the weather was foggy and he missed it. He sailed on and reached land which he explored and called Vinland. He then returned to Greenland.

Numerous tales and speculation have arisen over this short exploratory voyage. It seems almost certain that Leif reached the North American continent. He could scarcely have avoided doing so if he sailed far enough, for six hundred miles west of the southern tip of Greenland is North America and the continent is too large to miss.

Of course, Leif reported he found grapes growing in the new land, which is why he call it Vinland ("wine-land"). Due west of southern Greenland, however, is Labrador, on whose bleak coast grapes would certainly not be growing. For that reason, many suppose that Leif explored the coast southward and there have been speculations that have placed him as far south as New Jersey.

There is no sign that any colonies were founded in North America by the Greenlanders or that explorations inland were undertaken. Certain relics have been discovered here and there which some have ascribed to Vikings but all are doubtful cases. The most remarkable find is the so-called "Kensington Rune Stone" discovered near the village of Kensington, Minnesota, by a Swedish-born farmer in 1898. It was inscribed in runes (that is, in the form of the alphabet used by the early Scandinavians), dated 1362, and describes a small exploring party of thirty which met disaster, presumably at the hands of

Indians. Unfortunately, experts in the field seem just about certain the stone is a hoax.

More important, it was announced in 1965 that a map based on the Norse explorations seems to be genuine. It shows an island that has the indisputable shape of Greenland and to the west another island with two inlets that might well represent a first guess at the shape of the southern portion of Labrador. The most interesting part of this matter is that the map seems to be of the fifteenth century and early enough, conceivably, for Columbus to have seen it. If so, the Viking explorations could have been a direct factor in the later discovery and permanent European colonization of the Americas. (This is, however, by no means beyond dispute.)

To complete the story of Greenland, the Viking settlement persisted for four centuries after the time of Leif Ericsson. The weather grew gradually bleaker, however, and life more nearly impossible. After 1400 or so, no further news is heard of the Greenlanders. When, in 1578, the English explorer Martin Frobisher rediscovered Greenland, it was empty of Europeans once more. Only small bands of Eskimos occasionally summered on the island.

The tale of Leif Ericsson has periodically sparked controversies as to who "really" discovered America. That depends on what you mean by "discover." One might argue that the mere sighting of a new land or its exploration is ineffective and unimportant if the news is not generally published and if it is not followed by permanent colonization (assuming the land to be habitable). By this standard, the *effective* discovery of America was made by the 1492 voyage of Christopher Columbus and there is no arguing that.

But was Leif Ericsson the first to sight the Americas, even if only ineffectively? There is controversy there, too.

There is, for instance, a legend of an Irish monk named Brendan who had sailed westward into the Atlantic about 570, over four centuries before Leif's voyage, and discovered land. The tale of "St. Brendan's island" remained current until explorers finally emptied the Atlantic of unknown regions. This has been used to suggest that Irish monks discovered America. It is much more likely, however, that the tale of Brendan is a distortion of the Irish discovery of Iceland (an ineffective one since the colonization was not permanent and the land was forgotten once more).

Then, too, an old inscription in Phoenician characters was discovered in Brazil back in 1872, which purports to tell of a Phoenician vessel driven away from others in its company which were circumnavigating Africa. The vessel reached the bulge of Brazil (only sixteen hundred miles from the nearest part of Africa) and the inscription remains to tell us of the event. It was quickly dismissed as a hoax, but in 1968, Professor Cyrus H. Gordon of Brandeis University suggested it might well be genuine. In that case, Phoenician sailors would have seen the Americas at least a thousand years before even the legendary Brendan.

But all this is an exercise in unconscious racism for the argument is always about the first *white* man to discover the Americas, the natives of the continent being conveniently ignored. The true discoverer of America, after all, was some unnamed Siberian, about twelve thousand years ago during the Ice Age. Eastern Siberia and Alaska were relatively ice free at the time and the lowered sea level (thanks to the vast quantities of water locked up in glaciers) made a land bridge between them that is now drowned in the Bering Strait.

The enterprising Siberian crossed. Others came with him and they discovered America. What's more it was an effective discovery, for the continents were permanently colonized from end to end and the descendants of the original Siberians were the "Indians" who were there to greet all the Europeans who arrived from the Phoenicians onward. And still later descendants inhabit the continents to this day.

THE SON OF ALFRED

Let us return to England at the death of Alfred. There was a question of the succession. Alfred had been preceded on the throne by Ethelred, his older brother, and Ethelred had had young children. They were passed over as infants and Alfred had been made king, but now at least one of those infants, Ethelwald, was a grown man. As son of the older brother, he maintained he had a better right to the throne than Alfred's own son, Edward.

By modern standards, he was right. However, it was only centuries later that the notion of "legitimacy" arose. In the Germanic kingdoms of Alfred's time, all members of the royal family qualified as possible candidates for the throne and the nobles of the kingdom chose (in theory) the particular member they felt would make the best king.

In this case, there was no disputing the greatness of Alfred and his glory reflected itself on his son. The vote of the nobility, therefore made Edward the king.

There were to be other Saxon kings named Edward so this one ought to be called Edward I. However, the habit of numbering the kings of the same name developed only later. In Saxon times, kings were known in later chronicles by some descriptive adjective considered appropriate. Thus, Edward, as the first of that name, was called "Edward the Elder." I will follow this custom, which has the virtue of being colorful. However, it is also confusing for it is easy to forget which Edward comes after which, so I will use Roman numerals, too, where that seems useful. (But in the case of the Edwards, the use of Roman numerals has particular difficulties, for there were additional Edwards in post-Saxon England who *were* numbered. Thus "Edward I" would ordinarily refer not to Edward the Elder who began his reign in 899, but to another king of England who mounted the throne in 1272, nearly four centuries later.)

In any case Ethelwald, out of resentment (or, perhaps, to do him justice, out of a reasonable fear for his freedom and life) fled to the Danelaw. There, he occupied himself, as such exiles often do, in trying to persuade Danish leaders to invade Saxon territories on his behalf and place him on the throne. He would then, presumably, agree to reign as a Danish vassal so that the Danes would gain by it.

In 902, he succeeded in getting the Danes of East Anglia to play his game. In the invasion that followed, however, he was killed in battle. This effectively broke Alfred's old treaty and a new cycle of wars with the Danes began.

How conditions had changed in the past generation, though! Saxon England was much stronger now than Wessex had been when Alfred came to the throne, thanks chiefly to Alfred's own policies. On the other hand, the Danes had had a generation to settle down and to lose that fine barbaric fervor and delight in battle. Furthermore, unlike the Saxons, they had not united under a single monarch and could be picked off piecemeal.

Leading the Saxons was a remarkable brother-sister team, a situation not often found in history. Edward the Elder had a sister, Ethelfleda, who had been married to the nobleman whom Alfred had placed over the Saxon portion of Mercia. Ethelfleda was a strong personality, a worthy daughter of Alfred, and even before the death of her husband, she was the true ruler of Mercia. She is known to English legend, in consequence, as the "lady of the Mercians."

Together, Edward and Ethelfleda faced the Danes. They invaded Northumbria, badly defeated an attempt at a Danish counter-raid and by 910, the Saxons were in control of the region.

That still left the core of Danish power in eastern Mercia and East Anglia. Edward and Ethelfleda were careful not to hasten too quickly and stumble into a disaster that might lose them everything. They spent years in a cautious policy of fortification, building strong points on the Danish boundaries that would secure the Saxon territories in case failure at invasion brought about reprisals.

In 917, Edward was ready to make his move. He invaded eastern Mercia in strength and, beating aside Danish resistance, took their stronghold of Derby. By the end of the year, all of East Anglia was under his control.

The final campaign planned for the next year was delayed when Ethelfleda died suddenly in June, and Edward had to turn aside to take over personal control of Mercia. He did not want it to fall to some other leaders so that Saxon England would be once more broken up into separate kingdoms to the benefit of the Danes.

When he did return to the Danish wars, progress was again rapid and by the end of 918, the last piece of Danish territory owned him for its monarch. The first period of Danish domination over England came to an end only fifty years after the great Danish invasion had destroyed the Heptarchy.

To be sure, this did not mean that the Danes were driven out of England. They remained and intermixed permanently with the Saxon population so that the English of today are descended from both. In fact a number of Danish princes retained limited power under Saxon overlords.

Edward was now more powerful and ruled over a more extensive territory than any previous Saxon monarch. He was more truly king of all England than even Offa had been.

It is ironical, then, that in the course of the reign of Edward the Elder, when the Saxons were triumphing so significantly

over the Scandinavian descendants of Viking raiders, a new
gang of Vikings should be scoring a victory across the sea — a
victory that was to alter English history decisively a century
and a half later.

The scene was France, where the Viking raids had yet to be
met as single-mindedly anywhere as they had been in Wessex.
France was ruled in Edward's time by Charles III, usually
called "Charles the Simple" (the adjective meaning "foolish,"
rather than "unpretentious," and apparently aptly applied).
Charles, a great-great-grandson of Charlemagne but with
nothing of that king about him, was completely incapable of
handling the Vikings.

In 911 came a new great raid by the Vikings. A war band
had occupied the mouth of the Seine River and taken over a
section of land along the southern shore of the English Channel. Their leader was one Hrolf, or Rollo, usually called the
"Ganger" or "Walker." He was called this, according to the
story, because he was so tall and heavy that none of the northern ponies could carry him, so he had to walk. (He had left
Norway originally to get away from the same Harold the Fair-
Haired whose hard rule had led to the settlement of Iceland.)

To be fair, Charles the Simple had other problems at the
time. He was trying to extend his realm far to the east, over
lands ruled by a distant cousin who had just died. He was em-
broiled with numbers of his noblemen. He simply had no time
for the Vikings. All he wanted from them was peace — and
at literally any price.

He wanted to know what the Vikings would take for peace
and they replied they wanted permanent legal ownership of
the land they already occupied so that they might settle down
and live upon it.

Charles the Simple agreed, requesting only that Rollo go
through the motion of accepting Charles as his overlord. This
would save face for Charles and make the treaty look like one
in which Rollo submitted to the all-powerful Charles and re-

ceived a reward for it — instead of what it really was, an unconditional and disgraceful capitulation on the part of the French king.

There is a story that although Rollo agreed to accept Charles as overlord, he drew the line at going through the symbolic gesture of kissing Charles' foot. He ordered one of his lieutenants to do so.

The lieutenant, finding the task no less degrading for himself, seized Charles' foot and roughly raised it to his lips, so that he might go through the motion of kissing it without stooping. Charles fell backward in an undignified sprawl, a truly symbolic posture.

The region now occupied by the Vikings, or Norsemen, was given a new name — Nortmannia, soon slurred to Normandy. The Norse inhabitants came to be called Normans. Rollo allowed himself to be converted to Christianity soon after the treaty and took the name of Robert. By the time he died (931 at the latest) Normandy was well established and he proved to be the ancestor of a notable line of warriors and kings.

THE GRANDSON OF ALFRED

Edward the Elder must have known of the establishment of Normandy (although he could not possibly have foreseen its later significance to England) for by then, England was once more politically involved in Europe, as it had been in Offa's day.

Indeed, one of Edward's daughters had married Charles the Simple and the two had had a son, Louis, who was thus descended from both Charlemagne and Alfred. By then, though, the line of Charlemagne had dwindled to almost nothing. His descendants no longer ruled over the eastern part of that great king's empire, but over France only, and Charles the Simple could not even make that stick.

In 923, Charles was deposed by his fractious nobles, and his two-year-old son was taken for safety to the court of his maternal grandfather in England.

Edward himself is supposed to have had a romantic affair of his own, having fallen in love with the beautiful daughter of a cowherd. It is not certain whether he married her or not, but he had a son by her, Athelstan, who was brought up in Mercia under the eye of his forceful aunt, Ethelfleda.

This made him a kind of Mercian by adoptian which was a good thing, since Mercia still had a dim memory of its independence and greatness, a century and a half before, and sometimes showed perceptible resentment at Wessex' dominance.

When Edward the Elder died in 924, after a successful quarter-century reign, Athelstan was instantly elected King of Mercia and only in the following year became King of all England.

Athelstan built successfully upon the foundation laid by his father and grandfather. Where Edward had been content to accept an acknowledgment of overlordship and allowed Danish rulers to continue to possess a certain degree of independence, Athelstan proceeded to assume direct title over all the land. He took over in York, for instance, where a new immigration of men from Norway had recently strengthened the Danish position there.

What's more, Athelstan aspired to more than England. He wanted to rule all Britain. He insisted on the submission of the Scots to the north and the Welsh to the west. He forced them to pay tribute and to accept the boundary lines he drew for them. He called himself "King of all Britain" and put on a remarkable display of that fact in 934, when he sent his armies well north of the Firth of Forth and had his ships range over the full coast of Scotland to its northernmost tip.

Athelstan's action was bound to produce a reaction. During the half century after the foundation of the Kingdom of Scotland by Kenneth I, that kingdom had led a precarious life raiding Northumbria and trying to fight off the Vikings.

Finally, in 900 (the year after the death of Alfred the Great) Constantine II became King of Scotland. Under him, the Viking menace was brought under control for a time and Scottish dominion was extended to the northern tip of the land once more. Constantine could do little toward the south, however, in the course of his forty-year reign. First Edward the Elder and then Athelstan forced him into a subservient role. Athelstan's northward expedition in 934 served as a last straw and Constantine determined to strike back.

For this he needed allies. South of his own kingdom and west of Northumbria was the Kingdom of Strathclyde. (This is located in that area of modern Scotland which is directly south of Glasgow.) It had held itself free of both Scotland and England and had managed to preserve a precarious independence under Celtic rule. It gladly joined Constantine now and so did various Welsh princes.

Further reinforcements came from Ireland. There, the Vikings were still strong, and a horde of mixed Irish and Viking warriors came under Olaf Guthfrithson, whose family had recently held power in York, and who himself ruled over Dublin.

Allowing for the Viking admixture, it was a close approach to a united Celtic counterattack against the Saxon power, a striking demonstration that after five centuries of Germanic onslaughts, the Celts could still fight back.

Olaf, with a large fleet, sailed into the Humber in 937 and, joined by his Scots and Welsh allies, marched inland. Somewhere in Northumbria at a place called Brunanburh in the old poems written to celebrate the event (the exact site is unknown) the Celtic army met Athelstan's forces and after a long, hard fight, Athelstan won. Constantine and Olaf both escaped alive, but not very many of their followers did.

Athelstan's predominance was confirmed and this moment represents perhaps the peak of Saxon power in Britain. His place in the European family of nations was a proud one, too, and foreigners honored him. When the Normans expanded westward along the southern shores of the Channel and took Brittany, the son of the Breton duke fled to England where Athelstan welcomed him. Haakon, a son of the fearful Harold the Fair-Haired of Norway, also fled there when his brother, with the grim name of Eric Bloodaxe, seized the throne. Both joined Louis, the son of Charles the Simple and the nephew of Athelstan, who had arrived in England the year before Athelstan had come to the throne, and who had grown up in Athelstan's court.

All three eventually regained their thrones with Athelstan's help. Haakon returned to Norway in 935, for instance, defeated his brother, drove him into exile and became king in his place.

Then, in 936, a deputation of French noblemen arrived to ask that Louis return to France as their king in order to end a thirteen year period of anarchy. In the presence of Athelstan and his queen, they swore loyalty to the young teen-ager. He arrived in France as Louis IV, and was known as Louis D'Outremer ("Louis from Overseas").

Louis made an unexpectedly forceful king and perhaps the addition of a descent from Alfred had strengthened the thinning heritage of Charlemagne. However, France was disintegrating into an anarchy of squabbling nobility and no king could enforce much power. After Louis IV, there were two more kings of Charlemagne's line and then it came to a final end.

Three powerful Saxon kings reigning in succession over a total period of sixty-eight years meant that England's internal affairs were established and the government of the land assumed a reasonably efficient form. Wessex had been divided into convenient administrative districts called "shires" (from a Saxon word meaning "division"). As the Danish areas were conquered, they too, were divided into shires. These divisions were not only conveniently small in a time when transportation and communication were difficult, but also tended to break up local loyalties dating back to the days of the Heptarchy.

England is divided into shires (or counties) to this day. The largest is Yorkshire, which is six thousand square miles in area or somewhat larger than the American state of Connecticut. Most of the rest range between five hundred and two thousand square miles in area.

At the head of the shire was the "ealdorman" (a word which has become "alderman"). This meant, originally, "old man." In ancient times, the name applied literally, for it would then refer to the patriarch, the old man of the family whom the rest obeyed. It came to be applied to the chief representative of the ruling family of a district, whatever his age. His function was chiefly judicial and as the importance of the title declined it was replaced by "eorl," meaning nobleman, and this became "earl," a title of nobility peculiar to England.

The central authority in each shire was exerted by the representative appointed by the king, who was sent there to see to the collection of taxes and the execution of the king's orders. Such an officer is, generally, a "reeve," and one who is in charge of a shire is a "shire-reeve" which soon became "sheriff." *
This is the equivalent of the French "count" which gives a better notion of his status, particularly in these days when the American youngster's notion of a sheriff is that of a Western peace officer.

The officials ruling over the shires, as well as the various bishops and landowners, could not be utterly ignored by the king. Life was easier if they were on his side and it was customary for the king, in making decisions, to consult a council

---

* The best known of the sheriffs is, of course, the Sheriff of Nottingham who played the role of prime villain in the Robin Hood legends.

composed of some of these whom he selected for the purpose. This was the "witenagemot" (meaning "assembly of advisers"). They helped choose the new king after the old had died, assisted in making laws, imposing taxes, carrying on foreign negotiations, arranging for the national defense, bringing treasonable nobles to justice and so on.

The witenagemot was a source of strength to a strong king, who dominated it and used its acquiescence to show that the nation was behind him. It was, however, a source of weakness to a weak king, who was dominated by it and made the helpless pawn of conflicting interests.

6

THE SAXON FAILURE

DUNSTAN AND CONCILIATION

Athelstan died in 939, after a fifteen-year reign that had been uniformly successful, and was succeeded by his half brother, Edmund I, who had fought loyally at Athelstan's side at Brunanburh. (England had now become prosperous enough to afford a luxurious way of life for its monarch, and the new king was to be called "Edmund the Magnificent.")

The moment at which a strong king dies and his successor takes over is always a crucial one. Enemies who had been defeated by the old king (or perhaps who had not even dared try battle) are tempted by the confusion inherent in a change of reign and by the possibility that the new king is a weakling. They try again. In this case, the one who tried again was Olaf Guthfrithson, still ruling in Dublin.

Again he landed in Northumbria and to better effect, for it

took some three or four years for Edmund to drive him and his kinsman, Olaf Sitricson, out of the land.

The experience apparently sickened Edmund of the policy of military expansion followed in the previous two reigns. The time and blood required to subdue the Scots, for instance, seemed scarcely worth it, especially since the Scots could always turn to the Vikings for help.

It might be better to try conciliation or, to use a more modern term, coexistence.

In 945, Edmund made a daring move in this direction. He conquered Strathclyde and offered to turn it over to Malcolm I, King of Scotland. (Constantine II had died in 940.) The condition was a simple one, friendly alliance by land and sea. Malcolm accepted. The first step toward friendship between the two British nations had been taken, and while there were to be many, many wars in the next six and a half centuries, coexistence would win out in the end.

The policy of conciliation may have originated with a churchman, the most important man in the kingdom next to the king, in Edmund's time and during the reigns that followed. The man was Dunstan.

Dunstan had been born of good family about 909 near Glastonbury in Somerset, not far from the place where Alfred had made his back-to-the-wall stand. Dunstan had been well educated at Glastonbury Abbey, the oldest and richest in England and, as a young man, had appeared at the court of Athelstan.

At the court, his love of learning and the wide scope of knowledge excited the antagonism of the courtiers. (It is probable that, well aware of his own superiority, he tactlessly displayed it.) There are always handles that can be used against those who seem too brainy, and in medieval times a convenient accusation was that of practicing black magic. Dunstan was denounced as a magician and was forced to leave the court. He became a monk and lived as a hermit.

Athelstan's death changed all that. Edmund was now on the throne and he had been impressed with the young man. He felt a community of thought and decided he wanted the monk as counselor. In 943, Edmund made Dunstan the Abbot of Glastonbury and for a quarter-century afterward, Dunstan was to be uncrowned king and sometimes more powerful than the actual king.

Dunstan reformed and revitalized monastic life in England, following the sterner Benedictine practices that prevailed on the Continent at this time. He insisted on priests being celibate, for instance. He encouraged Edmund in following the policy of conciliating the Danish element of the population, making them partners with the Saxons in government. A full-blooded Dane, Odo, had even become twenty-second Archbishop of Canterbury in 942. And it was undoubtedly Dunstan's influence that was behind the treaty of accommodation with Scotland.

Edmund met his death unexpectedly and violently in 946. He was celebrating the feast of St. Augustine when a notorious outlaw entered the hall. The indignant monarch rushed over to order him out and received a mortal knife wound for his pains. The outlaw was promptly cut to pieces but the king was dead, too, and was buried at Glastonbury.

Edmund's oldest son was only five years old at this time and the reign of a child-king was not thought advisable. Edred, Edmund's younger brother, and the last surviving grandson of Alfred the Great, therefore succeeded to the throne.

He was a sickly man who was content to leave all matters not involving warfare to Dunstan. It was in Edred's nine-year reign that Dunstan had his chance to carry through his reforms which seemed virtually to wipe out the distinction between Saxon and Dane in England.

Once again, though, a new reign was the signal for troubles — and very much the same troubles. Eric Bloodaxe, who had been King of Norway for a time but had been driven from his throne by his brother Haakon, had lived the life of a pirate thereafter. Since Haakon had received help from Athelstan of England, Eric felt little kindliness for that nation. At Edred's accession, therefore, he tried to seize Northumbria.

Edred, like Edmund before him, and Athelstan before Edmund, had to begin his reign by reaffirming Saxon control of this area. This was done by 954, but Edred, conquered by his illness at last, died in 955. He was unmarried and left no direct successor.

Edwy, the oldest son of the previous king, Edmund I, was now a handsome young man of fifteen; so handsome that he is commonly called "Edwy the Fair."

He succeeded to the throne this time, but his reign was short and tragic. At the coronation feast, the young king tired of the festivities, which included much eating, drinking and horseplay. There was a young lady in the palace who was named Elfgifu and whose company he much preferred to the drunken nobility at the table. Discreetly, he retired.

His absence was eventually noted and Dunstan himself, a little the worse for drink, went in search for him. He found the new king with Elfgifu. It doesn't seem there could have been anything terribly wrong going on, for Elfgifu's mother was also there and Edwy's intentions were honorable. (He later married the girl.)

Dunstan, however, was enraged. He felt Edwy's leaving of the table to have been an insult to the nobility and to him and he must surely have felt himself to be much more nearly the King of England than this young man. He railed at the young king and at the women and dragged Edwy unceremoniously back to the feast.

Edwy would have had to be mean-spirited indeed not to resent this. Just as soon as he was settled on the throne, he accused Dunstan of financial irregularities during his control of the treasury under Edred. He exiled Dunstan and turned firmly against all of Dunstan's reforms, even to the extent of expelling unmarried churchmen in favor of married ones.

Unfortunately for Edwy, he was not strong enough to carry things off with quite so high a hand. The Danes of England were entirely pro-Dunstan, of course, and a large and vociferous party rose against the king, led by Odo, the Danish Archbishop of Canterbury.

Edwy didn't have a chance. Dunstan returned from exile in triumph after having been away for less than a year. The northern (Danish) half of England rejected Edwy altogether and accepted the rule of Edgar, his younger brother, instead. Odo then forced Edwy to divorce his young queen and had her abducted and taken away to Ireland. By the time Edwy died in 959, still a teen-ager, he must have had more than enough of the joys of kingship.

His tragedy was carried on beyond the grave, however, for the monkish chroniclers who wove the history of England took care to blacken his character and to make him out a monster.

After Edwy's death, Edgar ruled over all of England. He was a young man, too, but he apparently learned well the lesson of his older brother's life and death. He remained thoroughly subservient to Dunstan. He made the powerful abbot Bishop of London at the very start of his reign. In 961, he made him Archbishop of Canterbury (the twenty-fourth, for there had been an archbishop of short tenure between Odo and Dunstan). He also supported Dunstan's reforms completely.

His reign was most successful and so free of war that he is commonly called "Edgar the Peaceful." The monkish chroniclers attributed this to his support of Dunstan, but there were other reasons, too.

For one thing, Edgar had spent his youth in the Danish regions to the northeast and this made him popular with the

Danes who were therefore less likely to revolt. Secondly, he had a strong fleet which held off Viking troublemakers. And finally, in all truth, Dunstan was a capable ruler who held the affairs of the kingdom in good shape.

Dunstan's belief in coexistence with Scotland showed itself once more in 970, when Edgar peacefully ceded the northern section of Northumbria (the old Kingdom of Bernicia) to Kenneth II of Scotland, so that the boundary between the two nations became what it substantially is at present. Under Scottish domination, what had once been Bernicia came to be known as Lothian.

We don't have any record of the reasoning behind the move. The region, however, was never a firm appanage of England. Its own rebellions, and the frequent invasions of the land by the Vikings and the Scots made it a drain on English strength, for it stuck northward almost literally like a sore thumb.

If what could hardly be held was given up and if Scottish friendship were won thereby, it might be a good idea.

Actually, the farsightedness of the move could not possibly have been appreciated at the time. The Kingdom of Scotland, as originally founded north of the Firth of Forth, was purely Celtic. With the addition of Lothian, however, a region was added that had been under Saxon or Danish domination for nearly five hundred years. Scotland came, then, to be divided into the northern "Highlands" (primitive, tribal, Celtic) and the southern "Lowlands" (relatively advanced, citified, Saxon).

The advantage was with the Lowlands which represented far better agricultural opportunities and could support a denser population. Gradually, it came to dominate Scotland with the result that the Scottish speech became a dialect of English and her ways not too different from those of northern England.

Hostilities between the two nations continued, to be sure, but when the time and opportunity arose for the two to form a united kingdom, a common language made that step the easier.

ETHELRED AND CONFUSION

Edgar did not allow himself to be crowned until he reached the age of thirty in 973. Perhaps he wanted to be old enough to be able to run the coronation entirely his own way, remembering, as he must have, the tragic farce of his older brother's celebration.

Edgar put on a magnificent show that was better than anything of the sort that had ever been seen in Saxon England and did it only five years short of the centennial of the Battle of Edington. Through seven reigns and a full century, Saxon England had remained at the peak to which Alfred had raised it — but now everything started to go downhill.

Edgar died in 975, leaving two young sons. The elder, Edward, was only twelve. Another, Ethelred, was only six. They had different mothers, and the mother of the second, Elfrida, was still queen when Edgar died.

Elfrida, a ruthless woman of driving ambition, according to the chronicles of the time, wanted her own son to be king. She might have succeeded if he had been a bit older. Six, however, was too young, and Edward succeeded to the throne. He is Edward II in the Saxon line of kings.

The struggle between the parties of the two sons (who were themselves too young to take part in the quarrel) was escalated into a struggle over Dunstan's reforms. Elfrida, seeking allies to support her son's cause, took up a violent anti-Dunstan stand. This gained considerable support, for Dunstan, after twenty-five years of unlimited power (except for a short period under Edwy) had made many enemies.

Undoubtedly, Elfrida drew to her side those Saxon nobles who resented Dunstan's Danish policy. This meant that for her son's sake, she raised once again the spectre of racial animosity and stirred up the embers of anti-Danish prejudice.

The party of Edward and Dunstan grew steadily weaker and that of Ethelred and Elfrida steadily stronger until in 987, Edward was assassinated. Undoubtedly, the assassination was carried through by Ethelred's party and probably at Elfrida's instigation.

There was no choice but to make Elfrida's son king and he reigned as Ethelred II.

It was an extremely inauspicious start for what was to be a disastrous reign. Popular sympathy with the dead Edward was great. He was given the name "Edward the Martyr" by which he is known to history, and miracles were reported at his grave. Stories arose (probably false) detailing how Elfrida had stabbed him with her own hand and how he had ridden away, bleeding to death.

As Archbishop of Canterbury, Dunstan had to crown Ethelred, but he did so unwillingly, and retired afterward to Canterbury to spend the last ten years of his life in the quiet performance of his clerical duties. The anti-Dunstan party had won and Dunstan's power was gone, but he did what he could to sour the people against the king.

Ethelred lacked the good advice of Dunstan, which had so upheld the previous reigns. Nor did he have any other advisers who could take Dunstan's place; or if he was given good advice, he had the trick of paying no attention to it. The Saxon word for "counsel" or "advice" is "raed." Since Ethelred lacked advice he was "unraedig" meaning "unadvised" or even "ill-advised."

That came to be his common name, first applied to him, it is said, by Dunstan himself — Ethelred the Unraedig, or Ethelred the Ill-Advised.

Unfortunately, the Saxon word has been converted into a similar-sounding word in modern English, but a word which, despite the similarity in sound does not have the right meaning. The king is called Ethelred the Unready in all the history books. Perhaps, though, the mistake is not as bad as it might be, for Ethelred was also unready to meet the crises that dotted his reign.

The chief of them involved the changes that were taking place in Scandinavia. The old pagan Viking days were passing. In Denmark, a chieftain known as Gorm the Old began unifying the country, and his son Harold Bluetooth turned to Christianity and was converted about 960.

Harold Bluetooth had a son, Sven (usually written Swein, which, however, hides the pronunciation). In adult life he wore a long beard coming down to two points so that he is usually known as Sven Forkbeard. While still a youth, he quarreled with his father, went to war with him and kept it going till, in the course of time, his father died. In that year, 985, Sven Forkbeard became King of Denmark.

Meanwhile, Norway, the very heart and center of the Viking country, was turning Christian, too. First there had been a false start with Haakon, the young Norwegian prince who had been brought up in Athelstan's court. Naturally, he became a Christian, and a fervent one, too. When he returned to Norway and overthrew Eric Bloodaxe, he attempted to convert the country to Christianity, doing this too singlemindedly and too hastily.

There was a strong pagan reaction which was taken advantage of by the sons of Eric Bloodaxe. In the civil war that followed, Haakon (called "Haakon the Good" by the monkish chroniclers) was killed in 961 and, for a generation, Norway returned to its pagan ways just as Denmark was beginning to turn Christian.

One of the Viking chieftains who died at the hands of the sons of Eric Bloodaxe had a pregnant wife who gave birth to a son soon afterward. He was Olaf Trygvesson, who became one of the great Vikings of the age. He was brought up in the court of Vladimir the Great in Russia (where Viking influence had also penetrated). Vladimir was the first Russian ruler to turn Christian and perhaps Olaf gained a notion of Christianity there. Or perhaps he was converted in his later raidings against the British Isles. One legend, no longer believed, was that he was converted while visiting the Scilly Islands (the Tin Isles of the ancient Phoenicians).

In any case, he sailed to Norway in 995, where he raised a rebellion against the unpopular pagan king of the time. He had himself proclaimed king as Olaf I and under him Norway was permanently Christianized. Not long after, Christian influence became dominant in Iceland, too. (In Iceland, the wife of Eric the Red turned Christian, for instance, and when her husband would not follow suit, she left him.)

But Christianity formed, as yet, only a thin crust over the Viking. Both Sven Forkbeard and Olaf Trygvesson led raids against the English coast. These were not quite as horrendous as those of earlier days and churches and monasteries served as effective refuges now — but the raids were bad enough.

It may seem strange that England should suddenly seem helpless before Danish ships again when, for a century, they had been forging steadily forward at Danish expense. Partly the answer is that Sven and Olaf were exceptionally vigorous Viking leaders. An even more important answer was that England was reaping the reward of the anti-Danish reaction. The Danish nobility of the northeastern shores, smarting at the rising power of the Saxon nationalists, increasingly made common cause with the Vikings. (This, of course, fed the fire of anti-Danish feeling among the Saxons, and Dunstan's policy of conciliation was thoroughly and disastrously destroyed.)

By 991, the helpless Ethelred turned to the only course that seemed to be open. He bribed the Vikings to leave. This brought only a temporary respite, of course, and each time a new bribe was required the price was raised.

In 994, Sven and Olaf, working harmoniously together, ascended the Thames River to lay siege to London. London resisted successfully, as Paris had done, under similar conditions, a century before. The pirate-partners turned away and ravaged the southern provinces. It took sixteen thousand pounds of silver to buy them off and by 1001, the price had risen to twenty-four thousand pounds.

To raise the money a special tax on land had to be placed on the shoulders of the population. This was called the "Danegeld." It was levied on six separate occasions during Ethelred's reign and the proceeds handed over to the blackmailing Vikings. The total amounted to 160,000 tons of silver.

(As in the case of virtually every tax, the Danegeld was much easier to start than to stop. It was a good source of income and when the time came that there was no further need to pay the Danes, it nevertheless seemed a shame to turn it back to the people. It was continued, therefore, long after the Danish tribute ceased, and the last recorded collection was in 1163, a century and three quarters after it had first been imposed.)

The collection of the Danegeld was placed in the hands of the local nobles. The effect was to strengthen the position of those nobles at the expense of the people and the king alike, since the power to tax meant the power to control. The government was decentralized as it had been on the Continent for similar reasons. Such a decentralized government with the land-owning nobles petty kings over their own land is called "feudalism." As a result of the Viking raids, then, England began to go feudal in the reign of Ethelred II. The farmers were impoverished by the raids and by the Danegeld and were forced to hire themselves out to the local nobles if they were to survive at all. They became serfs.

What's more English cultural decline, arrested for a while by Alfred's efforts, now continued, and in Ethelred's reign England was an intellectual backwater. In comparison to

France and Italy, it was to remain so for over five centuries.

The reign, however, marked a turning point in the history of London. It had been a notable city in Roman times, England's biggest port, but it was only one of several notable cities.

In early Saxon England, it had the misfortune to be a border town that could not be used as a capital for the various kingdoms. Its location was almost precisely at the point where, in 700, the kingdoms of Essex, Wessex and Kent met. Therefore it was cities such as Canterbury and Winchester that had the prestige of being capitals.

Even in Alfred's time, London was the frontier city between Saxon England and Danish England.

During the tenth century, though, when Saxon kings dominated the Danish districts, London grew in size and by 1000 was probably the largest city on the island. Its successful defense against the Danes in 994 was a bright spot in a rapidly darkening scene and gave it the prestige it needed to become what it has remained ever since: England's great city; the one that put all others, however large, completely in the shade.

THE SECOND DANISH CONQUEST

Ethelred the Unready, unable to lead his nation effectively, or to control his nobles, or to counter the Danes by any means short of repeated, exorbitant bribery, managed to find time to embroil himself with the Duke of Normandy as well.

It had been less than a century since the savage Vikings under Hrolf the Ganger had settled in Normandy, but already a great change had come over the land. The grandsons of the Vikings spoke a French dialect and were difficult to distinguish from other Frenchmen. The frozen coast of Norway was forgotten and all that was retained of the wild old Viking heritage was an ability to fight like devils. Add to that a rather surprising ability to set up an efficient government.

The Normans were deeply involved in French politics and, for the most part, fought against the last kings of Charlemagne's line. Duke Richard I of Normandy (a grandson of Hrolf, and usually termed "Richard the Fearless" in the chronicles) was a strong supporter of the French nobleman Hugh Capet, who in 987 replaced the last of the line of Charlemagne and became the first of a new line of French kings.

Richard I was succeeded by Richard II (the Good) in 996 and it was with him that Ethelred quarreled over some obscure point. Ethelred even gathered ships with which to invade Normandy (as though they could not much better be used against the Danes) but his fumbling attempt was driven off by the competent Norman duke.

Ethelred may then have thought better of it, for he accepted papal mediation and ended the quarrel. Indeed, it may even have occurred to him that a capable enemy could become a capable friend if matters were handled properly, so a marital alliance was arranged. Ethelred was a widower, and Richard had a sister, Emma, who was unmarried. The marriage was arranged between the Saxon king and the Norman princess and in 1002 Emma arrived in England. She must have been quite young at the time, for though her birthdate is uncertain, she lived on for fifty years past the date of the marriage and it is reasonable to suppose she was in her teens at the time. She was called "the Flower of Normandy" and may well have been quite attractive.

However, any move made by an incapable monarch is liable to prove unfortunate, and this marriage, though it seemed a good move at the time, was eventually to have dismal consequences for the Saxons. Emma brought Norman followers with her, capable men whom Ethelred gladly gave office in England, since there were few of his own subjects he could trust. This began the growth of Norman influence in England, gave the Norman dukes a growing interest in the island and an increasing temptation to interfere in its government. The results would become painfully visible in half a century.

At the moment, though, Ethelred had a trick up his sleeve that was incredibly wicked and immediately disastrous.

He had gained power through the anti-Danish factions and these were growing stronger. The English humiliation at the hands of the Vikings, the Danes from overseas, had to be salved, and it was all too easy to blame it all on the stab-in-the-back from the Danes of England. To be sure, there had been Danish nobles who had sided with the Vikings, partly out of resentment against the anti-Danish policies of Ethelred and partly out of a need to come to some settlement with the Vikings since the central government could not protect them. But then, many Danes remained loyal and, for that matter, many Saxons also made an accommodation with the Vikings.

Mere logic, however, is no answer to prejudice, either then or now. Ethelred decided to throw himself into the arms of the extreme Dane-haters among his followers and to avenge the deeds of the Vikings on the heads of an unarmed and unsuspecting portion of the English population.

On November 13, 1002, only half a year after the marriage festivities with Emma had been celebrated, elements of the Saxon population of England rose at a given signal, and killed as many Englishmen of Danish descent as they could reach. Among the slain was a sister of Sven Forkbeard of Denmark — the sister had been living in England as the wife of an English nobleman of Danish descent.

Ethelred must have felt that by this horrible act he would at once show himself to be a strong king, remove a nest of treason from the nation and rouse all England behind him in a great wave of national pride.

It might have done all that if England had existed in a

vacuum. But it didn't. Beyond the narrow sea, unreachable by Saxon mobs, was that ferocious old fighter, Sven Forkbeard.

The news of the massacre (and of his sister's death) drove Sven into a fury, a fury that was all the more dangerous inasmuch as he was just then at the peak of his power. He had allied himself with Olaf Skutkonung of Sweden (that land's first Christian ruler) and together he had battled against Olaf Trygvesson of Norway. In a Homeric sea battle in the Baltic Sea, Sven had defeated his old fellow-pirate, and temporarily destroyed Norwegian power.

All of Scandinavia was now Danish-controlled and Danish-allied and Sven was the greatest power in the north.

With all the resources of Scandinavia behind him, Sven, swearing vengeance, quickly raised the largest fleet that he had yet taken against England and in 1003 landed at Exeter, far in England's southwest, managing to achieve complete surprise. The commander at that place was one of Queen Emma's Normans and he proved as completely able to turn traitor as any Dane or Saxon in the realm.

The following years saw English humiliation at its deepest. The massacre of the Danes had not removed the traitors at all, or given Ethelred one ounce more ability than he had earlier possessed. Nor was Richard of Normandy disposed to come to the aid of his brother-in-law. Rather, the treason of various Normans in England was the occasion for new quarrels between England and Normandy.

Ethelred could only continue to pay the Danes whatever he could scrape up and hope the storm he had brought upon himself would pass.

It didn't. It grew worse. An attempt by the English to raise a fleet miscarried through bickering and inefficiency. Alphege (al'fej), the twenty-eighth Archbishop of Canterbury was killed in 1012 by a Danish war band when he refused to give them the money they demanded. And finally, in 1013, Sven, fully assessing the utter inability of England to defend itself, decided to go all the way. He would take the kingdom and undo the work of Alfred.

The full effect of Ethelred's encouragement of the criminal massacre of the Danes now showed itself. The Danelaw still held many people of Danish descent and no one could possibly expect them to show loyalty to Ethelred. They joined the invading Danish forces at once. District after district fell to Sven without a fight and each bloodless victory by the invaders made other places the more reluctant to resist.

Ethelred was in London and only that city showed signs of wanting to resist. Ethelred, however, was no hero after the fashion of his great-great-grandfather, Alfred. Not for him the last stand. Quietly, Ethelred slipped out of London and fled southward. He had already sent his wife and children on ahead to Normandy, where her brother still ruled. He himself finally made his way there and was welcomed as a refugee king.

Sven Forkbeard of Denmark was now King of England. It was a climax to his hectic and violent reign of nearly thirty years, a reign that had been almost uniformly successful. And he stopped now at the very height of his career, for not long after Ethelred had fled, Sven died very suddenly. He had been King of England for six weeks.

CANUTE

Suddenly, all was in confusion. With Sven dead, the Danes fell back and the Saxon nobility saw their chance. They could offer to receive Ethelred back again, but they could also take advantage of his position by forcing him to meet a price. He would have to abandon certain practices of which they disapproved, grant more rights and privileges to the nobility, and promise to forgive and forget past treacheries.

This sort of thing fit the medieval notion of the king's position. The king did not succeed to the throne automatically; he had to be elected by the nobility of the kingdom from among the eligible members of the royal family. This meant that the king owed certain duties, in return, to the nobility, and if he failed in those duties, they could depose him.

Naturally, such a viewpoint could lead to anarchy. What were the king's duties to the nobility? Who was to say? Any nobleman who wished to revolt could always find some failure of the king to excuse his own treason.

Eventually, an alternate theory of kingship arose. The king was supposed to come to the throne not through any election, but simply by the right of descent. There was a fixed rule of inheritance ("legitimacy") and the new king became king according to that rule, whatever his qualifications or lack of them.

Such a king was king by the grace of God who had fixed him in the line of descent, and he owed no duties to anyone but God. The nobility or the people could not make any demands on him or rebel against him, without sinning against God. If the king were evil or incompetent, the only thing his subjects could do would be to wait till God in his own time reformed him or removed him by death.

For centuries, the European nations fought out these alternate theories of the kingship — whether the king was responsible to his subjects or only to God. Toward the end of the Middle Ages, the monarchy by grace of God was winning out everywhere, but in England that victory was less complete than on the Continent and the counterattack against it was more speedily and more effectively mounted.

One reason for that was that in England there was a particularly strong tradition of *written* agreements between the king and his subjects; agreements that made it plain that there was indeed a form of contract between monarch and people.

The first written document of this sort (or at least the first one of which we have records) was that between Ethelred and his subjects on that king's return from Normandy. This particular document turned out to have little value in itself, but it set an enormously important precedent that was to lead, by many steps (some wavering) to the Constitution of the United States and to our American form of government.

Sven's death and the sudden rallying of the Saxon nobility about Ethelred seemed to spell the doom of the Danish conquest, so recently achieved.

Sven had two sons, Harold and Canute. The former, as the elder, held dominion in Denmark itself. Canute, the younger son, had accompanied his father to England, and had commanded the navy while Sven had led his troops inland. Canute tried to have himself named King of England in his father's place. To put that through at the moment was, however, impractical. Canute decided to return to Denmark and gather a stronger armament.

The next year, 1015, Canute was knocking at England's door again. He found that Ethelred had easily managed to dissipate the goodwill that had been temporarily his. England was right back where it had been, with disaffected lords, discontented people and an incompetent king.

Canute might have effected the conquest of England as easily as his father had two years before, but unfortunately for the Danish cause, Ethelred died in 1016, after a thirty-eight-year reign of almost unrelieved disaster.

One relic of Ethelred's reign, however, may be considered as a still-living contribution of value to world culture. This is the epic poem *Beowulf*. It survives today because of a single manuscript, rather beaten-up and imperfect, which was still readable as late as the eighteenth century. That manuscript is almost illegible now but copies of it were made in 1787 and a printed version first appeared in 1815.

From the handwriting of the original manuscript, it is supposed that that particular copy must have been written about 1000, in Ethelred's time. Of course, it was not the first copy that existed (though all earlier copies have apparently been lost forever). The original written copy may have appeared two centuries earlier in Mercia and it must have existed in oral tradition for some centuries before that.

The story is placed in fifth-century Denmark. The Danish court is beset by a monster, Grendel, who carries off and eats men from the court every night, till Beowulf, a young hero from southern Sweden, confronts the monster and kills it. He must then fight the monster's even more fearful mother. Beowulf eventually succeeds to the Danish throne, rules fifty years, and, in old age, fights a dragon that is ravishing the kingdom, killing the dragon but dying of his own wounds afterward.

Ethelred's death was bad news for Canute, for the feckless old king had a hard-fighting son by his first wife (*not* Emma of Normandy). This son is Edmund II, though he is usually called Edmund Ironside because of his grim fight against Canute.

In the last years of his father's reign, Edmund controlled northern England and with restless energy tried to oppose the invading Danes. His generals deserted him or else refused to fight unless King Ethelred's own presence could be guaranteed.

Once Ethelred was dead, Edmund could do better. He fought Canute valorously, and won a few victories. Twice he came to the defense of London, which held out strongly against the Dane. Finally, he challenged Canute to single combat, pointing out that it was better that one man should die on either side than thousands.

A Viking of old might joyfully have welcomed the chance, no doubt, but Canute was no Viking of old. He was, in fact, a

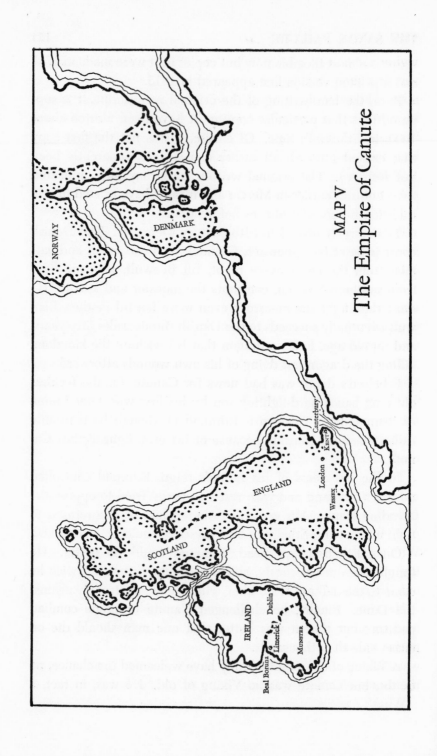

MAP V
The Empire of Canute

highly intelligent and realistic man who pointed out that he was of slender build while Edmund was a hardened hulk of a man. Therefore, Canute said, he himself would surely lose and he would not throw away Danish fortune in that fashion. He suggested instead that they should divide the kingdom as it had been divided in Alfred's day.

This was agreed upon, Canute took the north and Edmund the south. The arrangement could scarcely be a stable one, but at least it promised a breathing space in which each side had the chance to prepare for a better fight. But if Canute had had the bad fortune to see Ethelred die, he had much better fortune now.

Unfortunately for the Saxon cause, on November 30, 1016, not two months after the agreement, Edmund Ironside died, probably of natural causes, though afterward there was talk of assassination.

There was no one left to oppose Canute. Ethelred had two sons by Emma, the elder a fourteen-year-old boy named Edward, who couldn't possibly be counted on to lead an army. By the beginning of 1017, the discouraged Saxons accepted Canute as their king. The next year, Canute's brother, Harold, died, and Canute was sole King of England and Denmark.

To English surprise, Canute turned out to be a good king, miles better than incompetent old Ethelred had ever been. Indeed, Canute made every effort to soothe English national pride and reconcile them to his reign. He called together the Witenagemot and had them go through the motions of electing him king, so that he might not have it said that he ruled only by right of conquest.

He also married Emma, the widow of Ethelred, in 1017, to lend an air of continuity to the government. (And perhaps to please himself as she must still have been attractive; and if she was older than Canute — who was only twenty-three or so at the time — she was still young enough to bear children.)

What's more, Canute made no effort whatever to make England over into a Denmark, or set it under Danish laws. Rather the reverse — he kept England under its Saxon laws, and resided in England as a Saxon king. It was Denmark rather which was subjected to foreign influence. English priests flooded into the country, so that it soon lost its last traces of paganism. And it was Englishmen who were appointed to its bishoprics.

Canute was a pious Christian himself and pleased his subjects by taking a well-publicized pilgrimage to Rome in 1027. This effectively put to rest any Saxon notions of him as a "heathen Dane."

At first, Canute had a Danish bodyguard, but as little by little he felt the Saxons had grown to trust him, he sent his Danes back to Denmark and replaced them with Englishmen. He even accepted a Saxon, Godwin, as his chief adviser. In 1020, he made Godwin Earl of Wessex and Kent, and the Saxon earl became the greatest man in the kingdom next to Canute himself.

The reasonableness with which Canute refused personal combat with Edmund Ironside continued, if we are to trust the more famous story about him.

It goes as follows. Growing annoyed with the elaborate flattery of his courtiers, Canute decided to teach them a lesson. He had his throne set up on the seashore and took his seat on it as the tide was coming in. In grandiloquent terms, he ordered the tide to fall back, nor presume to wet his royal robes. He then sat there and the tide, uncaring for the monarch's pronouncement, rose and lapped about his rich cloak. Turning to his courtiers, he demanded to know where the God-like powers were which they had so loudly claimed were his.

(It is ironic that many people who tell this story mistakenly think that Canute was the vainglorious one and that he really thought the tide would stop at his bidding.)

However mild Canute might have been within England, he played the role of conqueror outside. He led an expedition into

Scotland in 1017, and forced the Scots to submit without a fight. In 1028, he took over a very restless Norway. For a brief few years, there was a Danish empire that included Denmark, Norway, England, Scotland, and even Iceland and Greenland — a political union never seen before and never seen afterward.

Ironically, at the very time the Danes were reaching the pinnacle of their success, the Vikings were losing their more than two-century-long foothold in Ireland.

The Irish hero of this struggle was Brian, who was born about 941, near a ford across the River Shannon, about ten miles north of the Viking center at Limerick. The name of the ford was Beal Boruma, and from its name, the Irishman was known as Brian Boru.

Brian began as ruler over a small territory, but little by little, through constant fighting, he enlarged his dominions, liberated Limerick and united all of Munster (the southwestern quarter of Ireland) under him. By 1002, the year of Ethelred's massacre of the Danes, he had defeated the Vikings of Dublin in battle and was recognized as "high king"; that is as overlord over all Irishmen.

But the Vikings were still in Dublin, despite Brian Boru, and the men of Leinster (the southeastern quarter of Ireland) were sufficiently antagonistic to Brian to be willing to ally themselves with the Vikings.

The final battle came in 1014 (at just about the time when Sven Forkbeard was dying). Brian Boru was an old man now, well over seventy, but he was on the scene of battle at Clontarf, on the outskirts of Dublin, to inspire his men, while his son did the actual leading of the Irish army.

In a twelve-hour battle, both Irish and Vikings lost heavily, but in the end it was the latter who broke and fled. Some were slaughtered and some escaped to the ships in the harbor. One party, in flight, came across the tent in which the aged Brian Boru sat. He was recognized and killed.

But the dead Brian had left an Ireland free of Viking rule as his legacy. Those Vikings who remained settled down and melted into the population.

One might wonder whether Canute might not have made some attempt to conquer Ireland if he had lived long enough. Perhaps not, for his empire was an unsteady one. Even in Canute's lifetime, Norway was in rebellion and when Canute died in 1035, about forty years old and after a reign of only eighteen years, Norway broke away at once and the brief day of Danish empire was over.

7

THE FINAL REIGN

EDWARD THE CONFESSOR

There were a number of possible choices for the throne of England after Canute's death. For one thing, old King Ethelred II had had two children by Emma. While she had remained in England as Canute's queen, the children, Edward and Alfred, were in Normandy with their uncle, Richard II.

At the start of Canute's reign, Richard had gone through the motions of demanding the throne of England for Edward, the elder child, but there was no chance of that while Canute lived, of course. The young princes grew to manhood in Normandy, therefore, half-Norman by descent and becoming all Norman in thought and feeling.

Edmund Ironside, the oldest son of Ethelred by his earlier wife, whose own rule had been so brief, also had two sons, Edmund and Edward. These had been hurried out of the nation after Ironside's death and were now in far-off Hungary, living in peace.

And in addition, there were two sons of Canute. One was an illegitimate son, Harold Harefoot (perhaps because of his fleetness). The other was Hardicanute (hahr"dih-kuh-nyoot'), Canute's son by his queen, Emma. At Canute's death, Emma, of course, did her best to see to it that her son by Canute became king, and in this she was joined by the powerful Earl Godwin of Wessex. The northern nobility, however, was unwilling to see Godwin become too powerful and they pressed for Harold Harefoot.

As it happened, Hardicanute was in Denmark at the time of Canute's death. He had to secure the throne of Denmark for himself and that made him slow in getting to England. That, in turn, made it possible for the party of the on-the-spot Harold to win out. He was elected king by the witenagemot in 1037 and became Harold I. Emma was exiled.

But then Harold I died in 1040 and Hardicanute became King of England as well as Denmark only to die himself in 1042. Both sons were incompetent, in any case, and rapidly grew unpopular. With them ended the Danish dynasty in England, less than thirty years after the successful invasion of Sven Forkbeard.

Now the problem of succession arose again. The number of possibilities had decreased. Neither Harold nor Hardicanute left descendants and more distant members of the Danish royal family were unacceptable. The princes in Hungary were too far away. What about the princes in Normandy?

Richard II, their protector, had died in 1028, but his son, Robert I of Normandy, was no weakling. Indeed, for his cruelty and self-will he was known as Robert the Devil. The English princes were his first cousins and he pushed for their succession (as his father had) even while Canute was still on his throne.

But when Robert I died in 1035, a period of near-anarchy

succeeded in Normandy. The fact that this happened just as Canute died also was a stroke of luck for England. The state of confusion over the English succession that followed, plus the two short Danish reigns, could have made all sorts of things possible for a vigorous Norman duke if one had existed at the time.

As it was, the younger of the two princes in Normandy, Alfred, was anxious to win back the throne of his father, Ethelred II, even if Normandy was in no condition at the moment to give him help. A little too anxious, perhaps. Not long after Harold I had been placed on the throne, a letter is supposed to have come to Alfred, urging him to come to England and overthrow the Danish monarch.

Perhaps it was a genuine call from Saxon nationalists planning an uprising, or perhaps it was a deliberately cast lure, designed to entice a possibly troublesome prince within snatching distance. If the latter, it worked. Alfred raised a fleet and sailed to England. He marched inland and, according to the story, was met by Earl Godwin, who greeted him in friendly fashion, quietly distributed the invading party over a number of houses and then captured them and had them killed. Alfred was taken to London where he, too, was killed.

That left only Edward, a quiet prince, much given to the religious life. In later years, he became known as Edward the Confessor, since he was so punctilious about attending confession and other rites.

In 1041, he was invited by Hardicanute to return to England. Hardicanute (unlike Harold) was a half brother of Edward's. The two had the same mother. Furthermore, Hardicanute had no heirs and perhaps expected none and was willing to make Edward his heir. Edward, who was now a mature man of nearly forty, was greeted with respect and friendship and was on the scene when Hardicanute died the next year.

Earl Godwin used his influence in favor of Edward's succession and so the son of Ethelred the Unready became king, as

Edward III the Confessor, a quarter-century after Ethelred's death. Thus began the last reign of a Saxon king of the line of Alfred the Great.

Edward was no strong king — he would have made a better monk. In fact, he was a monk on the throne.

Earl Godwin was the real King of England during the early part of Edward's reign, despite his role in the death of the king's younger brother, Alfred. Edward could not extort punishment for that because Godwin was too powerful to strike down just at first. Moreover, Godwin was perfectly willing to swear an oath that he had had nothing to do with Alfred's murder and was easily able to get other noblemen to bear him witness in this.

Godwin showed his power by forcing Edward to marry into his family. The king married Godwin's daughter, Edith, in 1045. If, by this, Godwin was hoping to have a grandson who would someday become King of England, he missed out. Edward had taken a vow of chastity and he meant it. Edith remained his wife in name only and they had no children.

There seems no question but that Edward harbored a serious grudge against Godwin and his house, either because of Alfred's death or because of the arrogant way in which the great earl displayed his power. This persisted to the very day of Edward's death and was to be of great importance to the course of English history.

Edward also made it perfectly clear that he was not fond of his mother, Emma. He may very reasonably have resented the years in which she was Queen of England without seeming to mind that her older sons lived in exile. Nor could he have felt kindly over the fact that after the death of her second husband, she should have labored to have her son by that husband become king to the exclusion of her older sons by her first husband. Edward may even have suspected his mother of complicity in Alfred's death. In any case, he seized her property and kept her in a convent till her death in 1052.

The chief point of conflict between Edward the Confessor and his Saxon noblemen lay in the fact that under Edward, the Normans were growing increasingly important in the kingdom. From our modern viewpoint, it is almost automatic to feel a kind of impatience with Edward. Surely it was not "patriotic" to bring in "foreigners." The Saxon lords who opposed the Normans, on the other hand, seem to be virtuous nationalists.

Yet one can see Edward's point, too. The Saxon lords were proud, contentious and grasping. The overbearing earl Godwin and his sons controlled virtually all of southern England. Another lord, Siward, controlled the north. Still another, Leofric, controlled the midregions that had once been Mercia.

All of these were self-willed. None of them were trustworthy. Godwin, the most powerful, had come to the fore as the favorite of a Danish king and had done his level best to assure a Danish succession, so how could he pose as a Saxon patriot anyway?

On the other hand, Edward had been brought up in Normandy, had learned to speak Norman French and to prefer the more elegant ways of Normandy to those of ruder England. He must surely have envied the way in which the dukes Richard II and Robert I had ruled powerfully and kept their own nobility under complete control.

It was only natural for him to feel kindness toward the Normans, to consider them a touch of the only real home he had ever known. What's more, the Norman functionaries he had imported he could trust to feel loyal to him since only in him could they be safe. It came about, therefore, that Edward introduced Normans and Norman customs, used Norman handwriting and adopted Norman styles of clothing. He introduced the office of "chancellor" after the Norman fashion. The chancellor was the king's secretary who took charge over internal affairs and became, in later reigns, the most powerful functionary in the land.

There were, naturally, many Saxon courtiers who tried to

curry favor with the king by imitating his Norman ways. This more and more irritated those nationalists who hated foreign ways and clung to Saxon traditions. Godwin put himself at the head of these, either out of conviction or out of a play for power.

Edward sought positions for his Norman favorites. He couldn't very well depose Saxon landowners and hand over their property to Normans. That would have meant a universal revolt at once. Church offices, on the other hand, were always available, and Edward began to fill them with Normans. He went too far, however, in 1051, when he appointed Robert of Jumiège, a Norman, to the post of thirty-second Archbishop of Canterbury.

At this Godwin moved into open revolt and raised an army against the king. Edward couldn't possibly have stood against Godwin without support, but it turned out to be easy to find such support. In any land in which a few great noblemen dominate the state, there is always jealousy among them. The most powerful of the nobles can always count on the combined enmity of the rest. Had Godwin beaten Edward, he might easily have made himself king and, to prevent this, the great nobles of the north, Leofric and Siward, promptly marched to the support of Edward.

Godwin and his sons were forced into exile, Queen Edith was placed in a monastery, and for a while Edward was triumphant — triumphant enough to make a real splash of his Norman bias by inviting the young Duke of Normandy to come visit him.

WILLIAM THE BASTARD

To see who this young duke was, let us go back to the time of Robert the Devil of Normandy. Robert had no legitimate children, but by a low-born mistress (the daughter of a tanner) he had a robust young son whom he named William.

In those days, the fact of illegitimate birth was not always taken seriously in connection with royalty, but the low birth of the mother gave ample room for snobbery on the part of the Norman nobility, and William must early have received such snubs as he was not to forget in a hurry.

In 1034, Robert decided to make a pilgrimage to Jerusalem. Such pilgrimages were popular in those days, but they were also dangerous undertakings and the chance of coming back alive was not great. Furthermore, if Robert were delayed in his return, the nobles would be quick to assume he was dead, and would snatch at the dukedom. So, for that matter, would the French king.

Robert, therefore, decided to make as sure as possible this would not happen by demanding that his nobles swear allegiance to his illegitimate son, William, before the pilgrimage began. The nobles swore as directed, Robert left — and never came back, for he died en route. The new duke, therefore, was William II, an eight-year-old boy.

The nobles had sworn and so the boy was accepted as duke, but he was a nonentity. The great question was who would exert the real control in the state and over this the Norman nobility squabbled and warred. Normandy was the scene of wild and unaccustomed anarchy. It was no surprise that a number of them left for England once Edward the Confessor came to power there.

The young Duke William passed through a most dangerous and hectic childhood. He was torn from one side to another as noblemen vied for the risky greatness of serving as Protector and ruling the duchy in his name. Three of these were killed, one after the other.

William's salvation may have been the French king, Henry I. Henry had a rip-roaring time handling his own nobility, so there was a certain bond of sympathy between him and young

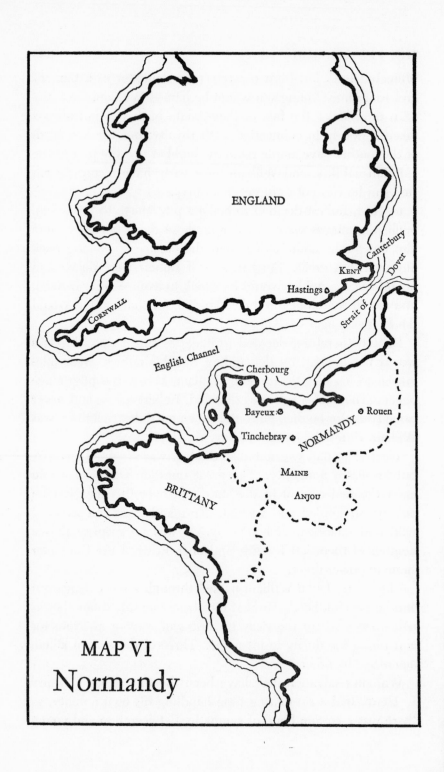

ENGLAND

Canterbury

Kent

Dover

Hastings ⊙

Strait of

Cornwall

English Channel

Cherbourg

Bayeux ⊙

Rouen ⊙

Tinchebray ⊙

NORMANDY

MAINE

Anjou

BRITTANY

MAP VI

Normandy

William. It may also have seemed to King Henry that in return for helping the young man, he would have a grateful ally
later on in his own fights with arrogant vassals. There was, after all, already a tradition of friendship between the Norman
dukes and the French kings.

Finally, William himself was a precocious youngster who, in
the course of his difficult youth, grew to be a hard and angry
man who acted quickly and with vigor.

Between his own ability and the French king's help, William made himself master. By the time he was twenty years
old, he was leading an army against the musters of the dissident
nobles. With Henry's help, William smashed his fractious nobility, then turned and helped Henry beat down a nobleman
whose land adjoined Normandy.

On one occasion, William took a castle whose defenders had
taunted him with his low birth, and the slaughter he visited
on them afterward in return for the insult made men no longer
eager to remember who his mother was. In fact, the battered
nobility discovered that in William they had a harsher devil
than ever his father had been.

William II despised pretense and showed a kind of arrogance
in actually flaunting his origin. On his official papers, he
signed himself "William the Bastard," but it is quite certain
that no one else would have dared call him that to his face.

The ruthless duke ground down his nobles in a way that was
unprecedented elsewhere in western Europe. To the last inch
he made them pay for every snub and danger they had visited
on him. He forced all of them to swear allegiance directly to
him in defiance of the ordinary rules of feudalism. He did not
allow them to build fortified castles without his specific permission — which was rarely given. He endowed monasteries
generously and kept the Church on his side as a strong and
useful ally against the nobles.

In short, he built up a centralized, efficiently organized
duchy that may have been small in area, but was one that made

its duke richer and stronger than any ruler in the west. He
made his nobles keep the peace and, with the waste of internal
warfare abolished, William had money to spare to hire
mercenaries and equip them with the latest and best in military equipment.

He built up a standing army of a thousand armed knights,
an enormous force for the time. Even the King of France (William's overlord, in theory) couldn't match that. England certainly couldn't, for in England at this time all was as inefficient
and as internally disorganized as Normandy was efficient and
organized.

In 1051, when Edward the Confessor invited young William
to England, the Norman duke was twenty-four years old and
already had a Europe-wide reputation. He was firmly seated
on his throne and the rough and rowdy Norman noblemen tip-
toed in his presence.

To Edward, William must have seemed everything that
could be desirable in a successor. They were cousins, for William was the great-grandson of Edward's grandfather, Richard
I of Normandy. If Edward died without heirs, the choice
would have to lie between William, the successful, powerful,
hard and intelligent Norman duke, or a period of anarchy in
which Saxon nobles fought over the throne with the hated Godwin possibly winning out.

Surely, it must have seemed to Edward that his own personal preference would serve the good of England as well and
he might have implied to William that he would be named
heir to the throne. This would have suited the proud duke well
for it would have given him the title of king, a title he could not
gain for Normandy itself.

But did Edward really make such a promise? If he did, it
would have been made in the strictest secrecy, so how could it
have become known? There is at least a good possibility that
the story of the promise is not true. It may have been invented
by the exiled Earl Godwin, seizing upon the occasion of Wil-

liam's visit to England, and judging shrewdly from his knowledge of Edward what Edward's feelings must be.

It would pay Godwin to put out the story (whether it was true or not) for though William of Normandy might be related to Edward the Confessor, the relationship was through Edward's mother. William of Normandy was *not* a member of the royal family of Wessex; he was *not* a descendant of Alfred the Great.

This piece of propaganda (like the earlier invitation to Alfred) worked out very well in the short run. All England was in a turmoil and Edward had never been so unpopular. Riding the wave of resentment that followed the visit of William the Bastard, Godwin returned to England in 1052, re-established his power as well as that of his sons and of his daughter, Edith, and was soon stronger than ever.

He was able to dominate the now-cowering King Edward to the point of forcing him to send some of his Norman favorites into exile. In particular, Godwin had the Norman Archbishop of Canterbury deposed and in his place there was appointed, as thirty-third Archbishop of Canterbury, one of Godwin's most important clerical supporters, Stigand, a Saxon who had served as chaplain to Canute and as adviser to Emma. It is hard to see how anyone could have been less palatable to Edward, but he was forced to acquiesce.

This, however, produced an unfortunate side effect. In replacing an Archbishop of Canterbury, it was, in theory, necessary to seek the agreement of the Pope. For nearly two centuries, however, the papacy had been in the weakest of hands and it had scarcely been necessary to pay much attention to it. Whatever figurehead Pope was in power would agree to anything, and so Godwin must have felt.

In 1051, however, a certain young and newly-appointed Cardinal named Hildebrand was making himself a power in Rome. For over twenty years he was to control the succeeding Popes until he himself was named Pope. In all that time he labored (and successfully) to restore the prestige and power of the papacy, and to do this he meant to keep the control of the appointment of bishops firmly in papal hands. Godwin could not be expected to know that this sudden change was taking place in Rome, and England suffered as a result.

Since Godwin had not felt it necessary to seek the Pope's approval, Pope Leo IX, on Hildebrand's urgings, refused to recognize the appointment of Stigand. Succeeding Popes continued Hildebrand's policy, and this was to play its role in the English disaster that was to come.

Godwin had little time to appreciate his return to power, in any case. He died the year after, on April 15, 1053, and his oldest son, Harold, succeeded to his title as Earl of Wessex and to his actual power as uncrowned King of England.

MACBETH THE USURPER

In the north, Siward, Earl of Northumbria (what remained of the old kingdom of Northumberland) performed a feat that was not terribly important in itself, but that, thanks to the writings of a great dramatist five and a half centuries later, is well-known to every educated Englishman and American.

The key event took place in Scotland.

Scotland managed to survive the new Viking onslaughts on the island of Britain. To be sure the northernmost part of the land was temporarily torn away by Viking raiders and became a virtually independent Earldom of Orkney. A Norwegian, Thorfinn, held this earldom during the reigns of Canute and of Edward the Confessor.

The rest of Scotland, however, remained under its native

kings. Malcolm II was King of Scotland during Canute's reign. While England was falling under the Danish hammer blows, Malcolm managed to tighten the tenuous Scottish hold on what had once been Bernicia and was now Lothian. It had been ceded to Scotland in Edgar's time a half century before, but the English nobility of the north had on various occasions tried to take it back. Malcolm managed to hold it against all comers. In 1031, he had to accept Canute as his theoretical overlord, but he held on to Lothian just the same.

Malcolm died in 1034 and was succeeded by his grandson, Duncan. The new king reigned for only six years. There was a blood feud between his family and that of Gruoch, the wife of his general, Macbeth. Gruoch's grandfather had been killed fighting against Malcolm II, who had been Duncan's grandfather. In the primitive tribal society that was Scotland at that time this was ample justification for Gruoch (Lady Macbeth) to try to kill Duncan. She persuaded her husband to rebel and in 1040, he rose against the king, and killed him in battle.

Actually, Macbeth was also of the royal family. Both he and Duncan were members on their mothers' sides and it is hard to say at this distance who had the legal right to the throne by later standards. By the standards of the Scotland of the time, the throne belonged to him who could seize it and that turned out to be Macbeth. He ruled for seventeen years, from 1040 to 1057, and on the whole was a capable king. There is no sign that he was considered by his people to be a usurper.

Duncan's son, Malcolm, fled to England and, as is usually the case with royal exiles, he did his best to find friends who would help him back to the throne. He found such a friend in Siward, the Earl of Northumbria.

Siward helped Malcolm because he hoped to profit by it; he expected to take back Lothian. He might have justified himself by stating that Macbeth was a usurper but, if so, it would have come with remarkably poor grace from his mouth. Siward had become Earl of Northumbria in 1041, the year after Macbeth had become king, and he had neatly brought about his own succession to the title by killing the previous earl, who happened to be his wife's uncle.

Siward beat Macbeth in battle in 1054, but not decisively. Then, in 1057, in another battle, Macbeth was killed and Duncan's son ascended the throne as Malcolm III. Siward died soon thereafter, without having managed to seize Lothian after all. That region was to remain permanently Scottish.

The material in this story, as embellished by later legends, was taken by William Shakespeare and made into *Macbeth*, his great tragedy of treason and murder which was first produced in 1606, five and a half centuries after the events it described.

In producing this masterpiece, Shakespeare managed to distort history utterly. Duncan became a hoary old king, renowned for his mildness and benevolence, instead of a comparatively young one, renowned for nothing but sloth and incompetence. Macbeth is pictured as treacherously slaying Duncan while the king was a guest in the general's castle, so that to murder and treason, Macbeth joined the still greater crime (to a primitive society) of violating the laws of hospitality. (Actually, Shakespeare borrowed this from a tale concerning an earlier Scottish king.) Macbeth is then pictured as a cruel usurper, haunted by his unprovoked and horrible crime, and hounded to his death by an enraged circle of virtuous foes, of whom Siward, pictured as the ideal, stoic English warrior, was one.

None of it is so, but the play is a wonderful one just the same, and while it exists (probably as long as civilization does) poor Macbeth will live on as one of the great villains of history.

Shakespeare also includes Banquo and his son, Fleance. Banquo is described as a fellow-general of Macbeth's who was assassinated at the order of the increasingly suspicious usurper. Fleance escaped and was supposed to have given rise to the kings who later ruled over Scotland and who, in Shakespeare's time, had come to rule over England, too.

Undoubtedly, Shakespeare wrote the play to please James I, the Scottish king who had mounted the English throne in 1603, not long before the play appeared. Since Banquo was James' ancestor (supposedly) and Macbeth was the slayer of Banquo, it was natural to blacken Macbeth's character by every possible means.

Unfortunately, there seems no historical reason to suppose that Banquo and Fleance ever existed, or that the royal Scottish line of later times could be traced back to such individuals.

Edward the Confessor does not appear in Shakespeare's *Macbeth* but he is spoken of. He is referred to as "the most pious Edward" by an unnamed lord who describes how Duncan's son has been received at the English court.

Later there is a scene before Edward's palace in England, when the Scottish lord, Macduff, strives to rouse Malcolm to lead an army back into Scotland against Macbeth.

At one point a doctor emerges from the castle and Malcolm asks if the king is coming, too. The doctor says:

> "Ay, sir; there are a crew of wretched souls
> That stay his cure . . .
>   . . . at his touch —
> Such sanctity hath Heaven given his hand —
> They presently amend."

Macduff, listening in wonder, asks Malcolm afterward what disease the doctor spoke of. Malcolm replies:

> " 'Tis call'd the evil:
> A most miraculous work in this good king;
> Which often, since my here-remain in England,
> I have seen him do. How he solicits Heaven,

Himself best knows; but strangely-visited people,
All swoll'n and ulcerous, pitiful to the eye,
The mere despair of surgery, he cures,
Hanging a golden stamp about their necks,
Put on with holy prayers; and 'tis spoken,
To the succeeding royalty he leaves
The healing benediction. With this strange virtue,
He hath a heavenly gift of prophecy,
And sundry blessings hang about his throne
That speak him full of grace."

The disease here spoken of as "the evil" or, sometimes more specifically as "the king's evil," is scrofula, a tuberculous swelling of the lymph glands of the neck, with a variety of unsightly side effects.

For some reason, it came to be believed that the touch of a king could heal the condition. The practice was most commonly followed in France, and in England the first practitioner was Edward the Confessor, who brought the practice from France. It was just another one of his Norman ways, but his ostentatious piety and holiness made his touch most desired. (Many legends of miracles grew up around his memory in after times and he was sainted in 1161, a century after his death.)

The custom of touching for the evil continued, on and off, in later centuries, and reached a new peak of popularity with James I and his successors. So pleased was James I at becoming King of England that he simply had to practice touching for the evil since that would prove him a legitimate English monarch. Shakespeare drags in the mention of it (for it has nothing to do with the plot) and specifically says " 'tis spoken/ To the succeeding royalty he leaves/The healing benediction" in order to please James.

Actually, James was a physically dirty individual of appalling habits; his touch was much more likely to give disease than cure it.

HAROLD OF WESSEX

The last thirteen years of Edward's reign belonged entirely to Harold, Godwin's oldest surviving son. He was about thirty-one years old when his father died. He succeeded to the title of Earl of Wessex and Kent, and strove mightily to seize control of the rest of England either in his own name or in that of one or another of his brothers.

Siward, Earl of Northumbria, together with his son, died in the course of the expedition against Macbeth, or soon after, and Harold's brother, Tostig, was granted the earldom.

The heirs of Leofric of Mercia were put aside on one pretext or another and their lands were parcelled out among Harold's other brothers. When some of the deposed lords sought the alliance of the Welsh, Harold and Tostig combined to march against them in 1063, and cowed them into sullen silence once more.

Meanwhile Edward was in his sixties, a great age for those days, and he had no children. The question of the succession was very much in the air. To be sure, Edward undoubtedly favored William of Normandy for the succession but, in these days of Harold's supremacy, he dared not make the suggestion openly.

As for the royal family of Wessex, the only members left were the descendants of Edmund Ironside who had been living in far-off Hungary. There had been two sons originally, when Ironside had died a half-century before, these were Edgar and Edward, nephews of Edward the Confessor. Edgar had since then died, but that still left Edward.

What's more, Edward had married the daughter of the German Emperor, Henry II (a good marriage indeed for an exiled and landless prince) and by her, had had several children, including a son, Edgar, and a daughter Margaret.

Edward had to be the answer. He was bound to be popular. After all, he was a descendant of the great Alfred, and also a son of Edmund Ironside, whom distance in time had converted into a great hero in the eyes of the English. Ironside had fought Canute fearlessly, saved half the kingdom, and, but for his sudden and early death, might have won back the rest. The English were probably sure he would have. Add to these ancestors, the personal tale of a tragically romantic exile, and what more could be wanted in an heir?

So in 1064, King Edward invited his nephew, the younger Edward (called "Edward Atheling"; that is, "Prince Edward," "Atheling" being used as the title of the heir apparent) to England. That proved to be a popular move. Edward Atheling came to England at once with his wife and children and was greeted with delirious joy.

Yet Edward the Confessor did not give him an audience immediately. Perhaps the king's secret yearning for William of Normandy as heir made him reluctant to confer his formal blessing on Edward Atheling. Or perhaps Harold, who wanted neither William nor Edward Atheling as king, maneuvered to keep the prince from appearing at court. It is hard to say.

The situation was bound to come to a crisis soon, but Edward Atheling solved matters by dying almost immediately after he reached London. There was some suspicion afterward that Harold had arranged the death, for it certainly fitted his ambition, but there is no proof of it and sudden natural death was quite common in those days.

That left only Edward's son, who was now Edgar Atheling, but he was a youngster of perhaps thirteen at the time of his father's death, and it did not seem the time to have a youngster on the English throne.

Some grown man would be needed for the next king and

there were only two who were strong enough and forceful enough to seize the throne, even though neither was a member of the royal family. These were Harold of Wessex and William of Normandy. Which was it to be?

There is reported now a famous event which may never have happened. That is, we get it from Norman sources and since it served to give William a kind of claim to the English throne, it may be nothing more than Norman propaganda.

The story is that Harold, in 1064, somehow got into a boat for some reason and was driven by a sudden storm to the coast of France. (Other versions were that he deliberately went to France on some errand but was driven off course by the storm and was wrecked.) In either case, he was seized by a local nobleman at the site where he came ashore.

Wrecked mariners, by the customs of the time, could be imprisoned and held for ransom, and Harold was a first-class prize. William of Normandy, receiving the news of this, forced the lord to disgorge his captive, partly by threat and partly by bribes, and soon Harold found himself in Rouen, William's capital.

There he was treated with the greatest friendliness and respect, and William, in most comradely manner, asked Harold to use his influence to help gain the succession to the throne for the Norman duke. Under ordinary conditions, Harold could scarcely think of anything he would less care to do, but there were Normans all around him and smiling coldly down upon him was the ruthless Duke William.

Harold had to agree. William then wanted him to repeat it before a council of his lords. Harold was required to place his hand upon a Bible and swear, which he did. The Bible was then removed from the table on which it lay, the coverings of the table were also removed and beneath was found a large container filled with bones of saints and other relics. This was supposed to make the oath more binding.

Harold was then allowed to return to England.

The tale of the oath, as I said before, comes only from the Normans, so that it is uncertain whether it is true or not. Even if it were true, an oath given under duress can scarcely be considered binding.

But now things were beginning to break badly against Harold. The Northumbrians had been under Harold's brother, Tostig, for some time, but they had no cause to be fond of him. He is reported to have been cruel and rapacious and the Northumbrians rose against him in 1065, and drove him out. They decided to choose an earl for themselves and picked Morcar, a son of old Leofric of Mercia.

In earlier years, Harold and Tostig had stood side by side in brotherly amity, but the present time was crucial. Edward the Confessor was clearly in the last months of his life and Harold knew he would have to face William of Normandy soon. He did not want a group of disaffected Northumbrians at his back.

So he decided to appease them at the expense of Tostig. He agreed to accept Morcar as the new earl. Tostig was furious. He felt betrayed and he determined on revenge. He left the country but, as events proved, not for long, and Harold was to end with precisely the situation he had sacrificed his brother to avoid.

Edward the Confessor was now dying and what his last wishes were, if he expressed any, are not known. The Normans later claimed that Edward, on his deathbed, insisted that Duke William was his heir; the Saxons maintained that he had named Harold. Looking back on the situation impartially, it seems much more likely that Edward would have chosen William than Harold, but it really doesn't matter. The decision was not to be made by Edward's word, but by force and, to begin with, Harold was right on the spot.

8

THE NORMAN CONQUEST

THE BATTLE OF STAMFORD BRIDGE

Edward died on January 5, 1066, and this opened the most important year in English history. Edward had ruled over England for twenty-four years. Through much of the time he had been little more than a body keeping the throne warm while others squabbled through the years to control the kingdom and decide the succession.

Still these had been rather peaceful years and though England remained a cultural backwater, it had become materially prosperous. London had grown to be an important center of commerce and was now by far the most important city in the land, and it was to maintain its primacy of place permanently. The total population of England at this time is estimated to have been 1,500,000.

Harold was at once proclaimed king as Harold II and, potentially, began a new dynasty. It was clear, though, that the start of his reign would be a most troubled one, for Duke William, receiving the news of Edward's death and Harold's accession, began at once to make preparations for an invasion.

He was, after all, cousin to the old king where Harold was no relative at all. William was also reasonably certain that he himself was the personal choice of the old king for the succession. And, if the story were true that Harold had sworn to help William become king, he might view Harold as a blasphemous oath-breaker.

But the rights and wrongs of the matter probably interested few. Duke William offered volunteers good pay, the chance at a good fight, plus the promise of glory, loot and land. Men flocked to him and William accepted them all.

All broke right for William. Those who had interest in opposing him found themselves impotent. Thus, Henry I of France had died in 1060 and had left the French throne in the hands of a child, Philip I. In 1066, Philip was still only fourteen and France was in confusion. There was no central power to exert pressure against William or to threaten Normandy with a takeover if William's expedition came to grief. (If there had been, William might have preferred not to take the gamble of an overseas invasion.) As a matter of fact, at the moment, one Baldwin of Flanders was regent of France. It was Baldwin who controlled the young king and supplied what central government there was, and this same Baldwin happened to be William's father-in-law and was kindly disposed toward him.

Furthermore, the County of Anjou which was just south of Normandy and which was in a state of chronic war with it, was itself tied into knots with internal fighting. It would have loved to interfere with William's project but at the moment it couldn't.

Then again, William gained an important ally in the Pope. The papacy, still guided by Hildebrand, remained bitterly offended over the appointment of Stigand to the Archbishopric of Canterbury. They had demanded Stigand's removal once again and Harold had firmly refused. Pope Alexander II therefore gave the papal blessing to William's project. That did much to hearten the men already under William and improved the chances of recruiting additional men.

The excitement of the time is reflected in a long tapestry (of which 231 feet still exist) twenty inches wide. This was kept in the cathedral at Bayeux, a Norman coastal town, during medieval times and it is therefore called the "Bayeux tapestry." Tradition has it that it was woven by Matilda, the wife of William and the Duchess of Normandy, in commemoration of this great time.

It begins with Harold's trip to France and the oath he took on relics to help William get the kingdom. It is also remarkable in that it shows men gazing in wonder up at a comet. A comet did indeed appear in that fateful year of 1066, the very comet known in later years as Halley's Comet. (The English astronomer Edmund Halley in 1705 demonstrated it to be a periodic member of the solar system, returning to the vicinity of the earth and therefore becoming visible every seventy-six years.)

In earlier times, it was widely believed that since stars and planets generally influenced events on earth, the sudden appearance of an unusual heavenly object could only be for the purpose of indicating some unusual or catastrophic event on earth. Since every year saw catastrophes on the earth, the prophecy never failed.

In this particular year, it was clear that either Harold or William was going to gain or lose a kingdom, so for one of them matters would be catastrophic. In the Bayeux tapestry, a courtier is shown hastening to tell Harold of the sighting of the comet and Harold is pictured as perturbed. Clearly, it would be the official Norman line that the comet would portend disaster for Harold, the oath-breaker.

It is easy for us to laugh, now, at such astrological nonsense, but we must not underestimate the effect of such matters at the time. If the Normans believed that the comet was a surefire indication that Harold was doomed, their morale would rise and they would fight all the harder. If the Saxons could be convinced that their king was an oath-breaker who was bringing down upon himself the displeasure of God, their hearts would sink correspondingly. Whether William believed such matters or not, it would clearly have paid him to make use of the comet to the full.

It might even be said, then, with literal truth, that the stars in their courses were fighting for William.

Yet Harold was no weakling or coward. He was a renowned warrior who had spent his years in the field. He knew of William's preparations and he took measures against them. He gathered an army in the south and he kept a fleet in readiness in the Channel. He was completely ready for all eventualities — in the south.

Unfortunately, he could not remain in the south. His brother, Tostig (surely the villain of the year from the Saxon standpoint) was still hankering for revenge at any cost because of Harold's willingness to see him ejected from Northumbria. He had been searching for someone to help him mount an invasion of his own to regain Northumbria and he finally found the man he was seeking in Harold Hardrada (Hawr'-ruh-duh), or "Hard-Ruler" of Norway.

Harold Hardrada had a life straight out of a historical novel. To begin with, he was the half brother of King Olaf II of Norway, who ruled in Canute's time. In 1030, Olaf II had been defeated by Canute, Norway had briefly become part of the Danish Empire, and Harold Hardrada had had to flee.

He went to Russia and served the Grand Duke Yaroslav who, at that time, ruled a vast eastern tract. Harold was a tall handsome man and the daughter of the Grand Duke is supposed to have fallen in love with him. Yaroslav was annoyed at this and Harold Hardrada found it advisable to leave the country in a great hurry. He moved southward to Constantinople, the capital of the Byzantine Empire (the fading remnant of the old Roman Empire) which was now in its last days of greatness.

At that time, the Byzantine emperor hired mercenaries to make up a personal bodyguard. These came from among the Swedish tribesmen (Varangians) who had invaded Russia and who now formed a ruling class there. Harold Hardrada joined this "Varangian guard" and soon became its leader. He was employed by the Byzantines in various parts of the Mediterranean world, with considerable success, and was even supposed to have made a journey to Jerusalem.

However, Harold Hardrada eventually got in trouble in Constantinople, too, presumably through the interest he roused in women's hearts. According to some stories, the Empress herself was attracted to him.

He left Constantinople in the usual hurry, retraced his steps through Russia, marrying the daughter of Yaroslav this time and taking her back to Norway with him. He had accumulated considerable wealth through his adventures and he had no difficulty, once he had returned to Norway, in having himself recognized as its king.

Yet the habit of adventure was fixed and when Tostig approached him with the suggestion that together they invade England, Harold Hardrada could not resist. He was over fifty years old now, but his joy in battle remained strong.

In September, 1066, the Norwegian force moved up the Humber and advanced into Northumbria. Harold, waiting anxiously in the south for William, left the defense of the north to Morcar, but that defense turned out to be inadequate. Harold Hardrada and Tostig were victorious and marched into York.

Harold was in a dreadful dilemma. William's invasion was delayed from week to week and from month to month and Harold's bored army was breaking up. The Saxon ships, consumed with useless sea duty were brought back to port, a number being lost in the process. And now Harold received the news of the Viking victories in the north.

He *had* to advance northward to meet this new threat, take care of it, and come back as quickly as possible in order to continue waiting for William. Gathering up his army, he swept them northward; moving so rapidly and skillfully that he was upon the invaders before they knew what was happening. The armies met at Stamford Bridge, eight miles east of York, on September 25, 1066.

Harold, desperately anxious not to ruin his army before it had to face William, offered Tostig the return of Northumbria, hoping to wean him away from Harold Hardrada and thus force the Norwegian to choose between retreat and sure defeat. Tostig, however, did not have the face to doublecross the ally he had brought with him and he therefore demanded to know what English territory would be ceded to Norway.

Harold, according to the tale, gave a ringing answer: "Seven feet of English ground for a grave; or a little more since Hardrada is so tall!"

Harold was as good as his word. Some of the army was detailed to help gather the ripe harvest but those who were left fought as though inspired and the invaders were utterly smashed. Harold Hardrada was killed and his thirty years of adventures across the length and breadth of the continent came to an end in seven feet (or a little more) of English ground at last. His son, however, was allowed to return to Norway, where he reigned as Olaf III. Tostig was also killed, and the north was secure.

It was Harold's finest hour; but not many more of any sort were left him.

THE BATTLE OF HASTINGS

Duke William's incredible luck continued to hold.

All through August, he had been waiting for winds to come tearing up from the south so that he might move his fleet northward across the Channel. Had the Norman fleet arrived in August, Harold would have been ready for it, defeated it in all likelihood, and then swept north at leisure to take care of Tostig and Hardrada.

Had the winds continued to be wrong through the fall, or even for another month, William's gathered forces might have broken up for the winter and to gather them in the spring once more might have proven impossible.

As it was, though, the wind might have done its work to William's order. It came from the south neither too early nor too late, but just, just right. It turned just in time to bring William to the southern coast of England on September 28, 1066, three days after the Battle of Stamford Bridge, when the southern shores were empty of an organized army.

The Norman expedition — of which only one-third was actually Norman, the rest being mercenaries — landed without opposition in Sussex, near the coastal town of Hastings. Harold, his army, and his fleet were two hundred miles away.

A story is told of the landing that reminds one of a similar story told of Julius Caesar when the latter led an expedition to Africa. As Duke William stepped off his ship — the last man of the expedition to touch English soil — he stumbled and fell. A deathlike hush fell over the army at this omen of ill fortune, but the Duke sprang to his feet, holding his arms high, each hand full of English earth, shouting, "Thus have I seized England!"

But William was cautious. He engaged in no sweeping moves inland. He had no intention of being caught by Harold's thunderbolt as the Norwegians had been. Instead, he fortified himself on the coast, within reach of his ships in case he had to retreat, and waited.

The news of William's landing reached Harold on October 2. Madly, he raced southward.

It might have paid Harold to do a little waiting himself; to let his army rest and regroup; to gather more men, and rally the countryside. William would keep for a while.

But this he did not do. Furious at the fortune that had taken him away from the south at precisely the wrong time and perhaps over-elated at the successful lightning march that had smashed the Norwegians, he could think only of a second lightning march. He passed through London with scarcely a pause to let his army draw its breath and was on the southern coast by October 13, eleven days after the news of the invasion had reached him.

The two armies faced each other, but with what a difference! William's force had had fifteen days of rest (except for a little joyous looting) and fifteen days in which to plan the battle and set up fortifications. The Saxon army on the other hand, had had a harrowing march northward, had fought a desperate battle, and had then had a harrowing march southward.

Saxon and Norman faced each other at a town called Senlac (since renamed "Battle"). The backbone of the Norman army consisted of fifteen hundred mounted knights, a tremendous force at the time, but one that wasn't as overwhelming as it would become in decades to come. The knights were still but lightly armored and the heavy armor that was soon to encase knights and steeds and convert them into precursors of the modern tank was yet for the future. These knights were strongly supported by archers, with their small crossbows,

(The deadly longbow that was to mark English battle tactics a few centuries later had not yet been developed.)

The Saxons, for their part, were expert wielders of the battle-axe, and any Normans who got closer than arrow range would be cleft by the whirling and deadly axe blade.

Harold had seven thousand men and they outnumbered the Normans, but that meant little since at least half the Saxon army consisted of green peasants who had been drafted on the spot. Again it would have paid Harold to wait. He was on his home ground. He could gather together a large number of men if he were patient, including those of the regular army who had not yet straggled in. He could have fortified himself in a strong position and waited for William to attack. William would have been forced to attack sooner or later, or his army would wither away and reinforcements across the Channel could not easily be counted on.

If Harold had waited and let his men rest, he would surely have won.

But to all the strokes of luck that William had so far had, there now came the greatest of all. Harold made the decision of a madman. With his army half-gathered and half-exhausted, Harold decided to strike.

Receiving the news, William hastened forward to force the battle before Harold had an attack of good sense and veered off. He surprised the Saxons, who managed hastily to form a defensive line at a place that was not ideal for the purpose.

Even so, had the Saxons held firm and steady, the battle might at least have been drawn and William's position was such that a bloody, drawn battle would have been no better than a defeat, and he would have had to leave.

William felt out the strength of the enemy. He sent in his cavalry and it was beaten off. He used his archers and they were countered by slings and spears.

So William decided to count on the Saxon's lack of judgment, already well-displayed. He ordered his men to turn and retreat quickly, and the Saxons with yells of premature triumph poured out of their line in pursuit. William held his retreat orderly, nor were his men panicked for they knew what they were doing. The maneuver had been carefully planned.

The Saxons, on the other hand, in wild jubilation dashed forward, each on his own, and when the Normans turned, with a snap, to fight again, they found themselves facing a disorganized horde they could easily cut down.

Twice this happened, and the Saxons were decimated. All they could hope for now was to save what they could, beat an orderly retreat, find some place where they could lick their wounds, gather reinforcements, and assemble to try a second battle.

But even that was denied them. Harold's brothers were killed and as the sun was westering, an arrow among many came flying toward the Saxons and struck Harold in the eye, killing him at once. He had been king for ten months.

The Saxons were now leaderless. The one man of resolution and courage, even if he had been wanting in judgment on this day, was gone, and the day ended in total victory for the Normans.

That one battle had swung the pendulum. What the Saxons had won in a century of warfare against the Britons; what they had saved in a century and a half of warfare against the Danes; they now lost to the Normans in a single battle in one morning and afternoon, in which the cream of the Saxon nobility was destroyed.

That one battle decided that England was to be Norman-governed; that it was to be knit, through Norman interest, to the Continent; that a new civilization was to be built up in the island, with Norman and Saxon finally melting together to form the English of today, and that out of the fusion would come a form of government not quite like any other; one that was to have its own peculiar weaknesses and strengths but which, with that of a daughter nation, was to dominate the world in the nineteenth and twentieth centuries.

If the Battle of Hastings had been won by Harold, how much of this would have come to pass? What might have happened that did not happen because William won? We cannot tell, and yet, considering the unusual history of England after the Battle of Hastings, it passes belief that the battle could have ended otherwise without altering world history drastically. That is why the Battle of Hastings can fairly be included on almost anyone's list of the decisive battles of the world.

Prior to the Battle of Hastings, England had been invaded over and over again. The Beaker People had come, then the Celts, and then the Romans. The Angles, Saxons and Jutes had followed them and after them the Danes and finally the Normans. I have mentioned six conquests of England in this book; the Normans were the sixth conquerors — and the last.

In the nine centuries since Hastings, no army has successfully carried through an invasion of England, and rarely has one even managed to make a respectable attempt. Our own century has witnessed the most recent threat, and its failure, in 1940.

The long period of security and freedom from the wars (except for occasional civil broils) could be attributed at least in part to the strong and efficient government given the island by its Norman overlords. And whatever the cause, the long stability gave England its chance to develop its own unique form of government.

THE LAST OF THE SAXONS

On the day after Hastings, of course, the importance of the battle was not yet apparent. William held only a patch of coast and England was still England, to all appearances.

The witenagemot (or what remained of it) gathered in London and selected Edgar Atheling as king. Once again, and for the last time, a descendant of the old royal house of Wessex, the grandson of Edmund Ironside and the great-great-great-great-great-grandson of Alfred, sat on the English throne.

It was an empty gesture, however. Edgar was still a youngster with no aptitude for the kingship. Worse still, the surviving Saxon lords, even in the face of total catastrophe, could not unite but thought their rivalries more important than combined resistance to the Normans. William could march north with impunity for none of the quarreling and disorganized lords could raise an army against him.

When Duke William appeared before London, Edgar Atheling gave in at once. The great Church figures, even Stigand, the Archbishop of Canterbury, did not have much heart for resistance, since William carried with him papal approval of his cause. The northern earls of Mercia and Northumbria were not anxious to fight for the south, preferring to withdraw that they might preserve their fighting strength and use it to keep their own lands intact.

London, therefore, in the end, did not resist. William sent in a contingent to build a fortress to house a Norman garrison and this was the nucleus of what came to be the Tower of London. When that was done, William entered, and on Christmas Day, 1066, was crowned William I, King of England. His career had reached a climax partly through his own very real ability and partly through an amazing combination of fortunate events in the course of this most extraordinary year.

The Duke of Normandy had become King of England and William the Bastard became what he has been known as in history ever since — William the Conqueror.

Saxon rule over England came to an end, after some six centuries, and in its place was the line of William I, which kept permanent hold of the throne. Some forty monarchs have reigned in England in the nine centuries since the Norman

Conquest, and every one of them has been descended from William I. The present English monarch, Elizabeth II, is twenty-ninth in one line of descent from William the Conqueror, and in that line of descent are included sixteen monarchs.

Yet the line of Alfred the Great did not die out altogether. Edgar Atheling and his sister, Margaret Atheling were, in 1067, taken to Normandy by William for safekeeping. They managed to escape and in 1068 arrived in Scotland. Malcolm III, the son of the murdered Duncan and the conqueror and successor of Macbeth, was still ruling there. The years he had spent in England had left him half a Saxon himself. On his return to Scotland he had introduced the Roman version of Christianity in full vigor and all but wiped out the remnants of the old Celtic Church that had lingered on in the far north ever since the Synod of Whitby had killed it in England four centuries before. Now Malcolm was, in his turn, the refuge of the Saxon royal line.

The Scottish king found Margaret Atheling to his liking, and was undoubtedly aware that if he married her, his successors might some day have a good claim to the English throne. He carried through the marriage, therefore, and, indeed, all later kings of Scotland could thus trace their descent from Alfred the Great. Since the kings of Scotland eventually became rulers of England as well (though not because of this marriage, after all) the same can be said of the English monarchs of the last three and a half centuries. Elizabeth II is thirty-sixth in line of descent from Alfred and included in that line are five Saxon rulers of England, ten rulers of Scotland and eight rulers of modern Great Britain.

Meanwhile, the northern earls were finally striking back at the northward tide of Norman conquest in the hope that they might at least keep their corner of the land free of Norman influence. With them, were two surviving sons of the dead King Harold.

To their aid, moreover, came Sven II of Denmark. Sven was a nephew of old King Canute and a grandson, through his mother, of Sven Forkbeard himself. He had been born in England and had become King of Denmark in 1047. He spent much of his reign fighting Norway under Harold Hardrada. After Hardrada's death and William's victory at Hastings, Sven bethought himself that he might easily claim title to the throne of England, and sent his fleet to help the northern earls against William.

Malcolm III of Scotland also sent forces to aid the rebels and Edgar Atheling served as titular leader of this contingent. Relatively weak Norman forces were overwhelmed at first, and in 1069, William was forced to hurry north in person.

He came with a strong army, bought off the Danish fleet, and fell like a thunderbolt upon the rebels. To make sure that the north would remain quiet thereafter, he deliberately devastated a sixty-mile stretch of territory between the towns of York and Durham. This "harrying of the north" resulted in a depopulation and famine that left its marks for decades, and even centuries, but it achieved its aim.

Organized revolt against William was impossible after 1070. The abortive Danish attempt at intervention was ended, and a still more bumbling attempt a couple of years later came to nothing. This was the final end of three centuries of Scandinavian raids on the English coastline. Never again were Norway and Denmark to be dangers to England.

William eventually raided Scotland and came to an understanding with Malcolm in 1072. Edgar Atheling had to get out of Scotland quickly, and he fled to Flanders to be out of William's power. (He spent a long and checkered life, thereafter, fighting here and there, sometimes even in the service of Normandy — for he was eventually reconciled with William — and sometimes as far as the Holy Land.)

Stigand, the Archbishop of Canterbury, had meanwhile been deposed, and Edwin, the last Saxon duke of Mercia, had been killed. Morcar, the last Saxon duke of Northumbria, had had to flee and join the final bit of resistance to William.

That final bit was no more than a guerrilla war, carried on with no real possibility of success by a Saxon named Hereward. He is usually called Hereward the Wake for some reason, possibly because he was thought to be related to a contemporary family of that name.

Hereward had joined the Danish expedition which had come to help the rebellion and when they left, he carried on unaided. He set himself up in the Isle of Ely, a swampy district some seventy miles north of London. There he maintained himself with the kind of romantic valor one often finds among guerrillas. Diehard Saxon rebels flocked to him in 1071, among them Morcar, as they had flocked to Alfred in his swampy stronghold two centuries before.

Norman forces trying to penetrate the bogs and rushes, the winding streams and trackless thickets of the area found they had to leave their horses behind and face men who knew every inch of the terrain. Time after time, they were cut down.

Finally, William threw a blockade about the entire district and slowly, step by arduous step, tightened it. As famine grew within, the monks of Ely, seeing no way out, offered to show William a path into the very heart of the resistance. William took that path and the guerrilla forces collapsed and had to surrender.

What happened to Hereward is uncertain. As the "last of the Saxons," romantic legends rose about him in later years. He was supposed to have escaped and carried on his guerrilla activities for several years with uniform success until William finally granted him a return of his lands and immunity from punishment in return for allegiance. That these legends represent the truth seems unlikely, for they are just the kind that would be invented by a defeated and humiliated people who would need some hero for themselves.

The even more insubstantial stories about Robin Hood and

his band of outlaws, which began to grow up some two centuries later, are sometimes viewed as still another set of Saxon daydreams of resistance. It is easy to view Robin and his merry men as Saxon guerrillas and his chief enemies, the Sheriff of Nottingham and the Bishop of Hereford, as Norman oppressors.

THE FIRST OF THE NORMANS

The Norman rule of England was distinctly different from the Danish rule. To be sure, William the Norman had some points in similarity with Canute the Dane. Both were of Scandinavian stock; both were good fighters and efficient administrators. Both had the intention of ruling England well and according to English laws and customs.

There was the question of language, however. The Danes and Saxons spoke virtually the same language and could communicate. Yet the Norman aristocracy, though they could trace descent from the Vikings and were only five generations removed from them, had thoroughly accepted the French language and culture. To English eyes, they were Frenchmen, whose language they could not understand and whose ways were abominable.

The Normans, for their part, faced sullen Saxons, speaking what seemed to them a barbarous tongue, and could not help but assume an arrogance that made them the more unpopular. When two people cannot understand each other's language, there is no chance of "soft words." Communication has all too often to be established by means of a shove or a blow, and it was the Normans who had the preponderance of force.

William himself tried to learn the Saxon language and wrote

his charters and decrees in Latin and in Old English, but in this he was exceptional. William's immediate successors, and his noblemen generally, refused to learn Old English. Norman-French became the language of the court, of law, of government, of literature and polite society. English was left to the peasantry.

Then, too, styles of warfare were changing on the Continent and William brought the new styles with him and had to change his English policy to suit. The armored knight was becoming more heavily armored and more elaborately trained. Hastings was only a beginning in this direction and soon it would be that an army of foot soldiers, wearing leather jerkins and wielding spears or axes could not stand for a moment against heavy cavalry, and William intended to have heavy cavalry.

But for a man to serve in such cavalry, and be a knight, he had to have ample revenue. It took money to buy arms and armor and train oneself to use them. It took money to raise a large horse capable of carrying armor for itself and an armed man to boot. It took a great deal of money to equip and train a whole squadron of knights under one's command.

The only revenue in those times was from land and this meant that William had to give land to those he felt would form his heavy cavalry. Since he could not trust the Saxons for understandable reasons, he had to rely on his Normans. This meant he had to give his Normans large tracts of land and the only land that could be had for the purpose belonged to the Saxon nobles. It followed, therefore, that the Saxons had to be evicted and the Normans put in their place, establishing an almost purely Norman aristocracy over a largely Saxon peasantry. By the time of William's death there were no more than six Saxon landlords of any consequence in all England.

Furthermore, the concept of the castle had been introduced in France some time before, a kind of fortified strong point, in which a lord might live in peacetime and which could, at a moment's notice, become an impregnable redoubt in wartime. Norman castles began to rise throughout England and the chance of victorious Saxon revolts diminished. An aroused peasantry might sweep all before them but sooner or later, their wave would break against the firm rock of a castle, where the Norman lord could outwait them until the deadly knights appeared in force.

Thus, even as late as 1100, the total number of Norman knights in England was only five thousand. Yet this sufficed, amply, to hold a population three hundred times as large in subjection. Against the armor that protected the knights and the stone walls that protected the castles, the flails and scythes of the peasants could do exactly nothing.

William went even farther. There was one institution that served Saxon and Norman alike and that was the Church. If the churchmen were allowed to remain Saxon they would keep Saxon culture alive for centuries and, in the end, would overcome the Normans. There was ample precedent for this in history. When the Germans took over the western provinces of the Roman Empire, the clergy of those provinces remained Romans and in the end the Germans were absorbed and learned to speak languages of Latin descent. The Vikings who settled Normandy turned French because they turned Christian first and the clergy were French.

So William decided to make the English clergy Norman. His chief ally in this was Lanfranc, a native of northern Italy who came to Normandy when he was about thirty-five and Duke William was still a disregarded teenager. When William married Matilda of Flanders in 1053, there was some technical opposition on the part of the Church. It was a case of Lanfranc to the rescue. He interceded with the Pope and managed to worm a papal blessing out of him. This gained William's lifelong friendship.

Once Stigand, the Saxon Archbishop of Canterbury was deposed by William, with papal permission, in 1070, the new king replaced him at once with Lanfranc, the smooth Norman of Italian birth, who now served as thirty-fourth archbishop. He was sixty-five years old at the time of accession but was destined to remain at his post for nineteen years, living to the patriarchal age (almost incredible for those harsh times) of eighty-four. Another Norman, Thomas of Bayeux, was appointed Archbishop of York.

Lanfranc, with the backing of William, undertook a thorough reform of the English Church, remaking it in the light of the doctrine of the powerful monk Hildebrand, who, after being mightier than the Pope for a quarter of a century, became Pope himself in 1073 as Gregory VII. Lanfranc also systematically replaced the Saxons among the higher clergy with Normans every chance he got. By the time of William's death, all the clergy save for two bishops and two abbots were Norman.

It was all this that made the Norman conquest a true conquest.

As William felt the land grow sullenly quiet under him, he could turn to internal administration and here he let nothing escape his restless eye. He meant to have his grip firm upon everything and for that purpose ordered a complete inventory taken of the landed property of the kingdom. It was a kind of census taken between 1080 and 1086 and was summarized in the course of 1087 in volumes called "Domesday Book." Nothing like this appeared anywhere else in Europe.

("Domesday" is a variant spelling of "Doomsday" and means "day of judging" because one of the purposes of the census was to settle, once and for all, the disputes that had arisen over land ownership in the wake of the wholesale shift from Saxon to Norman.)

Aside from settling the question of land ownership and getting it all down into writing, the Domesday Book made it possible to set up a rational tax program, so that money might be obtained with which to support the standing army that William was building. This tax was still popularly referred to as the "Danegeld."

William's thoroughness extended itself in another direction as well. He knew all too well, through much personal experience as a youth, how unruly an aristocracy could be. Now that he was king, he had no intention of following the usual practice of other kings.

In France, for instance, only the most important lords swore allegiance directly to the king. Each lord then had his own underlings swear allegiance to himself rather than to the king. The underlings had underlings of their own, and so on. In such a series of stages, characteristic of feudalism, it was easy to rebel. If a great lord broke his oath and fought against the king, he could call on his vassals to keep to their oath and fight with him. The vassals were not traitors for they had made no oath to the king directly.

William the Conqueror would have none of that. He would continue, instead, to use the system he had established as Duke of Normandy. He therefore gathered an assembly of landowners of all grades to a council at Salisbury, eighty miles west of London, in 1086. There he had all of them, large and small, swear a personal oath of loyalty to him. If any lord rebelled after that, he could only get his own vassals to support him by urging them to break their own oaths, something they might be very reluctant to do. (If the King of France had made use of such a system, William's own career as an arrogant and self-willed vassal of that king, might well have been impossible.)

Between the Domesday Book and the Oath at Salisbury, William laid the framework for a centralized and well-ordered kingdom. Unlike the other nations in western Europe, England was rarely to be in serious danger of breaking up in the pull of contending factions of the aristocracy.

William even kept a tight rein on the clergy. When he received the papal blessing for his projected invasion of England, there seems to have been some hope, on the part of the Pope, that William would place England under the overlordship of the Pope. This, however, William most certainly refused to do. Even the great Gregory VII found in William a rock that would not be moved. Firmly, William established the fact that Church policy could not be made in England without his own approval, and it was the Pope who had to yield.

On the whole, William — the first of the Normans — seemed a cruel tyrant to those Saxon earls whom he had dispossessed of their land. Nevertheless, wherever possible, William retained the customs and law codes of Edward the Confessor. More than that, he established a government that was efficient and reasonably just and the material state of England continued to improve. William had turned England from a backward disorganized realm to one of the best governed kingdoms in Europe, and though it would have been impossible to get a Saxon of the time to believe it, the Norman conquest was, in the end, a great good for England.

But William the Conqueror was almost sixty years old by the time of the Oath of Salisbury, and good living had had its way with him. He had grown grossly obese.

Yet he still retained his hasty temper. He had conquered the County of Maine, south of Normandy, in 1073, and was carrying on a desultory war against King Philip I of France in consequence. When, in 1087, he heard that the king had made a coarse joke concerning William's fatness, the Conqueror flew into a rage. He determined to raid the king's territory in such a way as to wipe the smile off the royal face.

His men advanced to the tune of much destruction and burned the town of Mantes which was just halfway between his own Norman capital at Rouen and the French capital at Paris. William pushed his horse forward to view the destruction and the horse stepped on a hot cinder. The horse stumbled and the fat Conqueror was thrown heavily against the pommel of his saddle. He was badly hurt.

He was carried back, in agony, to Rouen and there he died on September 9, 1087 at the age of sixty, and was later buried at St. Stephen's Church in the Norman city of Caen. He had been Duke of Normandy for fifty-two years and King of England for twenty-one.

9

THE SONS OF WILLIAM

THE SUCCESSION

One source of possible trouble for England, as a result of the Norman conquest, lay in the fact that the island was now firmly tied to the Continent. William was ruler in both England and Normandy, and it was Normandy that was home to him. He was vitally interested in the quarrels of Normandy with Anjou and with the King of France, and the interests of England had to be subordinated to that.

For a while, though, it seemed that this might end with the passing of the Conqueror, for he had three surviving sons and his kingdom was divided between two of them.

Actually, one might suppose that William would have been most reluctant to divide his realm. The division of an inheritance among sons was an old Germanic custom and Frankish kings, ruling over what is now France and Germany, had been doing this for five centuries, but the result of this practice had been civil war upon civil war, weakness upon gathering weakness.

William the Conqueror drove hard, however, for a strong, centralized realm at all costs, and did not hesitate to break feudal custom to get it, as in the Oath of Salisbury. Why did he not, then, strive to keep the kingdom united?

The answer seems to have lain in family friction. William's three surviving sons were Robert, William, and Henry. (A fourth son had died in William's lifetime.)

The oldest son, Robert, was a youngster of twelve at the time of the invasion of England and William, before making the Channel crossing, had arranged to leave his wife, Matilda, behind as a most capable regent and had further been careful to make his nobles swear allegiance to Robert as his successor — just in case.

But as Robert grew to manhood, he found himself opposing his father at every turn, and the short-tempered and aging William found it easy to return the dislike with interest.

It is not at all unusual for a king and his immediate heir to be enemies, despite the father-son relationship. The son, after all, can't help but want to be king and he can be so only through the death of his father. If the father lives on and on, the son grows impatient. In William's day, it was unusual for men to live much beyond forty, and as William himself moved into his fifties, Robert must have grown resentful. Would he himself die before his rock-hard parent? Would he be deprived of his own fair chance at kingship?

It is also customary for court officials of an aging king to have to take into account the chance of a royal death. It is necessary to make certain one is friendly to the son who is to inherit the throne. The heir would therefore develop what was almost a court-of-opposition, and members of such a group would be as impatient as the heir himself to see the old king dead.

The old king, for his part, would see the vultures gathering and would be bitterly resentful both of his son and of those around him. As the royal resentment grew and became obvious, it would be easy for calculating courtiers to insinuate to the son that if he didn't take speedy action, the king might imprison or even execute the hated heir. There would then follow, all too frequently, a rebellion led by the son.

This happens over and over again in the history of monarchies and there is no use being shocked at the "unfilial" behavior of the sons. It is part of the price of the monarchical system of government.

Naturally, if the king has a second son, this one is likely to side with the king. After all, if anything happens to the first son, the second is likely to become heir.

That was the situation, then, in 1077, when Robert, now twenty-two years old, finally made a move in open rebellion, after quarreling with his younger brother, William.

Robert had a certain military talent that seemed to consist more of sheer bravery than of strategic insight. (Such bravery was common to Norman warriors — and sometimes carried the battle.) He was unusually short, though, and was known as Robert Curthose ("Short-Breeches").

The Conqueror's second son, William, usually called William Rufus ("William the Red") because of his ruddy complexion, was also physically unattractive. He was bullnecked, sour of face, stuttered badly and, in later life, grew fat. However, he lined up with his father and earned the Conqueror's love.

Robert was defeated and exiled. Eventually, he managed to gain his father's forgiveness, but as the old king stubbornly insisted on continuing to live, Robert rebelled again in 1082, was beaten and exiled again. He was still in exile when the Conqueror died.

Had Robert been at home, and in his father's favor, William might have had him crowned king and duke in his own presence and during his own lifetime and then forced the nobility (usually referred to in England post-Conquest history as "the barons") to swear allegiance to him.

As it was, Robert hastened home to Normandy and managed to secure his position as Duke Robert II, but that was all. William Rufus had sailed just as hastily to England and there had himself crowned as King William II by Archbishop Lanfranc. He could do this because on his deathbed the Conqueror had indicated he wanted his beloved second son to succeed in England, and thus William's kingdom was divided. Henry, the youngest son, received a cash payment of five thousand pounds of silver to keep him from feeling too put upon in receiving no share of his own.

It was, all in all, a fair division, if the kingdom had to be divided. It might seem that the second son got the best of it, with the higher title and the larger territory, but that was not the way it looked at the time. Normandy was the conquering land, the imperial realm. England was a land of sullen serfs. Normandy was "home"; England was "exile."

It followed then, that it was not so much Duke Robert of Normandy who felt cheated as King William of England. It was not long before William Rufus dreamed of reversing the Conqueror's feat and of invading and conquering Normandy.

What made this notion tempting was that Robert did not make a capable duke. Sheer bravery was not enough when it came to ruling a strong and turbulent duchy and the Norman nobility, who had been cowed by the firm rule of William the Bastard, became difficult to handle once more under the funny-looking Robert Short-Breeches or Curthose.

And yet the barons were not pleased with the division of the kingdom either. Most of them had estates both in Normandy and in England and if the two lands were under separate rule, the individual baron might be frequently placed in a position where there would be a conflict of interest. He would have to make choices that would lose him his land in one place or another. The barons wanted a single rule, then, and if they had to make a choice they much preferred incapable but good-natured Robert to William Rufus, who was as short-tempered as his father but more cruel and far more greedy.

So William Rufus's plan to invade Normandy was blunted not by anything his older brother did so much as by a rising of the barons against him. The rebels were under the leadership of Odo, bishop of Bayeux and half brother of William the Conqueror. Odo had fought valiantly at Hastings (swinging a mace, rather than using a sword or spear, because his status as a churchman forbade his shedding of blood, though why death through a cracked skull should be any better escapes the modern mind.)

Odo held important offices under his brother and it was probably he who commissioned the Bayeux tapestry. Toward the end of the reign, however, he had fallen into disgrace and, undoubtedly, one of his motives in rebelling was to regain lost power.

If the war had been fought simply in terms of barons versus barons, William Rufus would have lost, for few of the barons were on his side. William, however, found he could count on the valiant help of his English subjects — not because they loved William, particularly, but because they thoroughly hated the rapacious and arrogant Norman barons, who taxed them heavily between kicks. Furthermore, William promised them concessions (which he later never delivered). The barons were defeated and Odo was allowed to retire to Normandy, where he remained in the service of Robert.

While the revolt was going on, Robert of Normandy had a glorious chance to take advantage of it, invade the island, and assume leadership of the forces against William Rufus. He did not take the risk of doing so; he lacked the trick of quick decision and swift action.

William did not give him credit for good intentions, however. Even though Robert had not taken action, the revolt had
been in his name and that was enough for the grim William.
He invaded Normandy in 1091, and years of rather small-scale
fighting took place — which finally came to an end for a most
unusual reason.

ADVENTURE IN THE EAST

In the 1090's, it seems, there was gathering enthusiasm in
western Europe for a war against the Turks who controlled
Jerusalem and the Holy Land. This projected war on behalf of
Christianity and the cross came to be referred to as a "Crusade" (through the Spanish from a Latin word for "cross"). Indeed, there was to be crusade after crusade for two centuries,
but the one being preached in the 1090's was the "First Crusade," the one that involved the greatest enthusiasm, that saw
the greatest folly, the greatest heroism, and that most captured
the imagination of later generations.

The Church was calling for a cessation of warfare among
Christian leaders and the turning of all efforts against the Turks.
To the kings of western Europe, the plea fell on deaf ears, but
many of the minor nobility seized on the opportunity to escape
from the narrowing horizons and limited hopes at home in
order to travel to a vague and misty East where both salvation and kingdoms seemed to lie beckoning.

The most highly placed individual to hear the call of the
Crusade was Duke Robert II of Normandy. He was heartily
sick of trying to handle his own nobles with half his limited
energies and fight off his brother with the other half. He was
not made to be a ruler; he was a military adventurer and mili-

tary adventure without day-to-day administrative responsibility was exactly what the Crusades offered.

In 1095, therefore, he announced he was going on the Crusade and William Rufus agreed to a truce. To have failed to do so would have risked papal displeasure and alienated the public opinion of Europe. Besides, getting rid of Robert on a crusade from which he might very well not return would be most convenient and the tight-fisted William was even willing to pay Robert ten thousand marks to finance his leaving. Undoubtedly, William wished him ill fortune with all his heart. Typically, William managed to raise the ten thousand marks out of added taxation rather than out of his private coffers. Odo of Bayeux, unwilling to remain behind and trust himself to the merciless William, accompanied Robert but died on the way and never reached the Holy Land.

Robert Curthose was by no means the first Norman to head east. His grandfather, Robert the Devil, had set off on a pilgrimage to the Holy Land sixty years before, and Norman nobles on similar pilgrimages commonly stopped off in Italy, where turbulent conditions made the land a good place for military adventure and the possible carving out of principalities.

Sicily, at the time, was held by Moslems, who had been in possession for two centuries. Southern Italy was part of the Byzantine Empire, that eastern remnant of the old Roman Empire, which was now entering its final (but prolonged) period of weakness.

Coming to southern Italy in the 1030's were the sons of a minor Norman nobleman, Tancred (tank'red) of Hauteville, a town about forty miles west of Bayeux. These sons were a notable band of hard-fighting rowdies, and the most notable of them all was Robert, the oldest of Tancred's seven sons by a second marriage (he had had five by a first marriage). This son was eventually known as Robert Guiscard (gees-kahr') that is, "Robert the Clever." (As a matter of fact, the old Norman pronunciation of the word was probably "wis-kahr," and that is somewhat similar to our modern "wise-acre.")

Robert's elder half brother had already carved out a duchy for himself in Apulia, the "toe" of Italy, and Robert now did the same for himself in Calabria, Italy's "heel." In 1057, when his half brother died, Robert seized Apulia as well and by 1060, the Byzantine Empire was reduced to the control of isolated strongpoints in southern Italy. All the rest of the region was Robert's.

Robert Guiscard then turned on Sicily, and its conquest he entrusted to his brother, Roger, the youngest of Tancred's twelve sons, who had come to join Guiscard in 1057. Roger had helped Guiscard beat the Byzantine forces in Calabria and in 1060, the younger brother led an expedition into Sicily. He began a slow conquest of the island, gaining ground steadily for twenty years.

Meanwhile in Italy itself, Robert Guiscard took Bari in 1071, the very last Byzantine stronghold in Italy. He then pursued the Byzantines across the sea, landing on the northwestern coast of the Balkans in 1081, and beginning a drive inland through the region now known as Albania. He might conceivably have reached the Aegean and annexed large portions of the Balkans had he not been called back to Italy by the necessity of defending his ally, the Pope.

The Normans in Italy were loyal supporters of the Pope in theory, though they often fought him in practice. The Pope at the time was Gregory VII who, while still the monk, Hildebrand, had supported Duke William's invasion of England. Gregory had opposed the Normans, at first, when it looked as though they were growing too powerful in southern Italy, but his main enemy was the German emperor, Henry IV. Gregory VII was forced to seek Norman help and Robert Guiscard loyally took up arms against the Germans. In 1084, he seized Rome, driving out Henry's forces and restoring the Pope (whom Henry had earlier evicted from that city).

Robert Guiscard died in 1085 at the peak of his success.

There is a remarkable parallel between the careers of William the Conqueror and Robert the Clever. Both were Normans, both contemporaries, both conquerors of large alien realms, both established efficient government and a notable line of rulers.

Guiscard's feat was actually the more remarkable of the two, for he had no powerful military organization at his back as William had had. Instead, he and his brothers had to begin their careers as little more than brigand leaders, enlarging their power, little by little, by all means from force to deceit.

And, in the end, Guiscard's kingdom was even richer and more cultured than William's. Guiscard had the advantage, to be sure, of dealing with a part of Europe that had closer and more direct connection with the ancient sources of civilization, but he made the most of it. Under the astute government of Guiscard and his successors, the Norman kingdom of southern Italy and Sicily became the richest and most cultured in Europe. Never before or after (down to this very day) was the region so fortunate.

Also, because a thin Norman aristocracy ruled over a complicated mélange of other races — Greek, Italian and Moslem — the land developed a religious and national tolerance that was quite uncharacteristic of this period of history in the west.

It is rather ironic, then, that the deeds of William the Conqueror should have remained so famous through all later generations while those of Robert the Clever should be so hidden in obscurity. Part of the cause, undoubtedly, lies in the fact that William's descendants have ruled ever since, over a land that made a tremendous mark in history.

In Italy, on the other hand, direct Norman rule continued only for a century and then (for lack of male heirs) the realm fell to Germans, Frenchmen, and Spaniards in turn, each of whom did their share in misruling the land into permanent poverty and misery.

While Guiscard was engaged on the Pope's business in Italy in the last years of his life, his army in Albania was commanded by his oldest son, Bohemund (boh'uh-mund). Bohemund had less success than his father, and was held off by the Byzantines.

He lost out at home, too. When Guiscard died, his younger brother Roger (Bohemund's uncle) retained control of Sicily. Only part of the Italian portion of the Norman holdings remained to Guiscard's own line and this was taken by a younger son, also named Roger.

Bohemund was left out in the cold altogether and an attempt at rebellion on his part failed. All he could extort was dominion over the city of Taranto on the Italian "instep." This was scarcely enough and when the siren call of adventure in the shape of the First Crusade sounded, he joined eagerly. Together with his nephew, Tancred, he marched off to become one of the most remarkable and glamorous adventurers in the East.

And so William the Conqueror and Robert the Clever were joined in another parallelism after their deaths. Robert Curthose, eldest son of the first, and Bohemund, eldest son of the second, were both among the leaders of the First Crusade.

The events of the First Crusade fall outside the compass of this book, but all three of the Norman leaders covered themselves with what passed for glory in those days. Bohemund was a leading figure in the capture of the Syrian city of Antioch, and became its prince. Tancred replaced his uncle in Antioch during the times when Bohemund suffered defeats and imprisonment, and for a time ruled large sections of Syria.

Robert II of Normandy also distinguished himself, fighting fearlessly in numerous battles and being present (like Tancred) at the successful siege and capture of Jerusalem in 1099. He had a chance to become King of Jerusalem (after all, he was the highest ranking nobleman on the scene). He preferred, however, to return to the west; one of the few leaders to do so.

THE SECOND WILLIAM

While Robert was off on his eastern adventures, William Rufus held England firmly. He also held Normandy under a kind of mortgage in return for the ten thousand marks with which he had financed his brother's crusade. In the last years of his reign, therefore, he ruled over the united kingdom of his father.

The King of Scotland after the Conqueror's death was still Malcolm III, son of the murdered Duncan. Malcolm's stay at the court of Edward the Confessor as a young refugee, and his marriage to Margaret Atheling, had combined to introduce a strong Anglicization into Scotland. He had done homage to William the Conqueror in 1072 and had thus retained his rule over Scotland at the cost of compromising her independence. He had even given his son, Duncan, to William as a hostage for his own good behavior and he made no trouble during the Conqueror's vigorous career.

Once the Conqueror was dead and William Rufus got himself entangled in Normandy, however, Malcolm thought conditions might now favor him. He began to raid northern England. When this went too far, William Rufus hastened angrily back to England from Normandy and marched northward. Malcolm quickly renewed his homage in 1093 but when he tried a new invasion later that year, when William had fallen sick, he was met in battle at Alnwick, some thirty miles south of the border. There Malcolm and his oldest son, Edward, were killed. Malcolm's thirty-five-year reign was over and his wife, Margaret Atheling, died very soon after.

There was a strong anti-English party in Scotland that had found Malcolm and his Saxon queen far too divorced from ancient Scottish ways for their liking. Malcolm's death was followed, therefore, by a Celtic reaction which placed his younger brother, Donalbane, on the throne, while Malcolm's remaining sons were forced to flee to England for refuge. (During Macbeth's reign, Donalbane had taken refuge in Celtic Ireland, and not in Saxon England.)

Donalbane was too preoccupied, during his five-year reign, with retaining power against internal rumblings to attempt foreign adventures. For what was left of the reign of William Rufus in England, therefore, Scotland remained quiet and, despite the temporary Celtic triumph, was docilely subject to the overlordship of the Norman king of England.

William was less successful in an invasion of Wales in response to rebellions there against the domination his father had imposed on that land. The Welsh, as had long been their custom, did not oppose the invasion directly. They retired to the hills and fought a guerrilla war that nipped the Norman knights to slow death. William Rufus had to leave the Welsh to themselves and contented himself with building a strong line of defensive castles on the border (along what had once been Offa's Dike, three centuries before) to keep them from raiding the western shires.

Internally, though, William fed the gathering hatred of all his subjects, English and Norman, lay and clerical, by the greed which caused him to subject them all to crude extortions that were almost insupportable.

And yet William's greed and frugality enabled him to gather a central treasure horde that led to the establishment of a stable financial regime, which encouraged trade and heightened prosperity. He put out coins of good weight and honest silver content which foreign merchants were delighted to accept. Some of these coins were marked with little stars "steorling" in Old English). The word "sterling" may have come from this to represent silver of high standard quality, first coins, then anything.

William the Conqueror had insisted on holding control over the English Church even against papal wishes, but had done so with skill and diplomacy and had made use of the clever Lanfranc as a kind of peacemaker and compromiser between himself and the Pope.

William Rufus showed no such skill in his dealings with the Church, but took an almost ostentatious delight in having his way in the crudest possible fashion. When Lanfranc died in 1089, William II calmly refused to appoint a successor. This arose out of no religious conviction of any sort. Rather it came about because as long as there was no Archbishop of Canterbury, William himself could dispose of the ample revenues of that office. He did this as well in the other lesser bishoprics which fell vacant for one reason or another.

Nothing could have been more calculated to infuriate the Church leaders. Yet it wasn't till 1093 that William could be persuaded to alter this policy, and then only through the immediate terrors of superstition. When William Rufus fell dangerously sick (the sickness that led to the final invasion of Malcolm of Scotland) the priests at once informed him that this was in punishment for his actions against the Church. He was absolutely certain, they said, to be plunged into hell at the moment of death. William, convinced he was dying, appointed a priest named Anselm as thirty-fifth Archbishop of Canterbury.

It was an excellent choice. Anselm was born in Aosta in northwestern Italy in 1033. He came to Normandy in 1056 to serve in the monastery at Bec, thirty miles southwest of Rouen, then presided over by his countryman, Lanfranc. In 1078, Anselm became abbot of the monastery and made it a center of learning, for he was the outstanding theologian of his time.

Anselm advanced the so-called "ontological argument" for

the existence of God (that is, an argument from the very nature of God) which had great influence for centuries. The argument goes as follows:

Everyone has an idea of God. Even a person who says boldly that there is no God, has a notion of what it is he is denying the existence of. The notion of God is the notion of a perfect Being, a Being who has every possible property required by perfection. But one of these properties must be existence, for a God who did not exist would be inferior to a God, otherwise identical, who did exist. Therefore, from the very nature of God, as a perfect Being, God must exist. (This argument was refuted in the eighteenth century by the German philosopher, Immanuel Kant, but to go into the philosophic obscurities of Kant's doctrines would take us too far afield.)

Anselm, now sixty years old, did not willingly accept the heavy burden of the Archbishopric of Canterbury. He much preferred his own quiet and scholarly existence at Bec. However, he saw his chance to introduce Church reforms into England, and he imposed a number of conditions on William, which the dying king grumpily agreed to.

Anselm then allowed himself to accept the post and William Rufus, perhaps to his own surprise, recovered from his illness. The king might have viewed this recovery as the direct result of his return to obedience to the Church, but the chances are that he decided, with sulky chagrin, that he would have recovered anyway and that he had been stampeded into giving up a most lucrative source of income.

The evidence for this is that William promptly demanded a huge sum from Anselm as the price of his post, which Anselm refused to pay. Another serious dispute arose at once. Anselm was a strong supporter of papal supremacy and would not accept the insignia of office from William's hand. He wanted to travel to the Continent to get it from the Pope.

William took every possible measure to prevent this and found a ready pretext for the purpose. There were two claimants to the papal throne at the time. One was Urban II, who had issued the call that had led to the First Crusade and whom Anselm recognized as the true Pope. The other was a claimant who called himself Clement III and who was recognized by some monarchs. William sardonically took the attitude that he could not decide such abstruse theological matters and supported neither. This freed him of papal control and made it possible to argue that Anselm must stay home and receive the insignia from the king's own hand.

For the rest of the reign of William Rufus there was relentless war between king and archbishop, which showed itself in even minor matters. The archbishop inveighed against what he considered dissolute customs of personal adornment, such as extreme points to shoes and the wearing of long hair. He managed to get Normans generally to cut their hair but William Rufus demonstrated his sullen opposition by continuing to wear his hair long.

It wasn't till 1098 that Anselm finally managed to worm his way out of England and after that he felt it prudent not to return while William was on the throne.

Outside the Church, William continued to impose taxes of all sorts and to levy higher and higher fines for all kinds of offenses. He increased the rigor of the law and where William the Conqueror had punished those who hunted deer and other game with blinding, William Rufus punished them with death. (Hunting deer was a royal sport and peasants weren't allowed to fill their famished stomachs with animals that the king might wish to kill — something that supplies part of the suspense in the Robin Hood tales whenever the outlaws killed deer.)

In 1100, the king went hunting in the New Forest. This was an area which had been created by the Conqueror near his favorite residence in Winchester (Alfred's old capital). The first William had deliberately emptied the countryside of people and demolished the buildings there without compensation, in callous disregard for the mountain of suffering that resulted.

An area about half the size of our state of Rhode Island was allowed to revert to forest in order that the king might go hunting there.

The victimized population found relief in ascribing a superstitious evil to the dark recesses of the forest. They told, with lurid relish, that it was haunted by the Devil, who would bring an ill fate on the Norman princes hunting there. Such superstitions made excellent cover, of course, for those who might seek to help out the Devil in his planned vengeance on the Normans.

For example, Richard, second son of the Conqueror, died in a hunting accident in the New Forest in the Conqueror's lifetime. Then, in May of 1100, another Richard, an illegitimate son of Robert of Normandy, had died of an arrow wound, also while hunting in the New Forest.

A son and a grandson of the Conqueror had died there, then; an elder brother and a nephew of William Rufus. And one thing we can be certain of, regardless of the tales — it wasn't the Devil who drew the bows that shot the fatal arrows.

In August, 1100, however, a bare three months after the second death, William Rufus prepared for a gay hunting party in the New Forest.

One of the party was William's younger brother, Henry, the youngest son of William the Conqueror. He had been born in England in 1068, the only one of the sons to be born after the Conquest. In the civil wars between his brothers, William Rufus and Robert Curthose, Henry had been sometimes on one side and sometimes on the other. He had ended, however, on William's side.

Since William was unmarried and had no children, Henry was the logical heir to the throne, provided Robert Curthose, the older brother of both William and Henry, remained in the East and, preferably, died there.

In 1100, however, the news may well have reached England that Robert, covered with glory as a result of his deeds in the

Holy Land, and entirely safe and whole, was on the way back.

This presented younger brother Henry with a crisis. If William died before Robert returned, Henry would surely become King of England. If William died after Robert returned, then Robert or a son of his might dispute the succession.

But how could William die before Robert returned? William was forty-four years old, rather advanced in years for the times but his health was excellent and his father had lived to be sixty. And Henry himself was thirty-two, no youngster by the standards of the time.

Henry, as youngest brother, had been fobbed off with nothing but a cash settlement at the death of the first William. Was he to get nothing at the death of the second William either? Not if the second William died quickly enough.

How much of all this was revolving in Henry's head is unknown, but it seems reasonable to suppose that he could not have avoided such thoughts. The question is: Did he act on them?

William Rufus was accompanied into the forest by his favorite hunting companion, Walter Tyrrel. The party separated in the search for game and, according to the tale that was later current, William Rufus and Walter Tyrrel gave chase to a deer alone. The king drew his bow, but the string broke. He had no second bow at hand and he hastily ordered Tyrrel to shoot, so as not to lose the deer. Tyrrel did so, too, shooting as quickly as possible, but the arrow was deflected by a tree and just happened to sink into William's heart. The king died at once.

Tyrrel stared a moment at the dead king, realized that any claim of innocence wouldn't stand the whisper of a chance of being heard, and departed immediately for the seacoast, heading for Normandy, then France and the Holy Land, where, he hoped, vengeance could not reach him. The body of the abandoned king was not found till later. A peasant came across it, heaved it into his cart and carried it to Winchester.

As soon as he heard of his brother's death, Henry spurred
to Winchester and seized the royal treasury. (This was important, for whoever controlled money, controlled the payment, and therefore the loyalty, of the royal bodyguard.) Three
days later he was crowned Henry I of England.

THE YOUNGER BROTHER

The question, now, is this: What did Henry have to do with
the death of his brother?

It came at an ideal time for him, and the tale of the acciden-
tally deflected arrow seems incredibly thin. Is it not more
likely that Tyrrel had been bought by Henry and had deliberately killed the king? It is very tempting to think so, but the
truth will probably never be known.

Robert Curthose was in Italy when the news of his brother
William's death reached him. He hastened back to Normandy
with all possible speed, sure that his crusading laurels would
make him the kind of glamorous figure to which the Norman
nobility would flock.

Henry, however, proceeded with perfect efficiency and
skill, for all the world as though he were prepared for William's
death and was acting out a carefully pre-arranged program.

He sent a conciliatory letter to Archbishop Anselm of Canterbury, urging him to return and promising his friendship.
In this way he gained the powerful support of the Church
and of its most eloquent spokesman in England. He arrested
Ranulf Flambard, the favorite of the old king and the one who
had executed the royal financial exactions. Flambard was the
man who, above all, was hated by the commoners and the
move was therefore enormously popular. Henry followed that

up by pledging no new exactions and by promising to rule according to the laws of Edward the Confessor (who was remembered with reverence by the peasantry and whose rule was looked back upon as the "good old days.")

Eventually, Henry granted charters to London and other sizable towns, guaranteeing them certain rights and allowing them to bargain collectively in case of any disputes. The towns, thus granted freedom from baronial interference and handed a bargaining leverage they could use to good advantage, flourished. Population increased, trade grew, money accumulated. The king benefited, since the towns paid more taxes as they grew richer, and were a more useful counterweight to the nobility as they grew more powerful.

Henry eventually brought the organization of the kingdom's finances to a new pitch of careful efficiency. Twice a year, a group of royal officials gathered about a table to receive the royal revenues and to audit carefully the books of the various tax-collecting sheriffs. The table was, according to tradition, covered by a checkered cloth. This trivial fact eventually led to the use of the term "exchequer" for the treasury.

Another popular move on Henry's part was to marry Edith, a Scottish princess. She was the daughter of old King Malcolm III and of his English queen, Margaret Atheling. This made Edith the great-great-granddaughter of Ethelred the Unready. The English commons had the feeling that if her children succeeded to the throne then the blood of Alfred the Great would once more flow in the veins of English kings. The marriage was made more palatable to the Norman nobility by the device of a name change. The queen dropped the Saxon name of Edith and adopted the Norman name of Matilda (which had been the name of Henry's mother). She is also known by the diminutive of that name — Maud.

Nor were the barons neglected. Henry promised to keep within the feudal laws and to avoid being as overbearing as William Rufus had been. To be sure, once he was firmly in the saddle, Henry ruled over the barons with an iron hand, and kept them as thoroughly under control as the Conqueror had —but he did it with a show of justice and without William Rufus's offensive arrogance.

Henry's concessions to the barons and the commons, made at this time in order to assure his succession over his older brother, had strong repercussions in later generations. It represented a recognition of the fact that the king had to obey certain rules; that his power was not unlimited. Many English monarchs of later times ignored this, or tried to, but the barons and, later, the middle classes, never forgot it. The concessions of Henry I (like those of Ethelred the Unready, a century before) were to be precedents leading to the demands for what turned out to be the Magna Carta a century later.

Henry's wisdom in all this was a tribute to his native intelligence and to his education, which was not at all like that of the usual run of Norman noblemen. The nobility tended to be strong in courage and action, but rather weak in calm consideration. Not so, Henry. It is not for nothing that, in later times, Henry became known to the chroniclers as Henry Beauclerc ("good scholar"). He was the first well-educated English king since Alfred the Great.

By the time Robert Curthose reached Normandy, he found Henry's program already well under way and himself completely outmaneuvered. His ingrained slowness nevertheless caused him to delay action still further, while each month made his situation less favorable. When he finally invaded England in 1101, he was in a completely untenable position. The English barons were firmly behind Henry and so were the Church and the commons. There was no use fighting. Even the not-very-bright Robert could see there was no future for him in England. With what grace he could muster, he accepted a 3,000-mark gift from Henry, renounced all claim to the throne of England, and returned to Normandy.

However, there could be no permanent peace between the

brothers just yet. Flambard, William Rufus' hated old favorite, had escaped from prison and had gone to Normandy where
he was constantly intriguing against Henry. What's more
Robert's loose rule in Normandy provoked anarchy and quarreling among his barons and those who were worsted were
bound to seek help from Henry.

In 1106, just forty years after the Battle of Hastings, a Norman army crossed the Channel in the other direction and
landed in Normandy. Battle was joined, according to the tale,
on September 28, at Tinchebray, a town forty miles south of
Bayeux.

Henry had laid siege to the town and Robert brought his
forces to its relief. The battle was hard fought but it ended
in a complete victory for Henry. Robert was taken prisoner
and was carried off to a life of impotent idleness in England,
where he remained till his death at the patriarchal age of
eighty, in 1134.

Taken prisoner in that battle, also, was a pathetic echo from
the past — Edgar Atheling, grandson of Edmund Ironside.
Through all his adventurous life he had been a dim hope for the
oppressed Saxons (a kind of "Bonnie Prince Charlie" of his
time) but he completely lacked the ability to lead a forlorn hope
to victory. Now he, too, retired into English imprisonment,
and died in 1130, also eighty, more than sixty years after his
few days as titular king of England.

After the Battle of Tinchebray, Henry was accepted by the
Norman barons as Duke of Normandy, and in this way England and Normandy were firmly united again for the first time
since the Conqueror's death twenty years before.

Robert Curthose's son, William Clito, occasionally disputed
this but never successfully and he died in battle in 1128. England's chance of independence from Continental entangle-
ments vanished for a century.

Henry's foreign policy with respect to Scotland was also
successful. Donalbane, who had ruled unquietly in the

Celtic interest after the death of Malcolm III, was overthrown
in 1098, and Malcolm's oldest surviving son, Edgar, was placed
on the throne. He had been in English exile and he brought
with him Anglo-Norman influence.

Matilda, Henry's queen, was sister of Edgar of Scotland, and
this forged another bond between the two nations.

Edgar died in 1107 and was succeeded by his brother Alexander I ("the Fierce"). He married an illegitimate daughter
of Henry's. Finally, when Alexander died in 1124, the last
surviving son of Malcolm III (there had been six altogether)
came to the throne as David I.

David I had spent most of his life in England and when he
become king there was a new influx of Anglo-Norman followers
who established much of the later nobility of Scotland. David's
reign, during which Scotland had peace and prosperity, marked
the final end of Celtic influence. Scotland became a kind of
diluted Norman in character and was a cultural appendage
of England.

Henry was less successful in his dealings with the Church,
partly because of a dispute that was Europe-wide. The point
at issue was the investiture of bishops. Kings and emperors
claimed the right to appoint bishops and then to invest the
bishops with the symbols of office in return for homage and the
swearing of fealty by the bishop to the king. The papacy, on
the other hand, found this horrifying because it seemed to subject the bishops to the king, making the secular power supreme
over the Church. The Pope insisted that only the Church
could invest the bishops with the symbols of office and that
no homage to the king was required in return. This, in fact, was
part of the quarrel between Anselm and William Rufus.

At stake were important practical matters. The Church was
bound to accumulate great wealth, for lands and property
were always being left to churches, monasteries and abbeys,
by pious kings and noblemen who sought in this way to smooth
their pathway to heaven. (It was the philanthropy of the age,

with soul-saving rather than tax-saving the practical motivation.) Since the Church was immortal and never relinquished property voluntarily, there was a tendency for the Church to grow ever richer and the state to grow ever poorer.

The balance was redressed by the fact that the secular power managed to find ways of squeezing money out of the Church. As long as the king could appoint bishops, he could charge them for the office, and heavily, too. (In a way, this was good for the Church, for if no financial leaks from Church to state were allowed, pressures might build up to the point where outright confiscation of Church property took place. This happened under a later Henry in the sixteenth century, for instance.)

From the Church's standpoint, though, "lay investiture" (investiture by laymen, even though the layman might be a king) was wrong not only in theory, because it seemed to make the State superior to the Church, but in practice as well, for if bishops depended on the king they would be likely to place the interests of the State ahead of that of the Church.

During the tenth and part of the eleventh century, the papacy was at a low ebb and most of the Popes were corrupt or weak or both. The various monarchs went their own ways.

Under the influence of Hildebrand, however, papal power revived and when he became Pope himself as Gregory VII, the struggle over lay investiture reached a climax. Gregory thundered against the practice and his papal successors maintained the firm stand against it.

Anselm of Canterbury had held to such a stand against William Rufus, and he maintained it just as firmly against Henry I.

Henry I was in a bad position. He had every reason to want to control his bishops, both for economic and political considerations. However, he was a religious man, and he had promised Anselm concessions in return for the support of the Church.

The king resisted as much as possible, almost to the point of having himself excommunicated (that is, thrown out of the fellowship of the Church and denied its sacraments — a fearful threat to men of that time). But then in 1107 (two years before Anselm's death) a compromise was reached. The Pope, not the king, would control the investiture. However, the bishop would have to do homage to the king.

As with all compromises, though, each side suspected it had conceded too much, and the dispute between Church and State was to break out again in a later reign.

10

CIVIL WAR

THE SUCCESSION AGAIN

Henry's queen, Matilda, died in 1118, leaving two children behind. One was a girl, another Matilda, who in 1114 (at the tender age of twelve) had been married to Henry V, Emperor of Germany. The other was a boy, William, Henry's only son and the idol of his heart.

William's importance lay in the fact that he was one of only two grandsons of William the Conqueror who were then alive and who could trace their descent through males only. The other was William Clito, son of Robert Curthose, who was, however, automatically excluded from the succession when his father had renounced all pretension to the English throne.

Prince William (or William Atheling, as he was sometimes called after the old Saxon style) was therefore the only heir to the throne; the only figure standing between the peace of an assured succession and the chaos of a disputed one.

In November 1120, Henry, his family and his retainers were returning to England from Normandy. He had been fighting a war there with Fulk V, Count of Anjou.* The County of Anjou lay directly south of the Duchy of Normandy, and the two regions had been long-time rivals. Wars had flared between them for a century and neither side could overcome the other. This war like all the others had ended in a compromise peace and now Henry was hastening back to England to tend to affairs there.

The party was large enough to require two ships. Henry sailed on one and young Prince William, then seventeen years old, sailed in a second named "Blanche-Nef" ("White Ship").

Gaiety on the White Ship was a little overdone. The happy prince ordered wine for all the crew and the festivities delayed the sailing till nightfall. This was imprudent for before moving away from the coast and into the open channel, it was necessary to skirt some rocks. With the light fading and the crew half-woozy with liquor, there was a serious misjudgment and the ship did not skirt the rocks successfully. Her side was staved in and she quickly sank. There was only one survivor and it was not the prince.

It was three days before anyone dared tell King Henry what had happened. Henry is supposed to have fainted at the news and, according to the story, he was never seen to smile again in the remaining fifteen years of his life.

Henry married again, but had no children. He was already in his fifties and he was outliving the other male descendants of William the Conqueror. When Robert Curthose died in 1134, Henry (now sixty-six years old) was the last male member of the "Norman dynasty" alive. That is, he was the last male who could trace his ancestry through males only back to William the Conqueror and beyond him to Hrolf the Ganger.

* Fulk was aided by William Clito, now nineteen years old, who had never reconciled himself to his father's renunciation of the English throne. In this attempt to reverse matters, as in all his others, William Clito failed.

The succession was now the supreme question in England and it had been concerning the old king for years.

For instance, he had an older sister, Adela, a daughter of William the Conqueror, and as capable as any man. She had been married to Stephen, the Count of Blois (a French region south of Normandy and east of Anjou) in 1080. This Stephen had gone off to the First Crusade (where his role was rather inglorious) and in his absence, Adela ruled the county efficiently and well. It was Adela, by the way, who had suggested the compromise of 1107 on the question of lay investiture.

Adela might conceivably have been considered as the next monarch, but her age made that impossible. She was already seventy-two when Robert Curthose died. However, she had a son, another Stephen (and known as Stephen of Blois to the historians) who had been brought up in Henry's court and who was in his middle thirties in Henry's last years.

It seemed that Stephen of Blois was the only possible heir to the throne. He was a grandson of William the Conqueror, on his mother's side, and a nephew of Henry I. Yet family names are inherited through the male line. Stephen might be a grandson of William the Conqueror through the female side of his family, but he was a member of the House of Blois through the male side. If he came to the throne he would not be a member of the Norman dynasty, but would found a new Blois dynasty.

The only other possibility was Henry's daughter, Matilda. If she were still married to the German emperor and had had children by him, German in language and culture, she would undoubtedly be unacceptable. Conditions had changed, however. In 1125, Emperor Henry V had died and Matilda, still only twenty-six years old, had had no children and was on the matrimonial market again.

The possibility of a remarkable coup occurred to Henry's agile mind. His old enemy, Fulk V of Anjou, had left for the Holy Land to become King of Jerusalem. Fulk's son Geoffrey IV (known as "the Handsome") ruled Anjou in his place and was only a boy. If Henry could swing a marriage between Matilda and Geoffrey and they should ever have a son, that son might succeed to a realm including Anjou, Normandy and England. This would end the long and futile feud between Anjou and Normandy and since Anjou was second only to Normandy in power among the French regions, the expanded kingdom would be powerful indeed. Stephen of Blois, on the other hand, did not rule Blois (he had renounced his claim there in favor of an elder brother who had no interest in the English crown).

Henry therefore was faced with a choice between his daughter and an expanded kingdom, and his nephew without expansion — and he chose his daughter.

In 1127, the marriage negotiations with young Geoffrey (still only fourteen years old) were going through and Henry at once called his barons together and forced them to swear allegiance to Matilda as their next monarch. Among those who swore was Stephen of Blois.

In 1133, Matilda had a son, whom she named Henry after her father. Henry must have felt some relief from the long-past tragedy of the White Ship. He called together his barons once more and forced a renewal of the oath of allegiance, this time to the infant as well as the mother.

Then, in 1134, Henry died at last, after a thirty-five year reign. His only grandson was two years old.

STEPHEN VERSUS MATILDA

Despite Henry's attempt to settle the succession, his disappearance from the scene led to instant anarchy. No sooner was

he dead when Stephen of Blois renounced the oath of allegiance he had twice sworn to Matilda. This was no light
matter, for an oath was to be taken seriously, of course.

Stephen had no trouble, however, in finding a pretext
for claiming the oath to have been invalid. The pretext lay in
the older Queen Matilda, the wife of Henry I. She had been a
Saxon princess, Edith, to begin with. In her younger days,
she had been placed in a nunnery where her aunt was abbess
as protection against Norman violence. To make the protection the more sure, the abbess kept Edith in a nun's habit.

When Henry I married her, the point about the nun's habit
was brought up and some claimed that this made Edith-Matilda enough of a nun to make it impossible for her to marry.
Henry, who wanted the marriage for political reasons as well
as out of affection, brushed that aside and no one dared
bring up the matter again during his reign.

Now that the old king was dead, however, Stephen brought
up the matter at once. Edith-Matilda could not marry, he said,
having been a nun, and her daughter Matilda was illegitimate
and could not inherit no matter how many oaths were sworn.
And in any case the oaths he had taken had been extorted under duress. He appealed this case to Pope Innocent II.

For the time, everything was in Stephen's favor. He was in
England, on the scene, having hastened there immediately after
Henry's death, while Matilda was still across the Channel.
Moreover, the Norman baronage was opposed to a woman on
the throne or, for that matter, to a two-year-old infant as monarch in her place. Furthermore, they were particularly annoyed at Matilda's marriage to the traditional enemy of Anjou.
Henry might have thought it a wonderful idea but the barons
felt that no oath ought to require them to serve a hated Angevin (the usual adjective derived from Anjou).

Stephen, on the other hand, was a grown man of impressive
appearance and of easy and affable manner. He was popular
with the Normans and the Saxons alike, and was a particular

favorite of the city of London. Furthermore, one of his brothers was Bishop of Winchester and this bishop helped Stephen
seize the royal treasury and then persuaded the Pope to decide
in his favor. On December 26, 1135 ("St. Stephen's Day," a
good omen, one would think, for a ruler named Stephen),
Stephen was crowned King of England in London by William
of Corbeil, the thirty-seventh Archbishop of Canterbury.

So far, all had been going marvelously well for Stephen, but
once he was king, troubles broke out at once.

There was still the oath of allegiance to Matilda. It remained
a perfect weapon in the hands of the barons, who could pre-
tend to be deeply concerned about it. If they insisted they had
great difficulty in appeasing their consciences, Stephen would
have to bid high to gain their support.

The new king did so. His easygoing nature was not such as
to allow him to engage in sharp bargaining. As a result, the
Norman barons gained concessions that none of the first three
Norman kings would have dreamed of granting them. Any
one of them, William the Conqueror, William Rufus, or Henry
Beauclerc, would have seen them dead and damned first.

But now the barons went off with permission to build
fortified castles for themselves and to gather men to defend
them, so that England became a nest of competing kinglets,
each avid to aggrandize himself at the expense of all the rest,
and feeling no great loyalty to either Stephen or Matilda. The
groundwork was well laid for anarchy.

Nor could Stephen consider his claim to the throne undis-
puted. There were still forces on Matilda's side. Henry I,
who had lacked legitimate sons borne him by his queen, had
had a number of sons by other women. All were illegitimate,
of course, and therefore incapable of inheriting the throne
despite the precedent of William the Conqueror's own
bastardy.

The chief of these illegitimate sons was Robert, Earl of
Gloucester. He had sworn allegiance to Stephen and that

easygoing monarch had let him keep his estates and power, something Gloucester now used to intrigue in favor of his half sister Matilda. (She was commonly called "Empress Maud" by the English, "Empress" because of her first marriage to the German Emperor.)

More open in his aims was David I of Scotland, who had a legitimate reason for his partisanship. He was the brother of Edith-Matilda and therefore the uncle of the younger Matilda. David invaded England in 1138 with a wild and savage army that threw themselves ferociously but hopelessly against the iron-encased Norman knights. The Norman swords and the English archers threw the Scots back with loss.

The Scottish invasion was, despite its failure, an invitation for the newly-strong barons of England to defect from Stephen and begin the game of playing the disputants against each other, with themselves the winner and England the loser at every stroke.

And in the confusion, the Scots slowly managed to establish a domination over England's northernmost counties.

CHAOS

In 1139, when Stephen had been reigning over three years, Matilda finally landed in England in an attempt to take the throne. Stephen, acting quickly, caught her in the castle in which she had taken residence.

Had he now taken and imprisoned her, all might have been well for him, but in a moment of mistaken gallantry, he made the grand gesture of letting her go free. If he felt that the nation would rally round such a generous and knightly gentleman as himself, he was reckoning storybook fashion. It didn't happen.

Matilda fled westward to her half brother, Robert of Gloucester, in Bristol, where she was too strong to be taken again.
Other barons, judging Stephen from his action to be either a
fool, a weakling, or both, decided to support Matilda for a while.

Now there was civil war, indeed, with the whole country in
flames, and the strife between Stephen and Matilda a mask for
dozens of petty raids of baron against baron.

In 1141, Stephen lay siege to the city of Lincoln, a Matilda-
sympathizing stronghold, 110 miles north of his own London.
Robert of Gloucester marched to its relief with forces that
were more numerous and more loyal. At the first onset, some
of Stephen's men ran off after having scarcely struck a blow.
Stephen himself fought valiantly — he was brave enough, as
were all the Norman princes — but was taken prisoner.

Matilda now had the chance of imitating Stephen's earlier
generosity but the thought undoubtedly never occurred to her.
She merely imprisoned him and probably thought herself kind
not to execute him out of hand. Or perhaps she considered
him to be more useful as a hostage.

She persuaded Stephen's brother, the Bishop of Winchester,
to do for her what he had earlier done for his brother. She took
over the royal residence with its treasury and regalia and assumed the role of Queen of England with the bishop's earnest
help. (The price paid the bishop was that he would serve
in the role we would call today "prime minister" and that he
would have, in particular, the disposal of any bishoprics and
abbacies that might become vacant — a potential source of
great income.)

But London was still heart and soul with Stephen and when
Matilda came to London as queen, she was greeted with sullen
displeasure. She might have won the Londoners over, but she
was an arrogant woman with the temper of her forebears. She
was furious with London for the support they had given Stephen and wanted to punish them, not conciliate them. She laid
new taxes upon them and curtly refused a petition that she

promise to rule by the laws of Edward the Confessor.

The Londoners thereupon rose against her with wild spontaneity and drove her out of the city before she could be crowned. The Bishop of Winchester at once changed sides again.

Forces sympathetic to Stephen, their morale bounding sky high, managed to reach Winchester and lay siege to it. Matilda had sought refuge there, and in the palace were many of her most highly-placed partisans, including David of Scotland and Robert of Gloucester. Matilda and David managed to escape, thanks largely to fierce fighting by Robert, who was taken in the melee and carried captive to Stephen's wife (still another Matilda.)

It was stalemate, and there was an exchange of prisoners. Robert of Gloucester was exchanged for King Stephen and then the civil war broke out again, more futile and wasting than ever. On the whole, the eastern half of the land was for Stephen and the western for Matilda, but the whole of the land went down the drain.

For a while, Stephen's persistence seemed about to pay off. Robert of Gloucester died in 1147. Matilda, deprived of the real military leader of her forces, was forced to leave England in 1149 after a decade of futile war. Stephen remained the only king in the land, but his was a feeble kingship indeed over turbulent barons, who were of no mind to obey him and demanded always greater privileges.

PLANTAGENET

Nor did Stephen control the Norman lands on the Continent. There Geoffrey of Anjou, the husband of Matilda, was master.

Little by little, while civil war raged in England, he took over Normandy, making most progress while Stephen was imprisoned and when it seemed that his cause was lost. He prevailed upon the Normans to accept his young son, Henry, as Duke of Normandy and thereafter, Stephen's power, such as it was, was confined to England.

Matilda wanted her husband to come to her aid in England, but this he steadfastly refused to do, using his preoccupation in Normandy as an excuse. Actually, his marriage to Matilda was a most unhappy one, for Matilda (twelve years older than he) was a termagant who took as little trouble to conciliate her husband as she had taken to conciliate her subjects. No doubt Geoffrey was quite content to have the Channel between himself and his wife.

At one time, Geoffrey had made a pilgrimage to the Holy Land. He had donned lowly garb as a gesture of humility and had carried a sprig of broom, a common shrub, in his bonnet as another such gesture.* The broom plant — the "planta genista" in Latin and "planta genêt" in French — gained Geoffrey a nickname. He became Geoffrey Plantagenet, and the nickname passed on to his son and eventually to his descendants generally, becoming a kind of surname. In English, it is pronounced "plan-taj'ih-net".

If Geoffrey did not venture his luck in England, his son, Henry Plantagenet did. He went to England first as a nine-year-old boy, while his mother held the western portion of the island and made war on Stephen. Henry stayed in Bristol, the very center of pro-Matilda sentiment and began there what eventually turned out to be an excellent education. While still in his teens he tried twice to lead armies against Stephen, but was beaten back each time.

However, he showed himself to be full of promise and gained

---

* The broom plant has long thin branches which can be tied in a bundle to a stick and used for sweeping. Such an instrument came to be called a "broom" eventually, no matter what it was made of.

the enthusiastic support of increasing numbers of people. Furthermore, he began to accumulate titles almost without trying. He had been accepted as Duke of Normandy in 1150, and when his father, Geoffrey, died the next year, Henry became Count of Anjou as well. Brittany was nominally independent but had accepted loose Norman overlordship since the Conqueror's time, so young Henry controlled the northwestern quarter of France.

He next made a most advantageous marriage that came about as follows:

Aquitaine is the name given to a region which includes much of what is now southern France, and which, in Norman times, included just about all of it. It was the pleasantest part of the kingdom and the most prosperous and cultured. It had retained much of old Roman civilization, and, throughout the Dark Ages, it kept more of what spark of learning still existed than did the northern section of the country.

In the eleventh century, Aquitaine did well under a series of dukes named William. The last of these, William X, died in 1137, leaving as his heir a beautiful fifteen-year-old girl, named Eleanor. She was easily the most eligible heiress in all of western Europe.

It was not possible that she would remain ummarried and the leading suitor was a sixteen-year-old boy, who was just coming to the throne of France as Louis VII (also called "Louis the Young").

The marriage took place in 1137, just three months after Eleanor of Aquitaine had become duchess and just one month before Louis the Young became king.

It was not, however, a happy marriage. Eleanor was gay, frivolous, and quite aware that she was a great heiress in her own right. She led a court of troubadours and pleasure seekers whom King Louis found distasteful.

Louis was a grave and serious person, very much involved in kingly duties. Undoubtedly, he seemed like a wet blanket

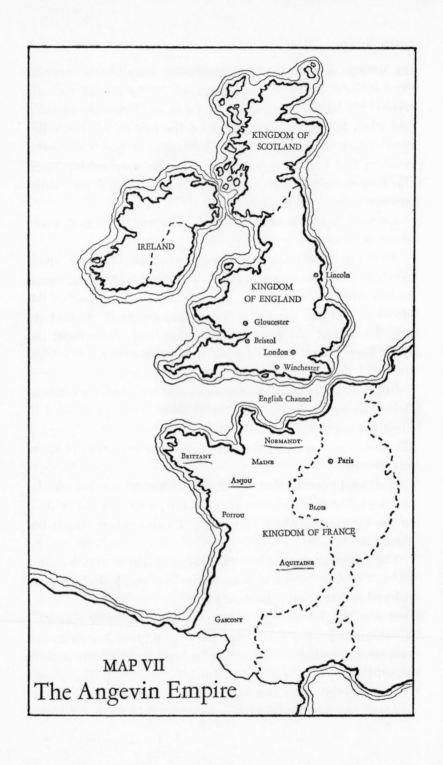

KINGDOM OF
SCOTLAND

IRELAND

Lincoln

KINGDOM
OF ENGLAND

Gloucester

Bristol
London

Winchester

English Channel

NORMANDY·

BRITTANY
MAINE
Paris

ANJOU

BLOIS

POITOU

KINGDOM OF FRANCE

AQUITAINE

GASCONY

MAP VII
The Angevin Empire

and spoilsport to his merry queen; undoubtedly she seemed like a feather-brained ninny to her hard-working king.

What was worse was that she bore two children to Louis, but both were girls, and by French custom, neither could inherit the throne either for themselves or for their descendants. Louis wanted a son and Eleanor wasn't giving him one.

The final straw came in connection with a crusade. The leaders of the First Crusade had established western power over the whole eastern coast of the Mediterranean, but their successors were now beginning to wilt under the Moslem counterattack. A Second Crusade was necessary and, in 1147, Louis VII volunteered to be one of the leaders. Surely, if the First Crusade, led only by second-echelon noblemen, had been so successful, the Second, led by a royal personage, would sweep the infidels aside.

But Queen Eleanor would hear of nothing but that she must go with her husband, complete with her court. The whole adventure was to be like a knightly romance, as Eleanor no doubt pictured it, with beautiful ladies watching their gallant lovers winning the colorful tournaments.

It didn't work that way. The Second Crusade was a costly and humiliating fiasco and Louis VII was forced to return home, a complete failure, with nothing whatever accomplished, not even a gallant try. He was aware of the miserable appearance he made before his scornful wife and he undoubtedly blamed her for weighing down the army and turning it into a woman's toy.

They were through as man and wife, and in 1152, Louis divorced her on the grounds that she was sufficiently closely related to him to make the marriage illegal. (He knew that all the time, of course.)

Eleanor was now thirty years old, getting on in years, but still capable of bearing children, and still the greatest heiress in western Europe.

Within two months, she was snapped up by Henry Plantagenet. He was only nineteen, but any woman who carried with her the rich south of France would have suited him.

From Louis' standpoint this was the worst possible second marriage Eleanor could have made. It gave Henry control of all of western France, making up at least two-thirds of the territory over which Louis was, in theory, overlord. Henry Plantagenet was now considerably more powerful in France than the king himself was.

Probably, Eleanor knew just how inconvenient such a marriage would be for Louis and found it all the more attractive for that reason.

Henry could now come to England as the powerful ruler of vast territories in France (which the Norman barons felt was worth more than English territory anyway). Indeed, Henry's French dominions were larger and richer than all of England and he had ample funds to support his armies and pay off those barons who chose to side with him.

He landed in England in 1153 and began instantly to make progress. Stephen was worn out with his long, useless striving. He had tried to get the barons to accept his son, Eustace, without much success. When, not long after Henry's landing, Eustace died, and when it was clear that Stephen's young son, William, had neither the will nor the ability for the kingship, Stephen gave up.

The two parties finally came to an agreement. Stephen asked only that he be allowed to live out his life as king. He was well past his fiftieth birthday and was ill. It did not seem he would last long and Henry conceded the point. In return, Stephen recognized Henry as his heir to the exclusion of his own torpid son.

Stephen died less than a year later and on December 19, 1154, Henry Plantagenet, still only twenty-one years old, became King Henry II of England. (He was sometimes called Henry Curtmantle from the short cloak of Angevin style he liked to wear.)

11

THE ANGEVIN EMPIRE

THE BEGINNING OF FUSION

Henry was great-grandson of William the Conqueror and the grandson of Henry I. But he inherited through his mother, and he is not therefore a member of the "Norman dynasty" which had given England three strong kings.

Henry II was the first of a new dynasty, called the "Angevin dynasty" after Henry's father, Geoffrey of Anjou, or the "Plantagenet dynasty" after Geoffrey's nickname.* This new dynasty was to give England fourteen kings and was to last for more than three centuries.

Henry's accession was like a great, fresh wind over England.

* Actually, the term "Plantagenet" did not become popular until the reign of Edward III, the great-great-great-grandson of Henry II, two centuries later. Edward III had ambitions to gain large holdings in France and deliberately harked back to Henry who had set the precedent for this.

It made everyone happy. The young, handsome king was descended not only from William the Conqueror by way of his mother, but also from Alfred the Great by way of his mother's mother. What's more he was ruler over a wider realm than any English king (except for Canute) before him — a realm that can be called the Angevin Empire.

To be sure, Henry II was a man of violent emotion who could roll on the floor in a passionate rage, or sink into the depths of a suicidal depression, but he was full of energy and firmness and he drove others as hard as he drove himself.

Henry made it his first task to seize and tear down the castles that had been built during Stephen's lax rule, and to put an end to the brigandage and petty tyranny that prevailed in the land. He accomplished that task with such grim dispatch that baronial opposition melted before him. He revived the notion of a standing army loyal to the king, and he began the slow change that would convert the quarrelsome Norman barons into the country gentlemen so characteristic of the England of a later age.

In a very few years, Henry II had raised the English crown to greater power than it had held before, and England was once again peaceful and in order. But although prosperity began to flow back, the twenty-year nightmare under Stephen remained to plague English memories for a long time.

Henry II also secured the northern border of England, which had caved in under Scottish pressure during the civil war. To be sure, Henry was under an obligation to David of Scotland for the latter's unending efforts to secure the throne for Henry's mother and himself. But he felt that this obligation did not extend to giving English territory to Scotland. The situation was eased for him by the fact that David had died the year before Henry's accession. Succeeding David was his eldest grandson, Malcolm IV. He was only twelve years old and so shy and timid that he is known in history as "Malcolm the Maiden." He could not stand against the forceful Henry;

indeed he found himself completely fascinated and dominated by the English king (who was his second cousin). Henry had no trouble, then, in restoring the northern border to what it had been under his grandfather, Henry I. Later campaigns in Wales (not uniformly successful against those hardy hill-men) secured that border, too.

The new order and new strength in England, and the presence of an educated king with an admiration for learning, meant that England was reaching out for new heights of culture, heights such as it had not seen since the Viking invasions had begun to disrupt the land three and a half centuries before.

It was now after all, a hundred years since the Normans had taken England. They had been more advanced, culturally, than the Saxons, but not very much more so. Their chief contribution to English culture was the introduction of a "Norman style" of architecture, which produced large, impressive churches, and gloomy, strong castles.

Slowly, however, as the decades passed, a kind of fusion of culture was beginning to make itself just barely visible. A language change was taking place, for instance.

The Old English ("Anglo-Saxon") of Alfred the Great was dying. It had become the rude language of an uneducated peasantry. Without a written literature to fix its forms, without schools to teach its subtleties, Old English became almost a "pidgin" language. All the fancy endings and declensions that are still to be found in modern German vanished. If the peasantry themselves didn't forget them, the Normans who were forced to communicate with those peasants ignored them. This was all the more true as the nobility developed the principle of "primogeniture" by which all land and title was passed on to the eldest son, exclusively. This kept estates and their power intact, but it created a class of younger sons who were "gentlemen" but who were forced into the middle classes where they had to learn the English language.

By 1100, Middle English had developed, a language that kept the basic Germanic grammar without the Germanic inflections, and adopted more and more of the French words spoken by the nobility. It became strong enough and flexible enough to gain an attraction even for the proud Normans. Little by little, English was becoming the national tongue, an English with such an unusual ability to absorb words from other languages and such a great versatility (owing perhaps to the very fact that it had spent so long a time away from the stifling attentions of grammarians) that it ended by becoming the most widespread and important single language on the face of the earth.

Naturally, the beginnings of a common language implied the start of a kind of fusion of nationality and culture. The distinction between Norman and Saxon under Henry II was a shade less keen than it used to be, and there was beginning to burgeon the faintest possible signs of a common consciousness of Englishness.

There were factors counting both for and against this. Against it was the perpetual involvement with France. The fact that the King of England was also the Duke of Normandy and that the Norman nobility had estates in both lands made it difficult for the barons ever to feel English. They were international.

This was all the worse in the time of Henry II since his French holdings were so far enlarged over those of the earlier kings. Indeed, before he had been king five years, he was distracted from his English duties by the necessity of leading an army into southern France to defend some of his wife's territory from the French king. He didn't do well there because he hesitated to attack Louis VII (his overlord) directly lest he set a bad example for his own vassals.

On the whole, Henry spent less than half his long reign in England and undoubtedly he considered the island as merely one of his many provinces and perhaps not the most important one.

Working for the fusion, however, was the beginning of a literature dealing with matters English.

The first important writer of the post-Conquest period is William of Malmesbury who was born in southwestern England about 1090, while William Rufus was still on the throne. He was educated at an abbey in Malmesbury, twenty-five miles east of Bristol. In the latter part of the reign of Henry I he began to devote himself to the writing of English history after the manner of Bede. He continued working down to his death, about 1143, in the depths of the civil war, during which he was on the side of Matilda.

William of Malmesbury dealt with events in England both before and after the Conquest and thus established a kind of continuity. It catered to Saxon self-esteem in that it did not consider the Saxon period as unworthy of comment. (It would be as though we began American history not with the first English colonists, but with the Indian tribal history that preceded.)

William dealt with actual history and was as accurate as the times permitted. Not so in the case of Geoffrey of Monmouth, who was about ten years younger than William. Geoffrey was from the borderland between England and southern Wales and was probably a Welshman himself. He must have been steeped in Welsh legends in his youth and his writings therefore go back even beyond the Saxons to the days when the Britons dominated the land.

In the late 1130's, when the civil war was in its early stages, Geoffrey published a Latin-language work entitled *The History of the Kings of Britain,* supposedly based on old records, but actually a tissue of myth and invented legend. According to the tale, Britain was first settled by a great-grandson of Aeneas of Troy. This great-grandson, named Brutus, gave his name to the island of Britain. Another Trojan, Corineus, gave his name to Cornwall. In this way, the Britons were made into a sister people of the Romans, who also traced their descent to Aeneas.

Later reigns are described including that of King Leir who was supposed to have founded Leicester and to have divided his kingdom between his two daughters — something which Shakespeare put to use in his great play *King Lear.*

The coming of the Saxons leads to an account of the Britonic king Uther Pendragon, followed by his conquering son, Arthur. This is the climax of the book. The kings after Arthur gradually succumbed to the Saxons until finally, under King Cadwallader, the Britons fled to Brittany and abandoned their island. The book also contains a kind of apocalyptic section supposedly by the magician, Merlin, who made all kinds of obscure predictions about the future and hinted at the eventual return of the Britons.

Geoffrey's history was enormously popular and other writers seized the opportunity to render it into other literary forms and languages thus increasing its popularity still further.

There was, for instance, the Norman writer, Wace, born on the island of Jersey, who put sections of the history into typical French poetic form of the time. He wrote the "Roman de Brut" in 1155 and dedicated it to Eleanor of Aquitaine, a known patroness of poetry of this sort.

The contemporary poet, Walter Map, wrote long poems on the search for the Grail, the cup Jesus drank from at the last supper. He tied it in with the Arthurian legend, giving the whole a religious cast.

A half-century later, another poet, Layamon, treated the same subjects in Middle English, so that it became available to the general public as well as to the aristocracy.

The Arthurian legend had its separate reasons for appealing to Normans and to Saxons. The Normans undoubtedly found it pleasant to have the Saxons the villains of the piece for it made their own seizure of the land seem like divine justice, a punishment for Saxon aggression. Besides, it is even possible that some Normans must have felt that they could be considered the heirs of the men of Brittany (a region which regularly paid homage to the Dukes of Normandy) so that they were taking back their own and fulfilling Merlin's prophecy of the return of the Britons.

To the Saxons, on the other hand, the Arthurian legend was a parable. It told of the resistance of the natives of a land against foreign aggressors and it was easy to translate this into the Saxon resistance to the arrogant Normans. The prediction of Merlin that someday the defeated would return to take back their own would seem to imply a final Saxon victory.

But these differing attitudes could not last. In the end, the ancient legends became the common heritage of England — of Normans and Saxons alike — and roused a common pride in their common land.

England also began to produce leaders in scholarship. Adelard of Bath, born in that city (twelve miles southeast of Bristol) about 1090, traveled widely during his youth through the lands of ancient learning — Greece, Asia Minor, northern Africa. He picked up Arabic and was one of the first of the medieval scholars to begin to study those fragments of ancient knowledge which had been preserved in Arabic books.

Once he returned to England, he translated the works of Euclid from Arabic into Latin, and Euclid thus became available to European scholars for the first time. He also picked up the use of Arabic numerals and helped them to European popularity. For the general public, he wrote a book called *Natural Questions* which contained a summary of all he had learned of Arabic science.

He was one of the teachers of young Henry Plantagenet, but he died in 1150, a little too soon to see his pupil become King of England.

A generation after Adelard came Robert of Chester (a city in western England, twenty miles south of Liverpool), who was born about 1110 and died about 1160. He was another of the indefatigable translators from the Arabic. He translated the works of the mathematician Al-Khwarizmi, thus introducing algebra to western Europe. He also translated many Arabic alchemical works, and even managed to produce the first translation of the Koran into Latin.

One cannot overestimate the importance of these English scholars to the gathering upsurge of knowledge that was putting an end permanently to the period of darkness of the past centuries.

Even more important than the existence of scattered individuals was the first coming to England of organized institutions of advanced learning. Soon after 1100, a school had opened in Paris, which germinated into the University of Paris. The youth of England went to Paris for training, a natural thing for a ruling class that considered itself French anyway. It is a sign of the growing feeling of Englishness, however, that a University, based on the French model, could be set up in England. Some time between 1135 and 1170, Oxford University came into existence on the banks of the Thames River, fifty miles west of London.

THE BECKET AFFAIR

Henry II, having tamed the barons and secured the borders, now aimed to settle matters with the Church. Under the lax rule of Stephen, the Church had asserted its independence and won for itself numerous privileges that had now made it virtually a state within a state. It had come to be accepted, for instance, that clerics could not be tried in the king's courts, but only by clerical courts — even for such heinous crimes as murder.

The clerical courts were always more lenient to priestly offenders than lay courts would have been. Since the Church could not shed blood, a cleric would not be executed for murder, for instance, but might be deprived of his clerical status. A second murder would then send him to the king's court. Henry II said, in disgust, "It takes two crimes to hang a priest," and not only priests, but anyone connected with the Church — monks, deacons, students, even sextons.

Henry's opponent in this was Theobald, the thirty-eighth Archbishop of Canterbury, who held firmly to the privileges of the Church. Theobald had been intimately concerned in the affairs of the civil war but unlike that other prelate, the Bishop of Winchester, he took care not to commit himself too far on either side. He had become Archbiship early in Stephen's reign and had neither opposed him too ostentatiously nor supported him too slavishly.

Only toward the end of the reign did he take a firm stand when he strove to keep Stephen from having his son, Eustace, crowned as his successor. Theobald then managed to arrange the compromise settlement between Stephen and Henry, and when the latter became king, Theobald was the most influential of his advisers, though his influence began to wane, naturally, as the Church-state dispute gathered force.

Even more important than Theobald himself were the men he patronized. He saw to it that men of learning were in his entourage and during his primacy, Canterbury was a small university. He brought a young Italian named Vacarius to England from the University of Bologna. Vacarius was the first to bring knowledge of Roman law to the land, lecturing and writing textbooks that were used at Oxford.

Theobald's secretary from 1150 to 1164 was John of Salisbury, a prime example of England's renewed prominence in scholarship. He was one of the most learned of his age and wrote the only important political treatise of the Middle Ages prior to the rediscovery of the political works of the Greek philosopher Aristotle.

But Theobald's most remarkable protégé was Thomas Becket.

Becket was born in London in 1118. There is an old legend that he is of Saxon descent, since this made his later tragic tale but one more romance of Saxon versus Norman, with right and justice on the side of the Saxon. But that is all nonsense. It is quite certain that Becket was of Norman descent on both sides. Both his father and mother were born in Normandy, though they migrated to London before Thomas was born. In his own time, Becket was called "Thomas of London."

Becket received a good education. He was not remarkable for his scholarship, but he was of most engaging personality and he had the knack of making himself liked. Theobald of Canterbury was attracted to the young man and took him in tow in 1142.

Becket proved of enormous use to Theobald. The archbishop sent his young aide to Rome to get papal backing for the stand against the crowning of Eustace and Becket got what was needed with ease and dispatch. He charmed the Pope as he had charmed the archbishop.

When Theobald felt old age making him unequal to the gathering fight with Henry II over the rights of the Church, he had what he thought was a true inspiration. He urged Henry to appoint Becket to the post of chancellor (which would make him the equivalent of a modern prime minister). If Henry did this, he would, of course rely on Becket to handle negotiations with the Church and Theobald was certain he could count on his protégé to make sure that the king saw the situation from the Church's standpoint.

It was done; Becket received the appointment. But now Becket labored to charm the king. He became his bosom companion, joining him in his pleasures and revelries and living in tasteful luxuriance. Becket advised Henry in peace and war and, to top it off, performed all his duties with great ability and efficiency. But to the old archbishop's horror, Becket took the king's side in the matter of legal jurisdiction over the priesthood and fought to bring about uniform justice for all Englishmen, lay or clerical.

Then, in 1161, Theobald died. He had been the greatest obstacle to Henry's religious policy and now he was gone. It would be Henry's task to find someone to succeed him who would be more amenable to the royal wishes. It was the Pope, of course, who appointed the new archbishop, in theory, but the Pope would probably see fit to appoint one who would please the king — if he also pleased the Pope.

And Henry had the same inspiration that Theobald had earlier had. As Theobald had made his loyal servant chancellor, so Henry decided to make that same loyal servant (now *his* loyal servant) Archbishop of Canterbury. To have a king's man in Canterbury would settle the whole matter at once.

Becket himself resisted the idea. It is hard at this distance to put oneself into someone else's mind, particularly someone as complex as Becket, but it appears he felt that whatever role he played in life, he would have to play it *well*.

As the archbishop's aide, he was a very good aide and did his duty to the archbishop in every respect. When he became the king's chancellor, he was very good at that, too, and did his new duty just as well, even to the point of taking stands he would never have taken in the performance of his old duty. If he became Archbishop of Canterbury, he would have to be a very good archbishop and do his still newer duty well, even if it meant once more changing his stand.

Either he didn't explain this carefully to Henry, or Henry shrugged him off. Thomas Becket became thirty-ninth Archbishop of Canterbury in 1162.

Becket changed at once. He resigned the chancellorship because he felt that he could not fulfill both duties at the same time: that of the chancellorship and that of the archbishopric. (This displeased and puzzled Henry, for he saw no conflict. As far as he was concerned, it was only necessary for Becket to do the royal will in both jobs.)

The new archbishop abandoned his old luxurious way of living and became the complete ascetic. To bring matters to a climax, he took up Theobald's old position with regard to the legal jurisdiction of the Church, and in an even more extreme and resolute form. The amazed and infuriated king pointed out Becket's own actions as chancellor, but Becket said in effect: That was my view as chancellor, but my view as archbishop is otherwise.

Henry found he had outsmarted himself and he was beside himself with rage. It was worse than a matter of mere opposition. It was Becket who opposed him; Becket, his own crony, his own creature, his own hand-picked appointee. To have Becket turn on him in this fashion went beyond all endurance. Friendship between the two men was destroyed forever and it was war to the death.

Henry insisted on having his way and as he multiplied the application of force and of royal anger, the priesthood began to fear and give way, and Pope Alexander III (who was having his own troubles with a competing claimant to the position and who wanted Henry's support) began to preach moderation to Becket. Even with the priesthood generally losing heart, Becket had stood firm and it was only the papal directive that caused him to agree to negotiate.

In 1164, a great council was held at Clarendon (just outside Salisbury). There Henry II pushed through an agreement with Becket and the other bishops that restored the situation between Church and state to what it had been under the Norman kings, particularly under Henry I.

The "Constitution of Clarendon" stressed the importance and power of the king's courts and limited the jurisdiction of clerical courts. In particular, clerics who were accused of crimes such as murder were to be deprived of clerical status and tried by the king's courts. Clerical murderers, in other words, were to be hanged for the first crime, not the second.

The Constitution also limited the Church's power of excommunication, for it could not act against the king's subjects in this respect without the king's consent. It forbade churchmen to leave the country or to appeal to the Pope without the king's permission (a limitation of churchly freedom that had been accepted under the Norman dynasty). As for the appointment of bishops and the question of homage, that was to follow the procedure settled upon by the compromise of 1107 under Henry I.

On the whole, it was a victory for the king, but once the Constitution was published, the Pope, now in a better position himself, refused to accept it, and Thomas Becket at once claimed that this relieved him of his own oath to adhere to the agreement.

The exasperated Henry struck back firmly. He instituted an investigation of Becket's financial affairs while he was chancellor, and the ex-chancellor's goods were declared forfeit because he had broken allegiance to the king. It was clear that the investigation was bound to yield results (the king would insist on that) which would enable Henry to take the sternest measures against Becket, and the Archbishop of Canterbury hurriedly got out of the country and fled to France.

From France, Becket labored to take the most extreme measures against his onetime friend: to produce wholesale excommunication in the kingdom, or to place the whole land under the interdict (that is, to forbid all priestly functions in the kingdom — the most terrible weapon in the armory of the Church).

Pope Alexander, although willing to support the archbishop, was not willing to go *that* far. He worked with all his might to bring about a reconciliation between king and archbishop before the quarrel grew so explosive as to inflict serious dam-

age on the Church generally. In 1170, a lip-service reconciliation was arranged, with both parties grim-mouthed and seeth-
ing with enmity.

Becket, back at Canterbury, had a new grievance, though
one that had no connection with legal jurisdiction or with the
Constitution of Clarendon at all. Shortly before he had returned, Henry II had decided to crown his oldest son and
have him accepted as his successor. Such coronation was
ordinarily the task of the Archbishop of Canterbury. Since
Becket was still in exile, Henry had the coronation performed
by the Archbishop of York.

But to Becket, this was an unbearable infringement on his
prerogatives. As soon as he was back in his cathedral, he excommunicated the bishops who had participated in the coronation. This was done on Christmas Day, 1170.

The news of this reached Henry II in his Continental domain
and he all but burst with fury. Had the reconciliation brought
only this? Had it brought instant renewed defiance and an
attempt to nullify the allegiance paid to his son and heir? He
cried out in agony against the archbishop and then said, in one
of his half-mad passions of rage:

"And not one of the cowards I nourish at my table — not
one will deliver me from this turbulent priest!"

It seemed a clear hint, and four knights, intent on earning
the king's gratitude, left at once. They did not consult the
king, who could have told them that any illegal solution would
only do him infinite harm and that he had spoken ungovernably
and while not quite in possession of his senses.

After all, the king was preparing to have Becket legally arrested for high treason, and he had a case for it, too. The archbishop would be legally convicted and legally punished, perhaps executed. What was the need for anything more? But
while he was planning all this, the four knights reached Canterbury and there, at the altar of the cathedral, on December
29, 1170, cut Becket down.

When the news reached Henry, he was horrified. It was an appalling event that might mean untold danger for him. It could be used against him; and indeed his royal enemy Louis VII lost no time at all in sending a messenger to the Pope demanding that Henry be excommunicated as having deliberately ordered the murder of a man of God.

There would be many among Henry's subjects who would consider him a creature of the Devil to whom all oaths of allegiance were suspended and against whom it was their duty to fight, as soon as an excommunication was announced. French intrigue would stir up Henry's vassals and the barons would eagerly accept God's permission to strike for more power at the expense of their lord. It would be the days of Stephen and Matilda all over again.

There was only one thing Henry could do. He had to convince public opinion that he had not ordered the murder; that it had been done without his consent; that it horrified him. He humbled himself completely, sent messages of contrition (and money, too) to the Pope, held a council at which he swore the most impressive oaths as to his innocence. He did all he could to testify to the holiness of the archbishop, and helped encourage popular opinion to revere that holiness.

In no time at all, reports of miracles at Becket's tomb were heard and by 1173, he was canonized and made a saint. A flourishing cult arose in his honor and spread over Europe, and it became fashionable to make pilgrimages to Canterbury to visit his shrine. (Two centuries later, when Geoffrey Chaucer wrote his *Canterbury Tales*, the pilgrims who told those tales were traveling to that shrine.)

The whole thing must have been endlessly humiliating to Henry, but he achieved his purpose. He deflected papal anger, held the allegiance of his vassals, the integrity of his kingdom, the security of the succession — but he had to give up much of what he had gained at Clarendon.

Clerics continued to be tried before clerical courts and were treated more leniently than laymen would have been. Since anyone who could read and write was presumed to have some connection with the Church, it sufficed to be able to read a verse of the Bible to escape the death penalty for a first murder — something called "benefit of clergy."

EXPANSION

Despite his failure with the Church, Henry II nevertheless labored to reform the legal system in those directions he could. Under the system of the times, each lord had the right to act as judge over his vassals. The result was that there were numbers of local courts, each with its own rules, and varying in harshness. No one could know all the local laws, and, in general, too much law was the equivalent of no law. There were few places the ordinary man could look to for quick justice or, too often, any justice.

Vacarius, having introduced knowledge of Roman law, had given the nation the idea of something that was a general law for all citizens, something that was more than local custom. This basic idea Henry seized upon. He was helped in this respect by his chief legal adviser, Ranulf de Glanville, who was the author of the first text describing and analyzing English law.

Henry II proceeded not by wiping out the local courts but by building a competing king's court that offered speedy judgment according to careful rules and precedents. He appointed judges who could travel to different parts of the kingdom, check on the doings of the sheriffs, and hear cases which could then be determined according to the "common law"; that is, the law which was held in common by the whole kingdom.

Since the traveling judges, in dealing with men accused of crime, had no personal knowledge of them, it became customary to collect local men to testify under oath as to the character of the accused. From this began the slow development of the English jury system.

On the whole, the king's justice was so superior to local baronial justice that all clamored for the former. This had an enormous influence in centralizing the kingdom and in preventing feudal disruption from ever playing quite the disruptive part in England that it did on the Continent.

It is no wonder that prosperity returned by leaps. Back in the time of Henry I, a new reforming order of monks had been introduced in England. It had originated in east-central France in a monastery at Cîteaux. From the older Latin name of the place, the monks came to be known as Cistercians. Labor on the land was one of their ideals, and the Cistercians of England began an extensive program of land improvement, road building and mill construction. They discovered that sheepherding could be made very profitable, and by the time of Henry II, England became an important wool-exporting nation.

As trade grew, the seaports expanded at the expense of the inland towns. London in particular became a commercial center with a population of forty thousand; a most respectable city for the times and a thriving and wealthy one. Merchants from the lowlands, from Germany and from Italy flocked into London which became then what it has remained ever since, a cosmopolitan city.

Yet although the nation was beginning to understand a great deal about law and administration, it still had little or no understanding of finance, of the way in which economic growth could be facilitated if some way were found to transfer the symbols of money rather than money itself.

Increasing trade made it essential that better financial techniques be introduced into the land, and this was something that the Jews did. They entered England from older lands with longer traditions of civilization. They had an international organization of sorts, for there were Jews in every European country and a common misery held them together.

The Christian laws that kept them from holding land or from engaging in any of the usual ways of making a living forced them to specialize in finance since that was permitted them. They developed bills of exchange and letters of credit, so that someone sitting in one place could raise cash in another place, and so that wealth could be quickly accumulated or dispersed.

They supplied something that England needed but didn't know it needed. They helped trade and the general welfare and also offered ready money to the Norman nobility when the barons needed it and could raise it in no other way. To be sure, they had to charge heavy interest for the loans they offered since there was never a sure guarantee that the money would be returned. In general, they were defended by the kings, who had financial need of them (but who might themselves default).

To the general population, the Jews were wicked men whose ancestors had killed Jesus and who had been rejecting him ever since, and were therefore under a curse. The interest they charged was abominable "usury" and they had no rights that anyone was bound to respect.

This was the general lot of the Jews of the period, not in England only, but throughout Christendom. They had already endured it for a thousand years and were to endure it for a thousand more. That they weathered it all and still exist and have managed to contribute as much as they have to mankind, in all fields, remains one of the wonders of history.

Henry's foreign policy continued to prosper, too. He was the first of the kings of England, either Saxon or Norman, to do more than merely look west to the other island — Ireland.

Since the time when Brian Boru had put an end to the Viking domination of the land in the time of Ethelred the Unready, Ireland had passed through a century and a half of tribal anarchy, the details of which are impossible to follow. Though the Irish were wild fighters and brave to the point of folly, they found themselves unable to unite or to organize themselves to fight in disciplined ranks. They could too often be beaten one group at a time.

William the Conqueror and Henry I had speculated on the chances of an Irish adventure and decided there was too much to do at home. Early in his reign, Henry II indulged in similar speculations. Indeed, he found himself with an unprecedented opportunity on his hands for an Englishman sat in an unusually exalted position.

The Englishman's name was Nicholas Breakspear and in 1154, the very year in which Henry II was crowned king, Breakspear was elected Pope, adopting the name of Adrian IV. He was the first Englishman ever to become Pope, and to this day the last. (Adrian was to remain Pope for five years only and was to be succeeded by Alexander III, Becket's ally.)

Henry II decided to take advantage of the understanding of national aims which he might expect in an English Pope. He quickly sent the learned prelate John of Salisbury to Rome to get Adrian's permission for an expedition to invade and conquer Ireland, as William the Conqueror had gained the approval of an earlier Pope for his invasion of England. Adrian gave the permission, but Henry then found that, as in the case of the earlier kings, there were too many projects at home clamoring for his attention. (John of Salisbury, by the way, became a strong partisan of Becket. He went into exile with Becket, returned with him, and was in the cathedral when Becket was murdered. He was not touched and lived on for ten years more.)

As is so often true, the prospective victim begged for the death-stroke itself. Henry might have continued to leave Ireland alone, but in the tribal warfare that continued interminably, some loser sooner or later was bound to cast about for outside help. In 1166, the King of Leinster, having been driven out of his kingdom, wandered abroad to France, where he waited on King Henry and asked for help.

Henry, busy about his own affairs, could do nothing in an official way, but gave him permission to raise mercenaries in England. This the Irishman did and soon Norman knights were freelancing in Ireland as a century before they had free-lanced in Italy, and with equal success. Such was their success in Ireland, in fact, that Henry became seriously concerned lest an independent Norman kingdom be set up there, one which by its efficiency and military discipline might prove a dangerous competitor, where the chaotic stumblings of the native Irish were no threat at all.

In 1171, therefore, Henry decided to take over himself. He landed near Waterford on the southeastern coast of Ireland, eighty miles from Dublin. There was virtually no resistance, perhaps because Henry made it plain he came with papal permission (harking back to the English Pope who had died a dozen years before).

He forced local chieftans to recognize him as their overlord, and when he left, the Norman occupation was in the name of the king. The Norman yoke was light at first and was chiefly confined to a section some twenty-five miles from Dublin in all directions. It was protected by lines of palings from surprise attack by the wild Irish tribes and the English area of Ireland came to be called "the Pale" in consequence. The free Irish were "beyond the Pale" and since they were considered barbarous the expression came to be used for anything not acceptable to polite society.

English control was established also in other coastal cities (much as the earlier Viking control had been) and it was many centuries before the island was completely subdued, if, indeed, it ever truly was — but from that day to this, a period of eight centuries, the English have continuously retained their hold over at least some part of the island.

In Scotland, Henry was equally successful. Malcolm the

Maiden had died in 1165, only twenty-four years old, and was succeeded by his younger brother, William. He is usually called "William the Lion" because of his courage, a common virtue but one which was not, in this case, alloyed by the somewhat rarer one of prudence.

He was the first Scottish king to attempt negotiations looking toward a French alliance as a counterweight to English influence — something the Scots were to continue to do for centuries.

He took pains to play the loyal subordinate to Henry, but when the English king grew involved in warfare elsewhere, he took his chance and invaded northern England.

The Scots tried this often in their history and were almost always beaten back with loss, but this time results were more than usually disastrous for them. William the Lion and a group of his knights were trapped in fog and when the mist cleared they found themselves nearly upon a group of English knights who were likewise wandering about. William took them for his own men at first and before he could find out otherwise, he was taken prisoner.

William was not released until he had signed a treaty in 1174 accepting Henry as overlord of all Scotland under firmer guarantees and more humiliating conditions than before.

Thus it came about that by 1174 Henry II ruled directly or indirectly over England, Wales, Scotland, the coast of Ireland and half of France. The Angevin Empire was at its height.

On top of all else, Henry had a flourishing family. Eleanor of Aquitaine had given Louis VII no sons, but she gave four to Henry. These were a younger Henry, born in 1154, the year Henry II became king; Richard, born in 1157; Geoffrey, born in 1158; and John, the baby of the family, and his father's favorite, born in 1166. Henry was almost fatuous in his father love, spoiling his sons completely.

He had daughters, too, for whom he arranged advantageous marriages that increased the prestige of his house. His daughter, Eleanor, he married to King Alfonso VIII of Castile, which then made up what is now north-central Spain. His daughter Joan, he married to William II of Sicily (still of the line of Tancred of Hauteville). His daughter Matilda, he married to Henry the Lion, Duke of Saxony and Bavaria.

Henry II was the most remarkable monarch in Europe and his connections straddled western Christendom. — And he was only two and a half centuries removed from that barbarous Viking adventurer Hrolf the Ganger.

FAMILY TRAGEDY

The very existence of the Angevin Empire was insupportable to Louis VII of France. As long as it spread itself over the map, he was belittled and humiliated, his position as King of France a mockery. Henry's continued success left Louis insecure on his throne and not even sure he would have a kingdom to pass on to his successor. (He had married again after his divorce from Eleanor and now had sons.)

To be sure, Louis had managed to hold his own without much actual fighting by playing his cards very shrewdly. Henry's long tangle with Becket was perfect for Louis' purposes and he did all he could to keep it going, protecting Becket and encouraging him in his extreme stand, doing his best to line up the Pope against Henry and generally playing the role of imp of mischief.

But it was not enough merely to hold his own, for his own was still less than half his own kingdom. What he needed was civil war within the Angevin Empire and that was difficult to arrange. Henry had his vassals so well-trained and well-tamed, it was hard to rouse them.

But Louis' shrewd and aging eyes turned elsewhere, to Henry's stalwart sons. It was already traditional in western Europe that sons rose against kingly fathers who lived too long and such cases were known among the Norman kings of England. Had not Robert Curthose risen against his father, the Conqueror?

Surely something could be done with four sons, of whom the three oldest were brave but not bright. (The fourth was still a baby and could be left out of account.)

In arranging the civil war, Louis VII had a most unlooked for ally, his own ex-wife Eleanor. Once she married Henry, she had what she wanted, a gay young king, as interested as she herself in amusement and pleasure. The only trouble was that the gay young king was not interested in Eleanor only, but was fond of other ladies as well. This Eleanor took extremely hard.

Out of her hatred (which Henry was soon returning with interest), she encouraged her sons to feel resentment toward their father and to rebel against him. Louis VII helped her out in this at every opportunity.

Henry II had tried to make provision for his sons. He had designated Prince Henry, his oldest son, as his successor, and indeed his crowning of the prince by the Archbishop of York was the occasion for the final and fatal quarrel with Becket. His second son, Richard, was made overlord of Aquitaine, his mother's inheritance, and his third son, Geoffrey, was placed over Brittany. The fourth son, John, was too young for an assignment and he gained the name John Lackland as a result.

As the boys grew older, however, Eleanor encouraged them to demand that their overlordship become real and not merely titular. Prince Henry, in particular, who was eighteen in 1172, wanted to share the kingly duties with his father at that time, or to be recognized as sovereign in Normandy at least. The younger brothers chimed in on behalf of Aquitaine and Brittany.

Henry II made it clear that he would allow no such nonsense

and the sons promptly showed their devotion to their father and to the lands they ruled by fleeing to Louis VII, Henry's worst enemy. Louis welcomed them, you may be sure, with the greatest pleasure. Eleanor, their mother, followed, but Henry managed to capture her, at least. He placed her in prison and kept her there.

It was clear, of course, that the sons would raise armies against their father, for Louis would surely finance them and it looked as though the realm would dissolve into civil war. It was at this time that William the Lion seized his ill-fated opportunity to invade the English north, while some of the English barons decided it might be well to try for what they had had in Stephen's time. By 1174, all was confusion.

Henry II reacted with the utmost energy. He made an ostentatious pilgrimage to the shrine of Thomas Becket, performing penance and permitting himself to be beaten with a knotted cord. In this way, he tried to show, once and for all, that he was innocent of the assassination four years earlier, in order that the common people might not feel that all that was happening was a judgment of God, and fall away from him in consequence.

With that done, his army marched north at once, defeated the Scots (this was the occasion on which William the Lion was taken prisoner) and crushed the English rebels. Henry then traveled back to France and, within a year, had brought his sons to the point where they thought it wise to seek his forgiveness. They were, in the end, forgiven, but Eleanor, their mother, remained imprisoned.

Though Louis VII had not succeeded in breaking up the Angevin Empire, he had forced it into a wasteful preoccupation with war that had weakened it, while his own French lands were kept safe and out of danger. Louis died in 1180, after a forty-three-year reign, but he was succeeded by his son, Philip II, who carried on his father's policies ably.

The new French king, only fifteen at the time of his accession, was even shrewder and more devious than his father, and more intent than he (if possible) on destroying the Angevin Empire. His eventual success in this direction led his admiring courtiers to compare him with the great Roman emperor of ancient times and to call him "Philip Augustus," by which name he is commonly known to historians.

Slyly, Philip encouraged any sign of trouble among the Plantagenets. Richard, the second son, who was showing himself an accomplished warrior, was enthusiastically beating down the barons of Aquitaine and earning their hatred (which was good for Philip). Richard's older brother, Prince Henry, worried over Richard's warlike proficiency and grew fearful that the younger brother would not consent to recognize him as king when the time came. Prince Henry prevailed upon his father to order Richard to do homage to his older brother. Richard refused and there was war between the brothers in 1183, with Philip's agents poisoning the atmosphere between them.

Henry II tried to mediate between the brothers and angered each of them since each was convinced he was favoring the other. The civil war might have grown worse but Prince Henry died suddenly and Richard became the heir. For the moment, that left him satisfied. Then, in 1186, Geoffrey attended one tournament too many (all three sons found jousting on horseback to be their notion of true fun). He was thrown from his horse and died of his injuries.

This left Henry with two sons: Richard, now aged twenty-nine, and John, aged twenty. Of the two, John was the king's spoiled darling, for he was the one who had never revolted. He was also the only one who had received no share in the kingdom. In 1185, Henry tried to make up for this by sending him to Ireland as its overlord. John showed no aptitude for rule, however. He could not keep the Norman lords from quarreling nor the Irish chieftains from growing restless. After nine months, Henry had to recall him.

He then tried to give John the Duchy of Aquitaine, reasoning that now Richard, as heir to everything, could give up a little. But Richard would not reason so at all. Aquitaine was his home and that of his beloved mother and he was going to keep it. When Henry showed signs of insisting, Richard's mind turned blackly toward revolt again.

Young Philip of France encouraged Richard in this thought and cultivated a friendship with him. Philip was eight years younger than Richard and at least eight years cleverer (for much of Richard's brains were in his shoulder muscles) and the French king had no difficulty in talking the English prince into an alliance. Together, they attacked Henry's forces and began to take his castles.

For once, Henry seemed at a loss. It was 1189 now. He had been ruling thirty-five years and he was fifty-six years old. He was tired and worn and there seemed no rest. What with his colossal reorganization of the kingdom, his Homeric feud with Becket and the seemingly endless family squabbles, it seemed to him he could fight no more.

He gave in, signed a treaty with the French king, and granted Richard all he wanted. He looked at the list of his own vassals who had lined up with the Frenchman and heading the list was his son, John; his last son, his favorite, who now turned out to be as false as the rest.

Henry said, "Now let the world go as it will. I care for nothing more!"

He never got out of his bed again and on July 6, 1189, he died. To the world, he had been a great king and a success, but in his own eyes, he died a despairing failure.

12

THE SONS OF HENRY

THE LION-HEART

Of all the kings of history, there are few who have so inflated a reputation as the Richard who succeeded to the English throne on the death of his father, Henry II. He is "Richard Coeur-de-Lion," or, in English, "Richard the Lion-Heart," a hero-king revered in hundreds of pieces of historic fiction.

To be sure, he was a giant in strength and in bravery, and an excellent leader of men where the victories went entirely to the stronger muscles. He could also sing and write verses and play the troubadour generally, something in which there was a hint of his formidable mother, still alive at his accession, a tough and wiry sixty-seven.

In all matters other than strength and physical bravery, however, Richard was quite a despicable person. He was a disloyal and treacherous son and brother and rarely saw farther

than the end of his nose. His notion of being a king was to engage in foolish knight-errantry. He was Don Quixote, sitting
on a throne.

He was not even a manly person, except for his ability to
fight. He lacked resolution and another nickname for him (not
as well known as Lion-Heart) was "Richard Yea-and-Nay"
meaning he could easily be swayed to either side of a question
and no one could rely on his staying on one side once he had
been swayed there. Nor (unlike his father) was he particularly interested in women; indeed, it seems quite certain he
was homosexual.

As for England, which worshipped him in the end, he took
no thought for it and rarely set foot in it. He was nothing to
England but a source of vast expense.

Immediately upon hearing of his father's death, Richard
seized the royal treasury and had his mother released from
prison. Then he set about the task that was to occupy much of
his reign and was to fix his false reputation with posterity.

The lands won by the First Crusade a century before were
in increasing peril. Louis VII's Second Crusade had done
nothing and now, on the side of the Moslems, rose a great hero,
Saladin, one who really was everything that Richard was
falsely supposed to be.

In 1187, Saladin had defeated and destroyed an army of
Crusaders and had taken Jerusalem itself. A thrill of anger and
despair swept over western Europe at the news. In the fury
and excitement of the moment, soldiers everywhere began to
take an oath to travel to the Holy Land and rescue Jerusalem
once more.

Old Henry II took such an oath. So did Philip II of France.
So did Prince Richard. Henry II, to raise money for the great
expedition, levied a special tax on his dominions in 1188. It
was called the "Saladin tithe" because it required each property owner to contribute a tithe, that is a tenth, of his rents and
movables. Additional funds in considerable quantity, were

beaten out of the Jews. (After all, Henry might have reasoned, why shouldn't infidels pay for the crimes of infidels — even though they were two different sets of infidels? In fact, it was the Crusading era that saw anti-Semitism reach its first furious peak in western Europe.)

But then, when all that was done, Philip and Richard went to war with Henry, and plans for the crusade had to be halted. The rescue of Jerusalem would just have to wait while matters concerning some castles in France were settled.

Once Richard was on the throne, however, he would wait no more. There was no knight-errantry in the world that could match the great eastern adventure. More than anything else in the world he longed to go eastward and have colossal tournaments with the Moslems and rescue Jerusalem and be the greatest knight the world had ever seen. (And perhaps it occurred to him that he might also please his mother in this fashion — and make up for her disappointment in the Crusade of her first husband half a century before.)

Richard needed money and to get it he went to England and sold everything he could. He sold church offices, secular offices, town charters, heiresses. He even sold the sovereignty of Scotland back to its king. And he squeezed the Jews once again. His actions here, combined with popular feeling against the Jews, resulted in dark deeds of riotous murder most uncharacteristic of English history. In York, Jews were slaughtered horribly and indiscriminately by the mob.

After four months, Richard, having obtained what he needed by means that were variously false, foolhardy and cruel, was ready to go off on a great adventure that was to bring him fame, but was to bring no permanent rescue to the Holy Land and no good of any kind to England.

Indeed, his leaving would have guaranteed the destruction of the Angevin Empire at the hands of Philip, but for the fact that public opinion forced the French king to go on the Crusade also.

Philip had vowed to do so, of course, just as Richard had, but the vow had been as a matter of policy and he had never intended actually to go. What he most wanted to do was stay at home while Richard was abroad, and quietly take the Angevin Empire apart. If he tried to do so, however, Richard would at once attack him as an oath-breaker and as a traitor to the general cause of Christendom. Philip's own vassals might desert him in that case.

Reluctantly, then, Philip went crusading. Whatever friendship there might have existed between the two men earlier, it existed no more. They were deadly enemies for the rest of their lives.

What followed is called the "Third Crusade" and Richard's eastward swagger represents the last great example of Norman freebootery, for the English king was indeed a kind of throwback to the days of Robert Guiscard.

Richard's voyage eastward was conducted without real strategic insight. He allowed himself to be delayed everywhere. In 1190, he reached Sicily and got into a quarrel with Tancred, the last Norman ruler of Sicily. When he finally signed a treaty with Tancred, it was the kind of treaty that offended the new German emperor, Henry VI, who disputed Tancred's claim to the Sicilian throne.

Richard next decided not to marry Philip's sister, to whom he had been engaged, and this insult served to alienate further the angry French king. Following that, Richard wasted two months and much energy by engaging in an unnecessary conquest of the island of Cyprus.

Richard reached the Holy land finally in June, 1191, nearly a year after setting out. The city of Acre, on the Palestinian coast, was then under siege by the Christians, and had been under siege for a long time without any signs of a Moslem surrender. The landing of Christian reinforcements under Europe's greatest knight was a tremendous boost to morale and Richard loved the adulation that was now his.

But Acre still held out just the same and it wasn't taken until many disgraceful events later which took considerable of the shine off Richard's glory. At one point, Richard showed the quality of his knighthood by slaughtering 2,600 Moslem prisoners in cold blood out of peevish annoyance with the Acre garrison for not surrendering.

As for Philip, who was constantly ill, he was less enthusiastic for the Crusade than ever and annoyed to death over the manner in which Richard insisted on hogging all the glory. The siege became only secondarily a fight between Christian and Moslem; much more so, it was a wary, circling dispute between Richard and Philip.

Then, when Acre fell at last, Richard performed an act of arrogant discourtesy. Leopold, Duke of Austria, led a contingent at the siege, and after Acre had fallen, he placed his standard on one of the battlements. Richard, seeing no point in giving credit to anyone else, ordered the standard removed and contemptuously had it thrown to one side. Some say that when Leopold protested, Richard, in a fit of anger, kicked him into silence. There was nothing Leopold could do at the time, but he did not forget.

After the fall of Acre, Philip left for home, pleading illness and swearing not to attack Richard's lands. Richard marched on toward Jerusalem, but never quite made it. He won victories, but those victories cost him men. The hunger and thirst, the heat by day and desolation by night, the cool flanking harassment organized by the shrewd Saladin, all wore him down. Richard penetrated to within sight of Jerusalem and, according to the romantic tale, covered his eyes, feeling he was not worthy to see what he was unable to take.

In 1192, having settled with Saladin for a three-year truce, Richard took ship for home, leaving behind several victories, many tales, a heroic reputation — and an overall defeat. It was Saladin who remained the real hero of the Third Crusade.

Richard realized that his homeward voyage was bound to be

difficult. He had managed to antagonize almost everyone in Europe and he lacked the army to force his way across the Continent against that antagonism. His ship was drawn ashore near Venice and he decided that the safest course was to complete the journey home by land and in disguise.

But Richard could not very well imitate a nobody. He was large, muscular and haughty. Nothing he could do could prevent him from appearing what he was — an arrogant knight of high estate. It was only a matter of time before he would be identified, and as luck would have it, he was recognized at the worst possible time.

Near Vienna, in December 1192, he was surrounded by armed men who were clearly intent on holding this obviously important personage for ransom. Richard drew his sword and said he would surrender only to their leader. When that leader appeared, it turned out to be none other than Leopold of Austria — the same Leopold whose standard Richard had thrown into the ditch and whose behind he had roundly kicked.

Leopold smiled grimly and set the highest possible ransom. But there were others more powerful than Leopold who also hated Richard. The Emperor Henry VI, who had been offended by Richard's policy in Sicily, forced Leopold to release the prisoner to him. Richard became Henry's prisoner and the emperor calmly threatened the English king with a further transfer to Philip of France.

The prospect of imprisonment by Philip was the last straw, for only to Philip was Richard's imprisonment worth more than any conceivable money ransom. Once in Philip's clutches, Richard couldn't possibly expect to get out without signing over most of the French provinces of the Angevin Empire. Richard therefore consented to an exorbitant ransom of 150,000 marks and a kind of formal (but essentially meaningless) recognition of the emperor as his overlord. (In theory, the emperor was lord over all of western Christendom, a tradition that dated back to Charlemagne, but of course, no one paid attention to that theory in practice.)

The money was raised by taxing Richard's subjects heavily (that was what the Lion-Heart brought England out of the Holy Land — a high price to pay for Richard's eagerness to kick an archduke) and in 1194, he returned to England. He stayed there just long enough to be crowned a second time and (what else?) to collect money; then he left for the Continent.

There he remained for the rest of his life, fighting Philip Augustus.

RICHARD AND JOHN

And what of England during Richard's absence? He had placed its administration in the hands of William Longchamp, his chancellor, who was also Bishop of Ely.

Richard also named an heir, in case he did not return from the Crusade. In the old days, any member of the royal family might have done, but in England the principle of primogeniture was continuing to grow in popularity and the notion of "rightful heir" was more and more important. The rightful heir was the oldest son and his line, or, failing that, the second son and his line, and then the third, and so on.

In the case of Henry II, the oldest son, Henry, had died, leaving no children and so the second son, Richard, had become king. Richard had no children and so the inheritance passed to the line of the third son, Geoffrey. Geoffrey had died in 1186 but his wife, Constance, the heiress of Brittany, gave birth to a son after his death. She named him Arthur, after the great hero of the ancient Britons (and therefore of Brittany). He is known to history as Arthur of Brittany.

By the principles of primogeniture, Arthur of Brittany was the rightful heir, though he was only three years old at the time Richard left for the Crusade, and so the king named him as his successor. As for younger brother John (who was next in line for the throne if Arthur died without children) he was restored to the old post that Henry II had given him — Lord of Ireland.

The post was intended to keep him out of England where he might create trouble through his ambitions for the crown. Richard made sure of this by having him vow not to return to England for three years after the royal departure, then topped it off by granting him the bribe of broad estates in England.

However, when Richard had been gone a year and a half Walter Longchamp was already proving to be unpopular with the English barons. John saw his chance and could not resist. He crossed into England in 1191 and began to gather a party who would favor him for the crown over Arthur of Brittany.

John was most unpopular in his lifetime and has had a "bad press" for a variety of reasons. To be sure, he was cruel and faithless, but no more so than Richard. What John lacked that Richard had was a fine appearance, bravery, gallantry and the ability to strike romantic poses. Most important of all, John was not much influenced by religion and in his lifetime got into enormous trouble with the Church. It was the churchmen who kept the chronicles of the time and they paid him back with assaults on his character.

But this is not to say that John was really admirable; he most certainly was not. It's just doubtful that he was any worse than Richard.

In any case, John lacked the gift of inspiring men to follow his lead. His efforts to take advantage of Longchamp's unpopularity, Richard's absence and Arthur's infancy made little progress. But then the news of Richard's imprisonment reached England. John hastened to France to come to some agreement with Philip, hoping to make sure that Richard would stay in prison (or, perhaps, be put out of the way altogether).

This also he could not manage. The tales of Richard's heroics in the Holy Land had returned to England and were greatly improved in the telling, so that Englishmen were eager to ransom their hero-king. John's attempts to supplant him only gained him odium in the eyes of the English.

Finally, when Richard returned, John had to leave England again. He was still Lord of Ireland (equivalent to a kind of Siberian exile) but most of his English estates were confiscated, and Richard still insisted that Arthur was heir to the throne.

On Richard's side through all this was Hubert Walter, one of the king's most important ministers. He was with Richard in the Holy Land and had represented the king in all negotiations with Saladin. He led what was left of the English army back to England, visited Richard in his imprisonment and in 1193 was active in raising the ransom. In that same year he was also appointed forty-third Archbishop of Canterbury.

Hubert Walter governed England in the last years of Richard's reign, while the king was fighting in France, and did it well. It was necessary for him to place stiff taxes on the people to raise money for the king's needs but he did this as justly as he could. Walter relied heavily on the "knights," the small proprietors who made up England's middle class at this time. Some were elected to maintain order in their districts and eventually developed into "justices of the peace." Others performed the duties of "coroners." When Walter raised money, he had the actual assessments made by juries of such men.

Such moves were of the greatest significance. When government was laid upon the great barons, each was powerful enough to have great ambitions. When the small knights were given responsibility, none could hope to achieve anything on his own; only in common action could they gain something and only the general peace would help them all. England continued to move toward its special form of government that was to bring it a remarkable stability and the kind of flexibility needed to adapt itself to changing conditions by slow growth and evolution rather than by sudden and radical changes.

Townsmen, too, were becoming increasingly self-conscious and were moving into positions where their political influence was growing. They formed "guilds" which were dues-paying organizations (the word "guild" means "dues" and is related to "gold") that saw to the common good of its members. Each group of artisans or merchants had its own guild that organized trading practices, regulated prices and wages, standardized weights and measures, and so on. And, of course, guilds could maintain the interests of the town against the landowners and the nobility with far more effectiveness than individual townsmen could. The first merchant guild was organized about 1193.

Meanwhile, in France, Richard went his knight-errantish way. He fought Philip II of France with enthusiasm, and usually with success as far as individual battles went, though Philip could always win back by intrigue and policy what he lost in the field.

Richard brought to the west new principles of fortification that he had learned in the east. In 1196, he began the construction of Château Gaillard ('Gallant Castle") on a promontory overlooking the Seine River, twenty miles upstream from the Norman capital at Rouen, and fifty miles downstream from Philip's capital at Paris.

It was skillfully designed to make it impregnable to the styles of attack of the time. Indeed, in a day when land warfare consisted chiefly in the attack and defense of fortified castles, the building of Château Gaillard was equivalent to the construction of a new and improved kind of battleship in more recent times.

Philip won a victory of a much different kind when he persuaded the Bretons to give up their prince, Arthur, to him.

Philip had a plausible excuse for this since he was Arthur's overlord, according to feudal theory, and he could argue that he was fulfilling his feudal duties by granting Arthur the very best possible education at the French court.

This was most unpalatable to Richard, however. It meant that Arthur, in due time, would come to the English throne as a full Frenchman, as once Edward the Confessor had come to the English throne as virtually a full Norman. Edward's reign had led to a Norman conquest and might not Arthur's reign then lead to a French conquest?

Prince John seemed the only alternative and, in 1197, Richard accepted him as heir.

This, of course, merely confused matters. The rightful heir had to be the rightful heir and no one else. Could even the king alter that? Could he designate as his heir anyone he chose? It was not the sort of thing that one could be sure about.

Unfortunately, the matter came up at once, owing entirely to Richard's continued folly. He lacked the ability to distinguish between an important fight and an unimportant one. Any fight would do. He further lacked the understanding to realize that it was more important to be a live king than a dead hero.

In 1199, some small sum was due Richard (so he insisted) from a minor nobleman. When the sum was denied him, he at once laid siege to the nobleman's castle. Richard refused a conditional offer of surrender for there was no fun in taking a castle without a fight. As he reconnoitered the walls, an arrow struck him in the left shoulder. He ordered an assault at once and the castle was taken. Only then did he bother to have the arrow extracted.

It was too late. The age was innocent of antibiotics or even of the notions of ordinary hygiene. The wound festered and the infection killed Richard. He was forty-two and had reigned ten years.

ARTHUR AND JOHN

John became king. He was on the spot; in fact, he was at
Richard's deathbed. Richard had named him heir two years
before and their mother, Eleanor of Aquitaine (still alive
though over seventy-five years of age) had always labored to
keep her two sons at peace. She strongly favored her youngest
son, John, over her grandson Arthur, whom she scarcely knew.
(Shakespeare's *King John* contains a stirring picture of the termagant enmity of the two mothers, Eleanor of Aquitaine and
Constance of Brittany.)

John was therefore recognized without difficulty in England
and in Normandy. Eleanor, who was still the legal ruler of
Aquitaine, turned that over to John, too. The only trouble was
that Anjou finally seized the opportunity to indulge in anti-
Norman activity again and recognized Arthur, and in this the
Angevins were strongly supported (of course) by King Philip
of France.

In the last analysis, though, Philip wasn't interested in hand-
ing the Angevin Empire over to Arthur, either. What he
wanted was to break it up altogether. Perhaps he took the
measure of John and saw that he was the best possible king to
have on the English throne since against him, Philip's measures
would be bound to succeed. (Some eventually called the new
king John Softsword, a name that explains itself.)

At any rate, after some fighting, Philip came to an agreement
with John in 1200 in which he sacrificed Arthur's interests in
return for considerable concessions (including a payment of
money and the giving up of foreign alliances on the part of
John). Philip, in return, recognized John as king and granted

Arthur only the title of Duke of Brittany. For that title, what's more, Arthur would have to do homage to John.

Once that was done, there remained for Philip only the necessity of picking a fight with John. He could then conquer the French sections of the Angevin Empire without having to turn them over to any competing Plantagenet such as Arthur. The excuse came soon enough.

In 1200, John had married, with considerable haste, a young lady (only thirteen years old in fact) named Isabella, who was heiress of Angoulême, a strategic county in the northern part of Aquitaine. The lady is reported to have grown up to be beautiful, but John might well have married her under any conditions, for the lands she controlled were important to him. He divorced his first wife, an Englishwoman, and it was with Isabella that he was crowned.

The trouble was that Isabella, at the time of her hasty marriage, had been engaged to a member of a powerful French feudal family. The family felt aggrieved and appealed to Philip II.

Philip listened gravely. As King of England, John was an independent sovereign, but as overlord of Normandy, Anjou, Aquitaine and all the rest, John was Philip's vassal, just as the aggrieved lord was. Philip, judging a quarrel between vassals, chose to remain strictly to the letter of the feudal law and summoned John to appear before him to answer the charges.

John would not, of course. His dignity as King of England made that impossible, and Philip knew he would not. When John failed to come, he was in contempt, and Philip could, again quite according to the letter of feudal law, declare John deprived of the lands he held as vassal.

Naturally, that meant nothing unless Philip was prepared to take them by force, but this was exactly what he planned to do, and with loud proclamations to the effect that he had right on his side.

The vassal warriors of the French portion of the Angevin

Empire now failed John. Many of them honestly thought Arthur was the rightful heir and hesitated to fight for John. Others honestly thought John was in contempt and was fighting in an unjust cause. And still others simply didn't like John (who had no trick of popularity) and were glad to use any excuse to drag their feet. As for John's English vassals, they had grown English enough to feel England was their home and to hate to cross the Channel in what was beginning to seem a foreign interest.

Nevertheless, John gathered the men he could and fought. He defended Richard's Château Gaillard well. When in 1203 his mother Eleanor (still alive) was besieged in Mirebeau, a few miles south of Anjou, John hastened to rescue her. The besieging army was led by his nephew, Arthur of Brittany, and in the battle that followed, John found Arthur to be one of the captives.

John carried Arthur off to prison in Rouen and the young man (only sixteen years old) was never seen again. It is presumed he soon died and it is almost universally accepted that John had him killed. He was accused of it at the time and if there was any way he could have denied it, he would have, for it ruined his cause.

Brittany was incensed at the apparent murder of its prince; its chief bishop accused John of murder; the King of France did his best to broadcast the accusation; and those of John's French vassals who had remained loyal now began to fall away in droves. Usurping the kingdom from the rightful heir was bad enough but *killing* the rightful heir was infinitely worse. Such a crime would have to be punished most fearfully by heaven and few wished to subject themselves to a share in the punishment.

John, who was not subject to spiritual fears, fought on, but now Philip went from one triumph to another. Château Gaillard fell; Normandy was penetrated; Rouen, the capital of William the Conqueror, was put under siege.

By 1204, John was thoroughly beaten. He had to agree to the loss of all his northern French territories and he retired to England without them. He was John Lackland in quite another sense than the one in which he originally earned the title.

Philip had triumphed amazingly and had consummated the ambitions of his father. He had destroyed the Angevin Empire after just half a century of existence. England still owned territories in the southwest but they alone (separated from the island by a broad band of French territory) could not serve as a threat to the very existence of the French monarchy.

Even Normandy was gone. It had been carved out by Hrolf the Ganger in 911 and had been held by his descendants for three centuries. From it, Normans had gone out to conquer England, southern Italy, Sicily, and sections of the Holy Land. Now John, the seven-times-great-grandson of Rollo and the great-great-grandson of William the Conqueror had lost it.

And Eleanor of Aquitaine finally died in 1204 at the age of eighty-two. It had been her marriage with Henry II a half-century before that had created the Angevin Empire and she lived just long enough to see it destroyed.

THE POPE AND JOHN

To be sure, John did not accept the end of the empire as final. For the next ten years he was to prepare carefully and single-mindedly for a return match with Philip. The trouble was, though, that he had been deprived of the proper means of doing so. The loss of large French territories was not merely a blow at his pride; it meant he was deprived of vast revenues. To win them back he needed money and this could not be obtained by regular means from his shrunken realm — at least not in adequate amounts. He was forced to increase taxes and use irregular means of raising money. His unpopularity, marked to begin with and increased as a result of Arthur's death and John's defeats, now reached a kind of fever pitch.

Worse still, trouble was brewing with the Church. In 1205, Hubert Walter, Archbishop of Canterbury, who had so skillfully handled English affairs in the latter part of Richard's reign, died. There was the question of who was to succeed him. King John naturally had a candidate. And under ordinary circumstances that candidate would have become the new archbishop and, in all probability, would have helped John raise money — even at the expense of the Church.

Unfortunately for John, the Pope at this time was Innocent III, the strongest and (from the political standpoint) most successful holder of that office in its history. Under him the papacy reached the peak of its material power and it was Innocent's firm desire to establish the papal office as supreme in Christendom and as superior to the various monarchs.

Innocent III saw a chance here to kill three birds with one stone. By preventing the appointment of John's man, he would prevent the possible plundering of the English Church and demonstrate papal superiority over the English monarchy. By forcing his own man instead, he would see to it that the English Church would be run in the papal and not the royal interest. And by choosing Stephen Langton as the man for the post, he would give England an Archbishop of Canterbury who was particularly well qualified, for he was a great scholar.

John was perfectly aware that Langton was a great scholar, but he was also aware that Langton would be a great enemy. Although he was English by birth, Langton had been educated at the University of Paris and had spent a quarter of a century in a French environment. He was completely unacceptable to John and, by modern standards, understandably so.

By the standards of the medieval Church, however, John's opposition was not only unreasonable, it was sinful. When John refused to allow the new archbishop to take his post, Innocent placed all of England under the interdict in March, 1208. This meant that all churchly functions were suspended (except baptism and extreme unction) and the population deprived of all spiritual succor. Even the church bells didn't ring.

This was a terrifying event for a medieval population, but John did not bend. By the use of force, he kept many priests at work, and maintained what he conceived to be his royal prerogative. (It was this, more than anything else, that caused the monkish chroniclers to vilify him and gave him his blackened reputation with posterity.)

After a year and a half of such a standoff, Innocent decided to use a more specifically aimed weapon. In November, 1209, John was excommunicated. It was not so much the kingdom generally that was being punished, as the king in person. He could not participate in any religious functions and his subjects were relieved of any duties they owed him. The Pope even went through the motions of deposing John and turning his kingdom over to Philip of France.

And still John held out. There were, in fact, several factors working on his side. There were many barons who resented dictation from an Italian Pope and a Frenchified archbishop and who remained on John's side. Furthermore, John had what we would today call "patronage." He had the money to pay soldiers, the lands with which to reward the loyal, and the ability to take land away from the disloyal. He could (and did) hold the children of some of his barons as hostages for their good behavior. In fact, he even seized Church property and used that as revenue, so that he could reduce taxes and gain somewhat in popularity.

On the other hand, there was a flight of clerics from England, for many did not want to remain in a land where they might be forced by the king to perform duties that they were forbidden to do by the Pope, and thus face either martyrdom or damnation. Their leaving deprived England of much of its administrative class and John found it harder and harder to govern the land.

It was a question of which side could outwait the other and as the months passed, John realized that Innocent III was not to be outwaited. The Pope could hold out forever, but there was a severe time limit for John. He was getting closer to the time when he planned to invade France to regain his empire, and he could not do that while he was under excommunication. As long as he was in England he could keep his barons loyal, but as soon as he was out of the country, and still excommunicated, they would surely rise against him.

So in 1213, he heaved a resigned sigh and decided to submit. Stephen Langton was allowed to assume his post as forty-fourth Archbishop of Canterbury and absolved the king. In return, John agreed to hand over his kingdom to the Pope, ruling thenceforth as a papal vassal. It was a great humiliation, but it had its value. John paid the Pope an annual tribute of a thousand marks and that was the full extent of the papal overlordship. In return, John had made sure that Philip could not invade English territory which had become the territory of the Church.

Now it was possible for John to try for his empire again.

For the purpose, he had been carefully building up a system of alliances, in particular with the German emperor, Otto IV. Otto was the son of Henry the Lion, who had married Matilda, the daughter of Henry II and the sister of John. The emperor was thus the nephew of the English king.

Henry the Lion had been driven from his lands by the vicissitudes of German politics and had sought refuge in Angevin territory. There his son Otto had been brought up at the court of Richard the Lion-Heart and had even reached the point of being made Duke of Aquitaine. In 1198, Otto's career had

had another startling reversal when he was elected German emperor.

Otto was thus united to John by blood and upbringing and Philip of France was their common enemy. Once the quarrel with the Church was out of the way, John prepared to attack France in concert with Otto and with as many lesser lights as could be brought in.

John's part was to attack from the lands he still held along the southwestern coast of France, while Otto IV invaded France from the northeast.

Unfortunately for the allies, they did not achieve synchronization. Had Otto and John acted together, Philip would have had to divide his forces and he would then very likely have been defeated. As it was, Otto delayed, and John found himself attacking in the southwest alone. There he was defeated.

When Otto finally moved, along with those English contingents that had joined his army, it had become a one-front war and Philip could move his entire force to the northeast.

The two armies met at Bouvines on July 27, 1214, a village ten miles southeast of Lille. It was a confused battle in which the knights made the air resound with the clash of metal upon metal but it was remarkably unbloody, at least for those knights. The development of armor had reached such a pitch that the individual knight was a kernel hidden in a very hard shell.

At one point, indeed, Philip II himself was seized and pulled off his horse. The enemy soldiers then tried to find some chink in his armor through which they could stick a lance and failed. Before they could do anything about the shell, Philip was rescued again.

In the end, the result of the mutual battering was that the emperor's forces were driven from the field. The victory of Philip II was complete and the Battle of Bouvines proved one of the decisive engagements of the Middle Ages.

Otto IV lost his imperial title and John his last hope of re-treiving the Angevin Empire. The return match had been lost and the decision was final.

Yet however much the loss might have offended those who longed for victory and broad realms, it proved a boon for England. John's failure did more for the nation than all the shrewd-ness of Henry II and all the knight-errantry of Richard the Lion-Heart.

While the aristocracy considered Normandy their true home and while the Angevin Empire existed, England was bound to seem a barbaric outpost to the Norman warriors. Henry II spent only half his time in England, Richard spent practically no time there. It was governed with one hand and half an eye and its interests were sacrificed continually to Continental intrigues.

But now England was not to be the island outpost of a Continental empire. It was to be a kingdom in its own right, going its own way, and making its own mark. John had to hold his state in England, perforce, and stay there. The Norman nobility in England now had only English estates and their interests became entirely English.

The slow amalgamation of Norman and Saxon, the gradual realization that there was such a thing as "English" began to advance rapidly from John's reign onward. It forged a common bond between lord and yeoman and united them against "the French."

It is from John's reign and the loss of Normandy that we can start speaking of England as recognizably the nation we know today. The English were not through with the Continent by any means. For centuries, the islanders would flood across the Channel in quest of those lost French territories, and meet with either victory or defeat, but they were to do so as Englishmen. Their wars in France would no longer be on behalf of a French duke against a French king; they would be on behalf of their own English king.

EPILOGUE—THE MAGNA CARTA

By now, though, John's unpopularity had reached a peak. His tax policies (and even those of Richard before him) had made the commoners increasingly restive. One William Fitzosbert, for instance, made rousing speeches against the rich and noble who did not bear their share of the expense of the war while the poor were ground down. He was treated as such "agitators" are usually treated by the comfortable and well-fed. He was arrested and hanged.

After the Battle of Bouvines, though, even the comfortable and well-fed deserted John. He had scarcely a friend left in England. John knew that his constant defeats in the field would lure the barons into combining against him and he was, at the moment, unable to fight them down by main force. He was a practical king who knew how to give in, whether to King

Philip, to Pope Innocent, or to his own barons. He prepared to consider concessions.

The barons had drawn up a kind of document which spelled out what they conceived to be their rights. It was not a revolutionary document; there was nothing high-flown in it about justice or freedom or liberty. There were no abstract principles involved at all. It merely dealt with specific redress for specific wrongs. It was an attempt to end what they considered a too-great increase in the royal power and to return to an earlier, less centralized situation.

If matters had been left to the barons themselves, the document prepared for John's consideration would have been purely feudal, for they were interested in their own rights and not in those of "the people." For instance, much of the document was concerned with widows and infant heirs, in order that it be made certain that the king could not alienate estates or take undue advantage of such as were not protected by adult males.

However, Archbishop Stephen Langton was on the side of the barons, as was the Church generally. They were the administrators of the land and were interested in law and judgment. They therefore inserted all sorts of clauses dealing with the freedom of the Church and with reforms in justice and law, which affected not only the barons, but the knights, the townspeople, the merchants and so on.

Thus, the very first clause says "The Church of England shall be free, and have her whole rights, and her liberties inviolable." Another clause says, "the city of London shall have all its ancient liberties and free customs." Still another says "No sheriff . . . shall take horses or carts of any freeman for carriage, but by the good-will of the said freeman." Rights to justice and to fair trial were extended to all freemen. (To the barons of the time "all freemen" undoubtedly meant "all the better classes" but in time it came to mean "all Englishmen.")

As security, the barons included a clause by which they

were to elect twenty-five of their own numbers to serve as a body to whom could be brought complaints concerning violations of the clauses of the documents.

It was this that King John was being asked to put his signature to. He didn't want to, of course, for it limited his powers over every class of society. Many of the barons weren't enthusiastic either. They wanted to grab what they could without a document that forced them to worry about the Church, and the city of London, and a freeman's horses and carts.

It was Langton, however, who was the guiding spirit throughout and who pushed on both sides for an accommodation. He even threatened John with excommunication again if he did not sign. Papal insistence on Langton as Archbishop thus had a consequence that Pope Innocent had not foreseen.

Finally, the issue came to a head. The barons under Robert Fitzwalter insisted the document (the "Magna Carta" or "Great Charter") be signed; the king resisted. Both sides made warlike feints. The barons gathered for war, with the Londoners clearly on their side. — And John gave in.

On June 15, 1215, John met the representatives of the barons at Runnymede, on the south bank of the Thames (just west of the present city limits of London) and signed.

That was by no means the end of it. John repented the signature. Pope Innocent opposed it and for a while suspended Langton for his part in it. There was a short civil war and even an invasion of England by Louis, the son of Philip of France.

But the Magna Carta remained, was amended and reissued, until in 1225 it came to have the version in which it now survives.

To be sure, the Magna Carta did not always govern the actions of English kings, and there were numerous periods in English history when it seemed as though the Magna Carta had never been issued.

Nevertheless, it was never entirely forgotten. It remained

always to the people of the land written evidence that the king's powers were limited, that there were rights of the subjects that could not be violated by the king. In short, the principle which evolved in England that did not evolve in other European countries of the time was that *the law was superior to the king*.

This is not to say that the internal history of the island was not without its oppression and violence after the time of King John; it even had its revolutions. But there was always the feeling that the relationship between monarch and subjects was governed by a contract which, like any other contract, could be amended by law and without violence. By and large, then, English history was quieter than that of other European nations and moved in a different and, many think, better direction.

For the first time, thanks to John's failures, a push began that was eventually to evolve the first approach to democracy on a national scale. (In ancient and medieval times, democratic or part-democratic governments flourished only in individual city-states.)

This approach to democracy on a national scale was inherited by the United States when it was formed out of what had originally been English colonies. By way of the United States, now the strongest and most influential nation on earth, the current of liberty that flows through modern history from the Magna Carta makes itself felt in many nations of the world and may, in the end, envelop all of them.

A TABLE OF DATES

B.C.

10,000 British Isles emerge from Ice Age

6000 British Isles cut off from Continent by rising sea level

2000 Beaker Folk invade British Isles

1750 Stonehenge built

1500 Phoenicians trade at the Tin Islands

1000 Celts invade Great Britain

300 Celts in control of all Great Britain; invade Ireland; Pytheas of Massalia explores northern seas

55 Julius Caesar's first campaign in Britain

54 Julius Caesar's second campaign in Britain

A.D.

43 Aulus Plautius begins Roman conquest of Britain

51 Caractacus captured

60 Boudicca's revolt

77 Gnaeus Julius Agricola consolidates Roman conquest of Britain

A.D.

84 Agricola defeats Caledonians at Mount Graupius; is recalled

122 Hadrian's Wall built

142 Antonine's Wall built

209 Septimius Severus campaigns against Caledonians

211 Septimius Severus dies in York

297 Constantius Chlorus in Britain

306 Constantius Chlorus dies in York

314 Britonic bishops attend church conference in Arles

367 Theodosius stabilizes Roman Britain for the last time

407 Roman legions leave Britain

429 Germanus preaches Christianity in Ireland

432 Patrick preaches Christianity in Ireland

450 Vortigern appeals for help to Jutes

456 Jutes land in Kent

461 Death of Patrick

A.D.

754 Death of Boniface

757 Assassination of Ethelbald of Mercia; succeeded by Offa

778 Alcuin head of school at York

781 Alcuin employed by Charlemagne as educator

787 Offa of Mercia forces establishment of Archbishopric at Lichfield; first Viking raid at Thanet

790 Irish monks reach Iceland; colonization not permanent

794 Monastery at Jarrow destroyed by Vikings

795 Vikings make first landings in Ireland

796 Death of Offa of Mercia

800 Nennius originates Arthur legend; Vikings ravage Dorset

802 Egbert becomes King of Wessex; founds greatest dynasty of Saxon kings

829 Egbert of Wessex in virtual control of England

839 Death of Egbert of Wessex; succeded by Ethelwulf

840 Vikings found Dublin

844 Kenneth I becomes first King of Scotland

851 Vikings sack Canterbury and London; defeated by Ethelwulf

858 Death of Ethelwulf; succeeded by Ethelbald

860 Vikings sack Winchester; Death of Ethelbald; succeeded by Ethelbert

865 Death of Ethelbert; suc-

A.D.

ceeded by Ethelred; Danish forces initiate first major invasion of England

866 Danes take York

871 Death of Ethelred; succeeded by Alfred the Great

874 Ingolfur Arnarson of Norway lands in Iceland; colonization permanent

875 Alfred's navy defeats Danes

878 Alfred reduced to near-ruin; recovers and defeats Danes at Edington

886 Alfred takes London; Danelaw established

899 Death of Alfred; succeeded by Edward I the Elder

900 Constantine II becomes King of Scotland

911 Hrolf the Ganger establishes Duchy of Normandy

918 Edward I the Elder in control of all England

923 Deposition of Charles III the Simple of France; his son, Louis (grandson of Edward the Elder) brought to England

924 Death of Edward I the Elder; succeeded by Athelstan

931 Death of Hrolf the Ganger of Normandy; succeeded by William I Longsword

934 Athelstan invades Scotland

935 Haakon the Good be-

A.D.

A.D.

comes King of Norway with Athelstan's help

936   Son of Charles III the Simple of France invited back to France to rule as Louis IV D'Outremer

937   Athelstan defeats Olaf Guthfrithson of Dunblin at Braunanburh

939   Death of Athelstan; succeeded by Edmund I the Magnificent

940   Death of Constantine II of Scotland; succeeded by Malcolm I

942   Odo becomes 22nd Archbishop of Canterbury. Death of William I of Normandy; succeeded by Richard I the Fearless

943   Dunstan becomes Abbot of Glastonbury

945   Edmund I conquers Strathclyde and cedes it to Scotland

946   Death of Edmund I; succeeded by Edred

954   Edred defeats Eric Bloodaxe of Norway in Northumbria

955   Death of Edred; succeeded by Edwy the Fair. Dunstan temporarily exiled

959   Death of Edwy; succeeded by Edgar I the Peaceful

960   Harold Bluetooth of Denmark converted to Christianity

961   Dunstan becomes 24th Archbishop of Canterbury

970   Edgar I cedes Bernicia to Kenneth II of Scotland

975   Death of Edgar I; succeeded by Edward II the Martyr

978   Assassination of Edward II the Martyr; succeeded by Ethelred II the Unready

982   Eric the Red of Iceland discovers Greenland

985   Sven Forkbeard becomes King of Denmark

986   Icelanders establish longterm colony in Greenland

991   Ethelred II institutes payment of Danegeld

994   London withstands siege by Sven Forkbeard

995   Olaf I Trygvesson becomes King of Norway

996   Death of Richard I of Normandy; succeeded by Richard II the Good

1000 Leif Ericsson discovers Vinland (North America?); Sven Forkbeard of Denmark kills Olaf Trygvesson of Norway in Baltic battle; approximate date of most ancient manuscript of *Beowulf*

1002 Ethelred II marries Emma of Norway; Saxons slaughter Danes of England

1003 Sven Forkbeard raids Exeter

1012 Danish raiders kill Alphege, 28th Archbishop of Canterbury

1014 Sven Forkbeard conquers England, then dies. Death

A.D.

1068 Edgar Atheling and Margaret Atheling flee to Scotland; Margaret Atheling marries Malcolm III of Scotland

1069 William I secures north of England

1070 Lanfranc becomes 34th Archbishop of Canterbury

1077 Robert Curthose rebels against his father, William I

1081 Robert Guiscard invades Balkans

1082 Robert Curthose rebels a second time; is exiled

1084 Robert Guiscard takes Rome

1085 Death of Robert Guiscard

1086 Oath at Salisbury

1087 Domesday Book. Death of William I; succeeded by William II Rufus in England and by Robert II Curthose in Normandy

1088 Bishop Odo rebels against William II

1093 Malcolm III of Scotland killed at Battle of Alnwick; succeeded by Donalbane. Anselm becomes 35th Archbishop of Canterbury

1095 Robert Curthose leaves on First Crusade

1098 Death of Donalbane of Scotland; succeeded by Edgar I

1099 Capture of Jerusalem by Crusaders

1100 Death of William II; suc-

A.D.

ceeded by Henry I Beauclerc

1101 Robert Curthose unsuccessfully invades England

1106 Henry I defeats Robert Curthose at Battle of Tinchebray

1107 Death of Edgar of Scotland; succeeded by Alexander I; compromise on lay investiture by Henry I and Anselm

1120 Death of Prince William on "White Ship"

1124 Death of Alexander I of Scotland; succeeded by David I

1125 William of Malmesbury writes *Acts of the Kings of the English*

1127 Matilda marries Geoffrey (Plantagenet) of Anjou

1128 Death of William Clito, son of Robert Curthose

1130 Geoffrey of Monmouth writes *The History of the Kings of Britain*; Death of Edgar Atheling

1134 Death of Robert Curthose

1135 Death of Henry I; succeeded by Stephen

1137 Death of William X of Aquitaine; his daughter Eleanor marries Louis VII of France

1138 Theobald becomes 38th Archbishop of Canterbury

1139 Matilda lands in England

1140 Adelard of Bath translates Euclid from the Arabic

A.D.

1193 Richard I ransomed. Hubert Walter appointed 43rd Archbishop of Canterbury. First merchant guild established

1194 Richard I returns to England

1196 Richard I has Château Gaillard built

1199 Death in battle of Richard I; succeeded by John

1200 John marries Isabella of Angoulême

1203 Death of Arthur of Brittany

1204 John loses Normandy to Philip II of France; death of Eleanor of Aquitaine

A.D.

1205 Death of Archbishop Hubert Walter

1208 England under Papal interdict

1209 John excommunicated

1213 John accepts Pope Innocent III as overlord; Stephen Langton assumes post as 44th Archbishop of Canterbury

1214 John and Otto IV of Germany defeated by Philip II of France at Bouvines

1215 John signs the Magna Carta

Note: Many of the dates prior to 700 are merely approximate.

Table I — The Saxon Kings of Wessex and England to 1000

Note:
In this and other dynastic tables reigning monarchs are indicated by the dates of their reign which appear below their names. The double line indicates a marriage and the dotted line an illegitimacy.

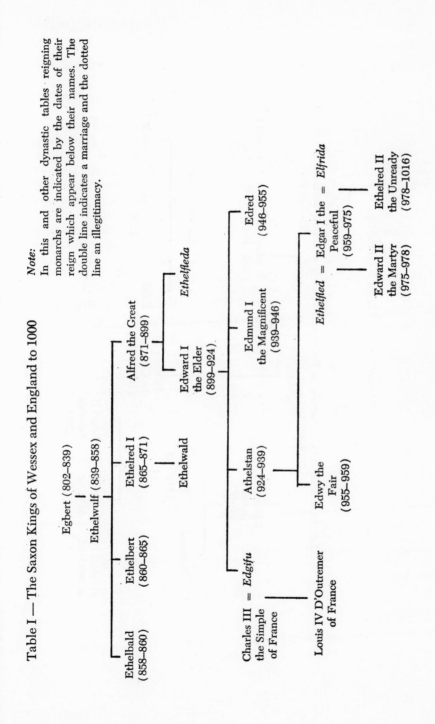

Egbert (802–839)

Ethelwulf (839–858)

Ethelbald (858–860)

Ethelbert (860–865)

Ethelred I (865–871)

Alfred the Great (871–899)

Ethelfleda

Ethelwald

Edward I the Elder (899–924)

Athelstan (924–939)

Edmund I the Magnificent (939–946)

Edred (946–955)

Charles III the Simple of France = *Edgifu*

Louis IV D'Outremer of France

Edwy the Fair (955–959)

Ethelfled = Edgar I the Peaceful (959–975) = *Elfrida*

Edward II the Martyr (975–978)

Ethelred II the Unready (978–1016)

Table II — The Kings of England from 1000 to 1066

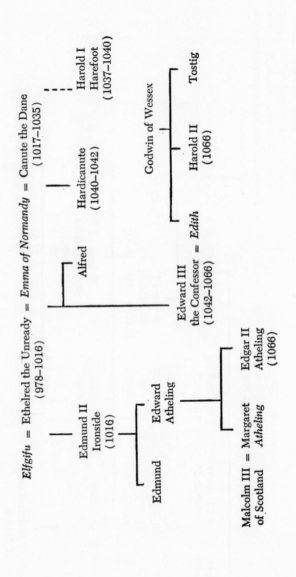

Table III — The Dukes of Normandy

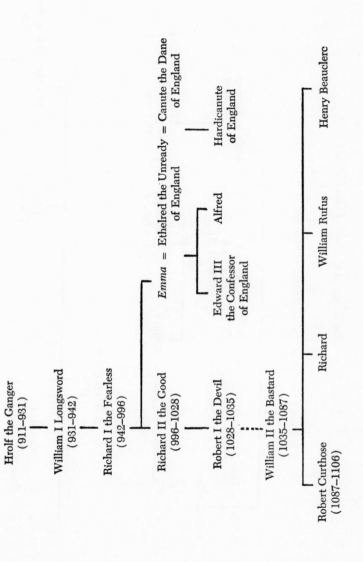

Hrolf the Ganger
(911–931)

William I Longsword
(931–942)

Richard I the Fearless
(942–996)

Richard II the Good
(996–1028)

Emma = Ethelred the Unready = Canute the Dane
of England   of England

Edward III
the Confessor
of England

Alfred

Hardicanute
of England

Robert I the Devil
(1028–1035)

William II the Bastard
(1035–1087)

Robert Curthose
(1087–1106)

Richard

William Rufus

Henry Beauclerc

Table IV — The Kings of England from 1066 to 1216

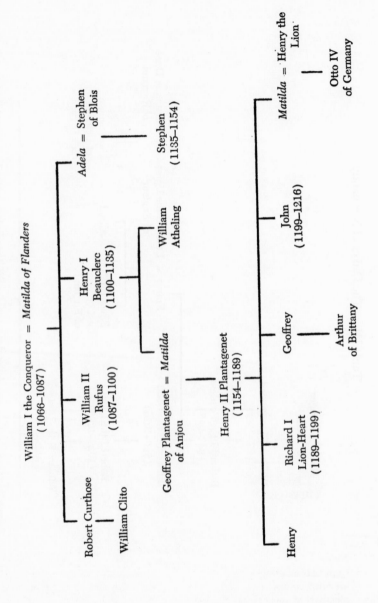

William I the Conqueror = *Matilda of Flanders*
(1066–1087)

Robert Curthose

William Clito

William II Rufus
(1087–1100)

Henry I Beauclerc
(1100–1135)

Adela = Stephen of Blois

Stephen
(1135–1154)

William Atheling

Geoffrey Plantagenet = *Matilda*
of Anjou

Henry II Plantagenet
(1154–1189)

Henry

Richard I Lion-Heart
(1189–1199)

Geoffrey

Arthur
of Brittany

John
(1199–1216)

Matilda = Henry the Lion

Otto IV
of Germany

Table V — The Kings of Scotland to 1214

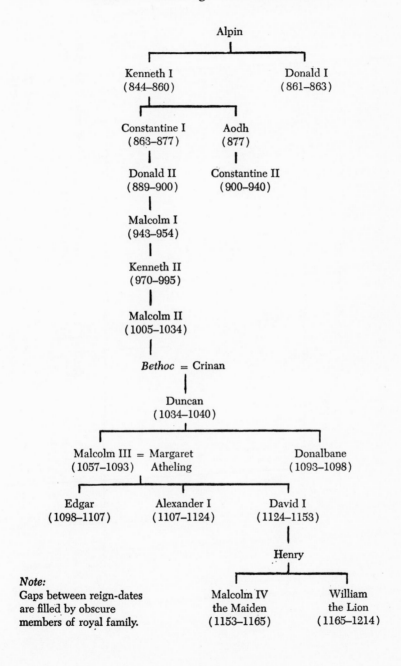

Note:
Gaps between reign-dates
are filled by obscure
members of royal family.

INDEX